Witch
Crafting

ALSO BY PHYLLIS CUROTT

Book of Shadows

Witch Crafting

A Spiritual Guide to Making Magic

Phyllis Curott, H.Ps.

BROADWAY BOOKS

New York

BROADWAY

Broadway Books titles may be purchased for business or promotional use or for special sales. For information, please write to: Special Markets Department, Random House, Inc., 1540 Broadway, New York, NY 10036.

BROADWAY BOOKS and its logo, a letter B bisected on the diagonal, are trademarks of Broadway Books, a division of Random House, Inc.

Visit our website at www.broadwaybooks.com

First edition published 2001.

Designed by Lee Fukui

Library of Congress Cataloging-in-Publication Data

Curott, Phyllis W.
Witch crafting : a spiritual guide to making magic / by Phyllis Curott.-1st ed.
p. cm.
ISBN 0-7679-0825-2
1. Witchcraft. 2. Goddess religion. 3. Magic. I. Title.
BF1571 .C88 2001
133.4'3-dc21   2001035376

10 9 8 7 6 5 4 3 2 1

For all of those who have come before,

those who will follow after,

and all who build the

magical bridge between them

Contents

Acknowledgments

Witch Crafting could not have been written without the gifts and assistance of many special people to whom I extend my heartfelt appreciation. First and foremost, I want to thank all of my patient, wise, and endlessly enthusiastic students who have taught me how, what, and why to teach.

My editor at Broadway Books, Lauren Marino, has once again been my champion. Her insight and savvy, commitment and verve have made all the difference in bringing this book to the widest audience possible. And of course, all the outstanding efforts of the great team at Broadway Books have helped this book to reach a growing and global audience: Steve Rubin, Catherine Pollock, Cate Tynan, Betsy Areddy, Lee Fukui, Alana Watkins, Brian Jones, and all the folks in marketing, sales, publicity, and design. Michael Windsor has created the most elegantly beautiful cover for any book on Wicca that's ever been published. I also want to thank Louise McNamara of HarperCollins U.K., and all my other absolutely wonderful foreign publishers, many of whom made my last book, *Book of Shadows*, a bestseller abroad, and who are helping the world to discover the spiritual gifts of Wicca.

This book could not have been written without the invaluable gifts of Nancy Peske—more than an editor, she has become a dear and valued friend whose talents and perspective have helped me to bridge the worlds of the magical and the mainstream. It is a service that only history can reward sufficiently, but she has my deepest respect and gratitude.

My agent, Joanna Pulcini, has once again brought her skills and enthusiasm and most of all her enormous heart to the manifestation of this vision. She shines with a light that brings radiance to all of her efforts. I'm also very grateful to everyone else at the Linda Chester Literary Agency: Linda Chester, Gary Jaffe, and Kelly Smith.

My dear friend and publicist, the very magical Arielle Ford, was and continues to be a gift of the Goddess in bringing this message of empowerment and reenchantment to a world in need.

I was very fortunate to have the insight of a fine group of readers and practitioners whose valuable feedback and generously shared stories have helped to shape this book. They have also nourished me, and this effort, with love and support: the members of my coven, the Circle of Ara—Charles Boyce, Jefferson Courtney, Gene Dratva, Bruce Fields, Tracy Grandstaff, Anna Hill, and Linda Magionico; the members of the Toronto Coven—Anne Gallagher, Kris Murdock, Barrie-Leah Gordon, Elizabeth Preiss, I.M., V.A., J.B., and the others; and Kirsten Rostedt, Allyson Edelhertz, George Darrow, Rhey Cedron, and Dr. David Oringderf.

Precious support and encouragement has also come from Ara High Priestesses Mikaela Pearson, Marilee Hartely, and Judy Landon and their hive covens Artemesia and SilverStar, all the members of the Ara Grove, and from Patricia Kennealy Morrison, Fiona Horne, Margot Adler, Starhawk, Z. Budapest, Janet Farrar, Patricia Telesco, Macha Nightmare, Selena Fox and the Circle Sanctuary Community, Lorenza Mengoni, David Hennessy, Deepak Chopra, Roseanne Barr, Bruce Springsteen for supplying the soundtrack, Michael Gross Esq, Rev. Laurie Sue Brockway, Shona Martin, Ornella Robbiati, Belinda Alexandra, Katherine Kellmeyer, Suzanne Colon and Jane Magazine, Ken Dashow, Buck Wolf, Art Bell, Whitley Streiber, Cynthia Wetzler, Randi Rhodes, Marlena Smith, Jeffrey Lyons, Koula Bouloukas, Kirsten Roy, Sirona Knight, Tara Lynda Guber, the Bodhi Tree, Women of Wisdom, the National Women's Music Festival, David Sirska and the Learning Annex Toronto, Paul Adamo and the Seminar Center, Justin Hilton and the Whole Life Expo, Janet Barres and the International Tarot Society, Doug Wilson and the Rowe Conference Center, Jeff Rosenbaum and Ace, BBMDC, Ed Hubbard and Telepathic

Media, Diane and Wade Berlin and the Phoeniz Fire family, Roger and the Florida Pagan Gathering, the OurFreedom e-list, the Religious Liberties Lawyers Network, Lisa Cady, Professor Robert Mathiesen, Professor Duncan Smith, Lorenzo Ostuni, Francesca Marino, Manuela Pompas, Rudy Stauder, Emilio Sioli, Morgana, Jan De Zutter, Circe and the Seattle Coven Seafire, Sally-Jo O'Brien, Debby Horton, Dan Gruber, Cory Rochester, Bruce Smith, Doug Sundling, Dr. Eleanor Rae, Rev. Darrell Berger, Leon Reed, Nymue, Gail Lamb Roddy, Angela Pope and Martin Isba, the fabulous Weber sisters, Jerrie Hildebrand, Lowell McFarland, Andrah Wyndfire, Jacque Zaleski, Joani Spadaro, Edith Deutsch and the Deutsch-Gross clan, Betty Jensen, Vera and Irv Schiller, Henry Jaglom, Zee Shakur, Grove Harris, Lorri Leighton, Victor Marsh, Tracy Baer, Rodger Parsons, Gloria Carol, Elspeth and Nibor, Angela Pope and Marin Isba, Deirdre Schweisow, Tempest, Laura Rodriguez and the Sarah Doyle Women's Center of Brown University, The Gay and Lesbian Center of New York City, Wisteria, Barnet Bains of Metafilmics, and my terrific lecture agent, Beth Elaine Carlson. I am also deeply grateful to the thousands and thousands of readers of *Book of Shadows* all over the world who have written to share their magic with me and to ask for more. No words can express how much your words have meant to me.

Finally, I want to express my gratitude to Bruce Fields for his support. And of course, Webster, the *sine qua non* who will have steak for dinner.

Introduction

WITCHCRAFT—this was once a word that conjured images of green-faced hags flying on brooms and worshiping the devil. But today, mainstream Americans can pick up a newspaper or book, turn on the radio or television, talk to their teenagers, or take a course to learn the reality of Witchcraft. Wicca (both a specific tradition of Witchcraft and a popular synonym for Witchcraft; I use the terms interchangeably in this book) is a beautiful, powerful spirituality that has much in common with Native American and other indigenous religions, and it's the fastest-growing religion in America.

As a Wiccan priestess for more than twenty years, and as an attorney, activist, and author, I've been very publicly devoted to transforming the negative stereotypes that burden this vibrant and authentic religion. With the publication of my first book—my memoir entitled *Book of Shadows*, in which I explained how I became a Witch—I sought to open a door to the hidden world of Witchcraft, to share its wisdom and power with a world in great need.

Witch Crafting: A Spiritual Guide to Making Magic was inspired by my adventures following the publication of my memoir. It was such a magical, joyful, transformative experience writing *Book of Shadows* that I was really looking forward to starting the sequel. But as I traveled all over the United States and much of Europe and Australia on my book and lecture tour, I increasingly felt that first I had to respond to what I was hearing from our community. Many readers who were enchanted by my descriptions of what it feels like to live a magical life asked me how they could

1

bring magic into their own lives. And both new practitioners and old told me they were looking for a guidebook that goes beyond the usual approach of "stand here, say this, and here are the altar tools you need, and be sure to have a supply of red roses and iron filings for spellwork." People are longing for something richer than just another recipe book; they are seeking a deeper exploration of our spirituality.

I decided I wanted to write more than just another mechanical course on "How to Be a Witch," so this is not your mother's Wiccan guidebook! I wanted to create an inspiring primer on how to live an empowered, divinely guided, magical life. I wanted to explore not just the "how" but the "why" of Witchcraft. Without understanding the "why do" behind the "how to," making magic is like driving a car without gas—you're not going anyplace. Or, like a lot of folks using all those mechanistic magic books, you may roll down the block for a while, but you're not going to reach your destination.

Understanding *why* unlocks the real power that makes magic happen. That power resides within all of us, and it's important for you to know, particularly if you are new to the subject matter, that you do not need special powers, psychic or otherwise, to be a Witch.

The real source of our power, which I will explore in Chapter 1, is the central spiritual principle of Wicca—that the Divine is present in the world, in ourselves, and others. Indeed, the goal in Wicca is not to do simplistic spellcasting, and it's certainly not to believe that God is out there somewhere. The spiritual focus of Wicca is to feel, to experience, and to *know* the Divine and the ecstasy of communion with that divinity. Our practices are what enable us to commune with the Sacred.

If you are not Wiccan, you certainly don't have to "convert" to Wicca, or accept all of Witchcraft's insights, to benefit from this empowering spirituality, and from *Witch Crafting*. You don't have to become a Buddhist to be moved by the words of the Dalai Lama, nor do you have to convert to mystical Hinduism to benefit from Deepak Chopra's Vedantic wisdom. *Witch Crafting* is ideal for all those who seek to experience a direct and personal revelation of the Divine, no matter what their age or gender, or whether they are practicing Wicca or another religion.

Witch Crafting's groundbreaking theories on the mechanics of magic—the laws of Nature behind the techniques, invocations of deity, rituals, spellcasting, potions, energy practices, divinations, uses of herbs and other aids—should stir your creativity and unleash newfound power to craft yourself as a Witch. And unlike any other guidebook, *Witch Crafting* explores the newly discovered laws of the hidden Universe where real magic rules. My goal in presenting some aspects of the new physics is simple: When we understand the laws by which the Universe operates, we are better able to make successful magic, for all magic works in harmony with Nature and her rules. It is neither "supernatural" (transcending Nature), nor irrational.

FOR THE BEGINNER

If you are a new practitioner, this book will introduce you to the magical richness of Witchcraft's spiritual principles and practices. It will describe the techniques and the tools that will help you experience and make divine magic, and it will explain, among other things, why we cast a circle, invoke deity, cast spells, work with Nature, do earth magic, use divination, and work with herbs, oils, and potions. You'll also find that *Witch Crafting* is uniquely helpful because it explores how important your feelings—emotional, physical, and spiritual—are in making magic. You will discover what you can and should expect when you use Wiccan practices, because without knowledge of what these feelings should be, it is impossible for you to know if you are cultivating the necessary skills to practice this amazing spirituality, especially if you are "book taught."

FOR THE EXPERIENCED WICCAN PRACTITIONER

All that said, *Witch Crafting* is *not* just another basic book for beginners. It is very much a book written for you skilled practitioners, who are the elders of this vibrant religion particularly with regard to the extensive theological discussions that weave both basic and advanced practices together. I have been privileged to travel all over the world giving lectures and workshops, and meeting, conversing, and working with Witches and

Pagans from many diverse traditions. I have found that over time, no matter what tradition they were originally trained in, serious and skillful practitioners are coming to similar conclusions about the core principles that we all share, and the key practices that really connect us to the Divine.

As I traveled, I was fascinated to find that many of you who have been doing this work for years are moving toward a more shamanic approach—with its emphasis on the sacredness of Nature, working spontaneously, making magic by connecting with deity, and communing rather than controlling. Most importantly, we are coming to a shared conclusion that our lives are our greatest magic.

While there are a number of additional characteristics of shamanism, the most significant in my work, and in this book, is the ecstasy of communion with deity. My own training began in a neo-Gardnerian women's mysteries coven, while I was simultaneously training in core shamanic techniques. The two have been intertwined throughout my adult life, resulting in a very experiential, Nature-based spiritual practice devoted to the magic of the Divine that dwells in all things. The perspective in this book reflects my experience as a philosopher, practitioner, Priestess, and teacher exploring this realm of sacred magic. And it reflects my tradition—the Ara tradition—which is distinctly shamanic.

Some of you may find this deconstructed approach disconcerting or seemingly undisciplined. I won't ask you to throw out all the techniques and elements of ritual, and I certainly don't mean to suggest that they are meaningless or useless. If they were, I wouldn't have included them in this book. In fact, you will find in *Witch Crafting* all the essentials that provide a common and useful structure for our spiritual explorations. What I will ask you to do is to question why we use these techniques, and to look beneath the surface to see the magical meanings of our practices.

RAISING QUESTIONS

This book is not the gospel according to St. Phyllis. Not everyone will agree with the conclusions I have drawn from my journey, and I'd be appalled if you did—I'd immediately feel compelled to start rethinking most of it. My goal is not to convince you that all of these ideas are right, but to stimulate dialogue, innovative thinking, and creative practicing—to stir the cauldron of magic. With our increasing numbers and our visibility, presence, and influence in mainstream culture, I believe we must explore the values and spiritual principles at the heart of our religion. This requires us to look at the contradictions in our practices, ideas, and vocabulary. So *Witch Crafting* challenges many of the assumptions that underlie aspects of Wiccan/Pagan thinking and practices, and disputes ideas that have started to become our own kind of dogma. This book invites all of us to free ourselves, and our religion, from outdated concepts and two-dimensional practices that limit us.

Witch Crafting also breaks new ground by offering radical new definitions of magic, spells, divinity, and who a Witch is. And this book deconstructs the remnants of patriarchal theology that distort the spiritual principles and practice of Witchcraft. I'm going to critique mechanistic spellcasting, abstract magic, and projections of power and divinity. I'm also going to challenge the false and inauthentic ethics of the Threefold Law, and propose an entirely different basis for the ethics of Witchcraft. And as I've said in the lectures where I've tested many of these ideas, if I don't provoke you at least once, I haven't done my job!

AN EVOLVING RELIGION

Contemporary Wicca is a modern, vital, dynamic religion. This statement flies in the face of the myth of our origin that many have subscribed to for a long time. A complete analysis of the history of Witchcraft's origins would require volumes to complete, and would still leave much to speculation. There has been some thorough and carefully researched work published recently (check the Resources section for titles of some of these books) that challenges the belief that modern Witchcraft is a historically unbroken, organized, hereditary tradition that can be consistently traced back to a golden era of matriarchy and worship of a single Great Goddess. However, there have always been individuals who claim they were initiated in traditions which remain hidden behind veils of secrecy—and there may indeed be hereditary traditions waiting for a safer time to emerge.

When I first found the coven that initiated me more than twenty years ago, I too believed that I was part of an ancient, unbroken lineage. But the sources of contemporary Wicca are far more complex, and in many ways more fascinating. The fact is that the origins of much of our current practice can be traced back to the creative genius of Gerald Gardner who surfaced publicly in England in the late 1940s and early 1950s following the repeal of England's Witchcraft and Vagrancy Acts. Although it appears he was indeed initiated by a Witch in England at the midpoint of the twentieth century, Gardner drew upon richly diverse sources, including a wide range of cultural and magical influences, to create many of the basic ritual structures most commonly used today.

This doesn't mean that there were not practitioners of Witchcraft, or *La Vecchia Religione*—the Old Religion. In fact, important and recent research by Professor Robert Mathiesen of Brown University provided in the new translation of *Aradia, or the Gospel of the Witches* has proven that the influential work of American folklorist Charles Godfrey Leland was indeed based upon material provided by a real woman, Maddalena, living in Florence in the late eighteen hundreds. She was a practicing *strega*, the Italian word for Witch, who provided him with chants, spells, invocations, and stories of the Old Religion which she knew and which she gathered from other practitioners. Today we know that, in fact, there were surviving pre-Christian religions, and that Leland's *Aradia* was a source for portions of the *Charge of the Goddess*, the most important and singular piece of contemporary Wiccan liturgy.

There were practitioners of forms of indigenous "Paganism" that preceded Christianity by thousands of years. The Witchcraft we practice today, however, is necessarily different from what we know of the practices of our forebears. It is a living, gloriously creative religion, a tapestry of rich threads with remarkable and fascinating influences that include Freemasonry, the elegant Golden Dawn, Leland's *Aradia*, mythology and folk practices, nineteenth-century American pantheism and transcendentalism, the Romantic poets, important figures such as Doreen Valiente and others, the countercultural explorations of the sixties that ushered in American feminism, spiritualism, yoga, Buddhism, shamanism, psychotropics, Jung . . . the list goes on and on. And archaeology, linguistics, mythology, and the remnants of ancient culture do show us that there were Goddesses, such as Isis, Inanna, Demeter, Persephone, and many others whose worship was, for a time, the central religious mystery of early Western culture.

We know that there were cunning men and women: *benadenti* and *streghe*, shamans and Priestesses. We know that the Witch persecutions that lasted centuries have had a devastating impact on the status of women and the public misperception of who Witches are, and what they believe and practice. We also know that we had pre-Christian ancestors, throughout Europe and the Middle East, who worshiped Goddesses, experienced the divine nature of the world in which we reside, and practiced shamanic techniques. These ancestors left behind a legacy of folklore and folk practices, invocations and charms, spells and cures, holy days and sacred sites that inspire us to dig more deeply to retrieve our heritage. And this may be their greatest gift to us, for we are spurred to greater activism in discovering our past as we take responsibility for creating our future.

And this may be one of modern Wicca's greatest gifts—it is a deeply personal spirituality crafted by each of its practitioners. By embracing our diverse influences we are inspired to greater creativity in shaping our future. For Witches, the unfurling truth of who we are and where we come from is liberating, inspiring, and empowering—and it is filled with magic.

So I want to suggest something radical, realistic, and re-directing: The legitimacy of modern Wicca as a meaningful, powerful, and real religion does not depend upon unbroken, hereditary, organized lineage. The fact is that the greatest and most profound cultural and historical phenomena is the birth of a new religion. Witchcraft may, in a real and romantic sense, be the rebirth of an ancient religion, but ultimately the phenomenon of modern Witchcraft is the birth of a new religion.

WHY WICCA?

A new religion occurs when the old religions no longer explain reality, nor meet the needs of people. With modern Witchcraft we are collectively creating a religion that specifically addresses our needs and this makes Wicca one of the most dynamic, exciting religions of this post-Christian era.

It respects and affords genuine empowerment to those who have felt powerless. Women have found a spiritual home in Wicca because it is the only Western religion that has a Goddess, as well as a God, and because it honors women as spiritual leaders and priestesses.

Another reason for Wicca's growing popularity is its reverence for the Earth as sacred, a spiritual value that addresses the terrible environmental crises we face today. Like our ancestors, we learn from the greatest teacher, Nature, and we recognize Her intrinsic value.

In a psychological age, Wicca requires us, and inspires us, to bravely acknowledge the shadow self (our fears, inhibitions, conflicts, neuroses, and destructive patterns) and to learn from it, rather than repress it. It is a religion of joy not punishment, love not fear, practice not belief. It's a personal path of self-exploration, growth, and responsibility, helping us to understand that our lives are spiritual journeys, and providing a genuine and intimate experience of the Divine.

Wicca is a spirituality well suited to the modern temperament. There are no gurus, no hierarchy, no dogma. Instead, there is a system of effective practices, which anyone can master, that opens the door to the divine world in which we live. Witchcraft does not defy our rationality, and in a rational world people need to *experience* the Divine rather than have faith in a far-off deity.

Personally, Wicca directly addresses things I've known since I was a child, that the Divine is present in Nature and its cycles, that it also dwells within us, and that the power of love is magical. And this is perhaps its greatest appeal. It is a spiritual practice anyone can master to reconnect themselves to divinity and to empower their lives. Wicca is a religion that recognizes the innate divinity of the world in which we live, not as an abstract principle, but as a living experience. That is what crafting yourself as a Witch is all about.

Today we are taking Witchcraft to a new level. We have come to recognize that our religion is, like Nature, our great teacher, ever evolving. I am deeply proud of participating in this world-transforming event. And I hope that you will find *Witch Crafting* a worthy contribution to this historic process, and to your own spiritual journey.

—Phyllis Curott, New York 2001

How to Use This Book

Witch Crafting is written for two audiences simultaneously: both skilled and new practitioners.

Many of you are coming to this book following *Book of Shadows* and, naturally, you may be expecting the same kind of reading experience that evokes what it is like to be in circle, cast a spell, encounter the Goddess, and make magic. But the key to *Witch Crafting* is that this book requires your interaction. You can't just read it—you've got to *do* the practices and the exercises in order to experience the feelings that the *Book of Shadows*'s narrative style created. Ask yourself, "Am I just reading this and believing it, or am I doing it and experiencing it?" Reading is not practicing, and thinking is not feeling. When you get to a practice, stop, close the book, and do it before reading on. If you do, *Witch Crafting* will help you to make those experiences uniquely your own. Also, if you are a new practitioner, you may be tempted to skip over the explanations—the "why do"—and rush to get to the "how to," but I urge you not to do so. Understanding *why* unlocks the real power behind Wiccan practices. You may wish to do the advanced practices as well, but before you do, I urge you to master the basic practices in this book.

If you are an experienced Witch, you may be tempted to skip over the familiar "basic" practices and exercises, but I ask you to return to them as if it were your first time. By approaching these practices in the context of spiritual principles and working in Nature, I hope you will find your experiences deepened and enriched. In fact, I've labeled many of the practices "basic to advanced" because I've either added a new perspective to them, or they will be completely new to you. Also, as skilled practitioners you know the real joy and illumination of always being at the beginning—one reason we end circle where we begin. Then too, I've provided strictly advanced practices for you that require a true mastery of the basic practices.

And if you have ever read or worked with the many Wiccan guidebooks available, you are probably used to an approach that allows you to stay in your head by imagining, visualizing, and working in your living room. *Witch Crafting* has a much more visceral and Nature-based approach. Instead of asking you to imagine the breeze on your face, I'm asking you to go out on a windy day and experience it. Even if you are a seasoned practitioner, I am hoping that this shamanic and often deconstructed approach will help you to more fully experience the practices that are so familiar to you. I've presented the material in a way that I think will help you break out of the mechanical approach of "stand here, say this, do that" and into a creative, spiritually driven, divinely empowered practice. The magic and spirituality of Witchcraft can't be experienced vicariously or abstractly. *This book, like our spirituality, is experienced by practicing!*

And whether you have been practicing for two years or twenty, I also ask you to keep a magical journal—a diary of notes and descriptions of your magical experiences, your dreams, divinations, intuitions, synchronicities, and your reactions, as you work with *Witch Crafting*. Many exercises involve journaling as part of your magic, and this writing will help you to see the patterns and lessons in your experiences and the progress you are making in your growth. I also urge you to begin creating your own Book of Shadows (information on how to do this follows this section).

Witch Crafting is intended for use by the solitary practitioner as well as by study groups and covens. If you are working in a group, I suggest you do one exercise or practice per meeting. As you continue working, you can integrate more than one—for example, you can begin by casting circle hand to hand, continue with a grounding and centering exercise, and then run energy. And even if you are working with a study group or coven, you should do those exercises that are intended for personal practice as well.

Finally, the Resources section in the back of *Witch Crafting* will provide recommended reading, websites, organizations, and other valuable sources of guidance.

I hope you find this journey magical. If you'd like to share your experiences and insights with me, or are interested in initiatory training programs, or in subscribing to a future newsletter, please enclose an SASE and write to me at:

>Phyllis Curott
>P.O. Box 311
>Prince Street Station
>New York, NY 10012
>www:WitchCrafting.com
>www.bookofshadows.net

Future lectures and workshops will be posted on the websites.

Beginning Your Own
Book of Shadows

CREATING YOUR OWN Book of Shadows is an ongoing, creative, magical process that will accompany you through your entire life as a practitioner of Wicca. Within the community, covens and traditions record their rituals, initiation rites, Sabbat ceremonies, and collected wisdom in a Book of Shadows that is shared with other members of their group, usually after initiation. But in contemporary Wicca, each Witch also crafts her or his own magical book. A Book of Shadows is your personal compilation of invocations, rituals, spells, and magical techniques with which you work, and which you find powerful, meaningful, effective, and evocative.

I also write down in my Book of Shadows poems, songs, and chants; wisdom imparted to me by my power animals and spirit guides; what I am able to remember after Drawing Down the Moon, and spiritual wisdom I have received from others.

After more than twenty years of practicing, I have many magical diaries and several Books of Shadows—some are spiral-bound notebooks, others are looseleaf, others are beautiful books bound in silk or tooled leather. My practice in crafting my Book of Shadows has been to work first in an informal book, and then to carefully transcribe my rites and rituals, by hand, into a beautiful bound book. This takes much more time than simply typing into your computer (which is also a fine way to record your magical efforts), but writing by hand helps you to memorize and also infuses your book with your magical energy.

In the beginning, you will write your rituals before performing them. You can copy them from other sources such as this one, and combine and rewrite as you use them. Over time, you will cast many circles and have many magical experiences spontaneously, both within your circle and as you live your life. Whenever possible, try to write down what you did and said and experienced as shortly thereafter as you can. Don't wait too long, or think you'll simply remember—I made the mistake of assuming I would remember, and I certainly wish I had recorded more of my magic!

Below is a simple outline of subjects to help you organize your Book of Shadows:

- Title Page: "This Is the Book of Shadows of [Your Name]"

- Dedication Page: Here you should record a simple statement of your spiritual commitment. Write down what it is that draws you to Wicca, what it is you hope to learn, and what you hope to create with your spirituality. Note the date and astrological aspects and consider this first writing the beginning of your book. Read it periodically, and on the anniversary of beginning your book. It will be an important touchstone on your journey. You may wish to rewrite it as you grow and mature.

- Invocation of the Goddess: Many people begin with the *Charge of the Goddess* adapted from Leland's *Aradia* by Doreen Valiente and Gerald Gardner (see page 142). You will also find numerous invocations in *Witch Crafting*. Write your own invocations as soon as you feel ready. And write down any that come to you spontaneously or from other sources.

- Invocation of the God: as above

- Diagrams for your altar, and markings for your working tools

- In Sacred Space:
    Purification of Self
    Purification of the elements
    Purification of the Circle with the elements
    Grounding, centering, meditation
    Casting the Circle
    Invocations for the four directions/elements
    Invocation of the Goddess and God
    Statement of Purpose
    Magic/Ritual/ Spell/Divination/ Journey, etc./ Taking in and
        raising and directing of energy
    Grounding
    Libation—cakes and wine

- Closing Circle:
    Giving thanks
    Thanking and banishing the four directions/elements
    Sealing the Circle with fire
    Farewell

- Rituals. These should include:
    Consecration of tools, jewelry, and other magical objects
    Cleansing and Purification
    Healing
    Peace and Protection
    Inspiration
    Honoring the Divine—in Nature, oneself, etc.
    Creativity, prosperity, fertility
    Love—in all its wonderful forms
    Communion
    Guidance
    Giving thanks, making an offering
    Banishing and binding rituals, etc.

- Esbats: lunar rituals, dark moon, waning moon, waxing moon

- Full Moon rituals: Drawing Down the Moon

- Eight Sabbats: the Wheel of the Year

- Self-dedication and/or initiation ritual

- Chants, dances, songs, prayers, invocations, words of wisdom, and quotes from others

- Wisdom and insights that have been given to you in ritual, meditation, etc.

- Tools of the Craft and their markings: List each tool and its magical purpose and connection to the elements, as well as how they are to be marked.

- Magical information: Table of Correspondences, spells, potions, talismans, sigils, symbolism, and information about herbs, oils, gems, candles, crystals, magical alphabets, and methods of working magic such as elemental, knot, trance, and others. It may also contain dream symbolism and methods of divination such as scrying, reading signs, using runes and tarot cards. All of these should be enumerated; for example, each rune should be drawn and its meaning and interpretation written next to it. (These are often collected in another volume called the *Witch's Grimoire*.)

Some of the above may be unfamiliar right now, but you will learn about all of these aspects of Witchcraft as you read this book.

Above all else, enjoy yourself! Writing a Book of Shadows is a magical experience.

Your Magical Diary

I suggest you start keeping a magical diary, whether it is part of your Book of Shadows or separate. This is where you can write about your magical experiences as you work through *Witch Crafting*, and during your magical career as it unfolds. You may even wish to have several journals—one for working with *Witch Crafting*, another for dreams, one for tracking whether your intuition proves true, one for divination, another for evaluating your magic. It is particularly important for you to have at least one journal to record some of the exercises and practices in this book and your reactions to them so that you can see the progress you are making in your growth.

In your magical diary, write about your dreams, journeys, synchronicities, magical experiences, and divinations—this is where you should write down the results of throwing the I Ching, drawing runes, doing a tarot reading, or other form of divination. As with your intuitions, it is important to review these later and note what came true, what didn't, what you misinterpreted. Patterns will begin to appear and they will help you to realize your deepest spiritual nature. I have many notebooks filled with my experiences over the years and they have helped me immeasurably in discovering how my everyday life is filled with magical experiences of rich spiritual meaning.

Real Magic

"*Bring me the love that is right for me now. There's someone out there longing for me. Bring us together so we can be happy. And give me a sign, so I'll recognize him.*"

With these words I ended my love spell and watched the smoke from the attraction incense I had made carry my spell into the future. I blew out the red candles, put the cap on the Aphrodite oil, and closed my magical circle.

Eight months passed and nothing was materializing, but I remembered the advice I always gave others: You have to be happy with yourself before you can be happy with someone else. I threw myself into my work, which was always a source of personal growth for me.

And then one night, it happened. The sign I had asked for appeared in a dream. It was a waking or "big" dream—the kind that's so vivid you feel as if you're awake. And it was very cinematic: I was standing in the midst of the most beautiful clouds—all brilliantly lit by enormous klieg lights—when suddenly, a dark-haired man wearing a black leather motorcycle jacket and black jeans stepped out of the clouds. I couldn't see his face because he was lit from behind.

A motorcycle appeared next to him. It was black with lots of dazzling chrome shining in the light. I found myself climbing onto the back of the bike, and magically, he was seated in front of me. He gunned the engines and we took off into the clouds.

I woke up to the sound of the phone ringing, and I answered it, even though I was still half asleep. It was my best friend Mitchell, calling to persuade me to go out with a friend of his. He sounded like an interesting guy—a successful photographer with a studio in SoHo and a house on the ocean in the Hamptons. Mitchell said he was smart, funny, attractive, a "real man" —and, Mitchell added, "he rides a Harley."

"What color is it?" I asked, sitting bolt upright in bed.

"Black," he replied. "With a lot of chrome."

"I'll meet him."

Our second date was on the bike, and we were married a few years later.

Is the world really filled with magic? If you experience falling in love, you know the mystery, promise, and power of magic are all real. You feel as if you've been given a key to an enchanted kingdom where anything is possible, where dreams come true, and your heart's desires are yours for the asking.

But in our everyday lives, we find it hard to believe in such things. Look around you: turn on the television and watch the evening news, walk down the street and see the homeless folks, look at a strip-mined hillside, dolphins dying in a trawler's net, or another bloody war and it's not just hard, it's impossible to believe the world is filled with magic. There's no doubt that we humans treat the world as if it's the complete opposite of magical. In fact, we pretty much use it like a combination supply depot and garbage dump. And our own lives seem ensnared in endless details and responsibilities that couldn't seem further from magic.

We live in a world of sophisticated skeptics, where the word "magic" is dismissed with a sneer. It's a silly childhood belief that Hogwarts School can teach us to fly on brooms. We know it's just Hollywood special effects that enable beautiful babes to make furniture fly and demons explode. And it's elaborate props and mirrors that allow a Las Vegas lounge act to make a tiger "disappear." We enjoy the illusion, but we tell ourselves real magic is impossible, because we've been taught to believe in scientific, rational explanations. We've been told that magic is just a superstitious and illogical belief, defying science and the harsh realities of grown-up life. Yet, deep down inside, everyone longs for the power to heal the wounds of the world and to make their dreams come true.

The irony is that even when we've been told that it's foolish, even demonic, to believe in magic, the dominant patriarchal religions in our culture tell us that we should believe in their "miracles" —Moses parting the Red Sea, Jesus rising from the dead or walking on water. The difference, apparently, is that their "miracles" come from their "one true God." But this distinction is just an example of one religion demonizing another.

Throughout history there have always been magicians and mystics, and modern Wicca is one of the world's most magical religious traditions. Divine magic is an integral aspect of this spirituality, but what we practice is not your childhood abracadabra. So how do we make real magic?

To answer that, we have to look first at the traditional definitions of magic, see how they work, and then consider a new one.

THE TRADITIONAL CRAFT DEFINITIONS OF MAGIC

Over the years, two definitions of magic have had a major impact on the development of Wicca. "Magic is the science and art of causing change to occur in conformity with will," wrote the controversial Aleister Crowley, enfant terrible of early twentieth-century magic. In keeping with this view of magic, practitioners of Wicca learn to visualize their goals, create thought forms, raise energy, direct that energy into the thought form, and project, direct, or will the energy into taking form—first in the realm of pure thought, and then in the realm of material manifestation. Mental focus and the projection of will are key to this magical approach. And it certainly works. But not all the time, and often not in the ways that one expects.

Another very popular definition of magic was provided by Dion Fortune, author and member of the Golden Dawn, a magical order from the early 1900s in England and Ireland. Her definition has had an enormous impact on contemporary Wicca and was later popularized by Starhawk: "Magic is the art of changing consciousness at will." And, once we have entered an altered state of consciousness, magic is then the art of changing events in the world by using heightened consciousness.

Wiccans employ a wide variety of simple yet very effective techniques to shift their consciousness from the mundane to the magical. It's one of the first things you learn in crafting yourself as a Witch, and something you will continue to explore for the rest of your magical life. Below are some basic, but critically important, Wiccan practices designed to "flip the switch" and get the part of your brain that you need to make magic working.

BASIC PRACTICE
CHANGING CONSCIOUSNESS AT WILL THROUGH MEDITATION

Here's one of the easiest and most important of all Wiccan techniques for changing consciousness: basic meditation. It has many elements in common with the practices of yoga, Buddhism, and transcendental and other meditation traditions.

The actual meditation need not take more than five minutes when you first practice it. As you become more able to relax and focus, work on gradually increasing the time you devote to meditating. A half an hour is ideal.

If at all possible, find a secluded spot outdoors, or at least in a place where you can see and hear nature. If you are indoors, turn off your phone ringers and lower the sound on the answering machine.

Sit comfortably. Next, relax your muscles—begin by tightening the muscles of your face, then releasing them. Continue to tighten and release your muscles, as you gradually work down the length of your body to your toes. Exhale. Take a deep breath slowly, breathing in through your nose, and hold it for a count of three. Exhale slowly through your mouth. Take another breath through your nose, fully expanding your diaphragm as you inhale, hold it for a count of three, and exhale slowly through your mouth. Repeat one more time, and then continue to breathe deeply, slowly, and fully throughout this meditation, inhaling through the nose, exhaling through the mouth.

Feel yourself growing quiet, centered, peaceful. Thoughts may enter your mind. Let them float by, like a cup floating in the ocean. Don't be distracted by them—just concentrate on your breathing, on how it feels as the divine energy of life enters and moves through you. And as you exhale, release the tensions of the day. As you inhale, feel the tranquility flowing through you.

Continue breathing, deeply and fully, allowing thoughts to float by. If your mind starts to wander, bring it back by concentrating on your breathing. Feel your inner stillness, your peacefulness. As you sit, focusing only upon your breathing, you may also begin to experience a wonderful sense of freedom and joyfulness. Allow these feelings to rise and flow through you.

When you are ready, open your eyes. Sit quietly for a moment, observing your surroundings. Stretch, and enjoy your energized and calm state.

You may wish to write about your experience in your magical journal.

Why shift your consciousness? The simple answer is because it helps you to focus and to manifest your desires by projecting your will into carefully visualized thought forms. There are actually other very important reasons for shifting your consciousness from the daily cares we carry around with us to a magical form of consciousness, and we'll be exploring them a little further on in this chapter and throughout *Witch Crafting*.

The next step common in Wiccan magical training involves mastering practices that enhance your ability to create clear thought forms.

VISUALIZATION AND CONCENTRATION

Visualization

This first practice will help you to focus on specific images; to visualize them with precision, clarity, and confidence; and to concentrate on them without distraction. You should try to set aside about fifteen minutes a day, or at least every other day, to practice these visualization techniques. If you practice regularly, you'll find your skill growing quickly. But don't try to spend too much time each day—this exercise seems to work better when you practice it for a few minutes regularly than for longer stretches infrequently.

Don't worry if you find it difficult to see images in your mind's eye. Learning to visualize takes time, like appreciating art—the first time you saw a Picasso you probably said, "What's that?" So give yourself time to develop this skill. And because it's difficult for some folks to visualize, I've added tactile experiences to the learning process, which should make it much easier to master this important practice.

Begin with your basic meditation practice, keeping your eyes closed. When you feel yourself relaxed and your mind quieted, imagine a circle. See it clearly in your mind's eye. Next, with your eyes still closed, concentrate on the shape of a triangle, then a square. See them floating in space before you.

As you are able to hold the image without becoming distracted, try spinning or moving it in space. Turn the two-dimensional circle into a sphere, the triangle into a pyramid, the square into a cube. Visualize a star, and then visualize it in different colors—beginning with silver, then moving through the spectrum from red to orange, yellow, green, blue, indigo, and finally purple. You may also reverse the order of visualizing colors.

When you feel you have mastered geometrical shapes and basic colors, visualize a variety of organic objects such as an apple, a tree, or your pet.

Concentration 1

This next step is particularly helpful if you have trouble visualizing. You are now going to add more sensations to your visualizations. Start with a distinct physical experience, then re-create it with your imagination. Light a candle and stare into it for several seconds. Now close your eyes and see the flames dancing, see the color and shape and movement. Repeat this until you can see the candle flame clearly and hold the image in your mind's eye. Next, work on imagining heat by placing your hands near the candle so that you can feel its warmth against your skin. Be careful not to burn yourself! Move your hands away, close your eyes, and imagine the feeling of heat on your skin.

Concentration 2

The next time you practice your concentration and visualization skills, don't light the candle—just visualize and experience the feeling. Retrieve your memories as clearly as you can, and concentrate on them.

You can work with other sensations too, imagining the way an orange feels, tastes, and smells, for example. Peel the orange, inhale the fragrance, and taste it. Then remember/imagine the sensations and, on another day, imagine peeling and tasting an orange without holding the real orange first.

Creative Visualization

When you feel confident in your ability to visualize and concentrate on shapes, objects, and colors, taste, smell, and other sensations, it's time to begin creative visualization involving visionary experiences. This process is greatly enhanced by working with someone else (usually a Priestess or Priest) who can lead you through the technique that we call guided or creative visualization. (You can tape these for yourself.) Try to leave a half hour for these experiences.

First, decide where you will go in your creative visualization. Then close your eyes, meditate, and begin. It's often useful to start by visualizing yourself opening a large wooden door. Next, visualize a beautiful countryside before you. See yourself walking through green grass, sitting beneath a great tree, bathing in a pool of crystal clear water.

Now concentrate on the feelings you are experiencing—smell the fresh grass and flowers as you walk, feel the warmth of the sun on your skin, feel a cool breeze as you sit beneath the tree, hear the birds singing, the leaves rustling, feel the refreshing silkiness of the water as you step into the pool. Pay careful attention to how each of these experiences affects and transforms you—how the warmth of the sun energizes you, how leaning against the tree gives you strength, how bathing in the pool refreshes and restores your sense of peace, well-being, and joy.

As you become more accomplished at creative visualization, allow yourself to wander and explore. Visit your place of power, a sacred grove, or a temple. You will begin to have genuinely magical adventures and receive extraordinary insights from the images and events that appear spontaneously.

The practices you're mastering will enable you to develop the skills necessary to make real magic. You can't manifest a desire if you can't visualize it first. And to visualize clearly, you must first learn to quiet your mind. You are learning to create a thought form on akashic, or psychic, planes of spiritual and magical energy. Once a thought form has been created there, you'll learn to animate or fill it with energy so it can manifest on the material plane.

Even if you don't have immediate and powerful experiences, with time and repetition eventually these techniques will enable you to experience the nonordinary aspects of reality, so be patient and keep practicing. You'll discover that what many think of as "supernatural" powers, such as receiving messages from the dead, having precognitive dreams, or knowing what's going to happen before it happens are not supernatural at all. These are natural abilities that we all have and can develop further through Wiccan practices.

A New Definition of Magic

The two traditional definitions of magic—that magic is the science and art of causing change to occur in conformity with will (Crowley) and that magic is the art of changing consciousness at will (Fortune/Starhawk)—are helpful in understanding basic aspects of Wiccan practice. But they are incomplete. Real magic is more than just changing consciousness at will or projecting will into thought forms, for magic doesn't just occur in your mind, or on akashic planes. And it is far more than just something we do to control the world, or manifest our desires.

I want to propose a new definition of magic: *Magic is what happens when you have encountered the Divine.* It is the life-altering experience of connecting to the divinity that dwells within yourself and in the world. It is all of the extraordinary events and manifestations that flow from your union with a real and present divinity. *Real magic is your relationship with immanent divinity, and it is how you craft yourself as a Witch.*

Making magic is like making love, and your partner is the Divine. Together, you share and express mutual pleasure and appreciation. *Making magic is a dynamic process by which you co-create reality with deity. And ultimately, all real magic is a manifestation of the Divine.* This connection means that you approach making magic as a spiritual practice, with respect and reverence, joy and gratitude, and, you may be surprised to learn, humor and spontaneity.

This definition of magic really resonates for me. And because the practice of magic *is* a centerpiece of Wiccan spirituality, it only makes sense that our most important spiritual practice should reflect our most important spiritual principle. Among the many diverse traditions of Witchcraft, and other magical traditions within the broader neo-Pagan or Pagan communities, it's common to hear many people say we have no common spiritual principle. I disagree. I think immanent divinity is a profound precept that unites us.

What is immanent divinity? It means *the Divine is everywhere present in the world**. Everything that exists in the natural world—you, other people, plants, animals, earth, sky, air, water, weather, moon, sun, stars, galaxies, everything—is a form, an embodiment, of divine energy. And *everything is interconnected by that sacred energy.*

"But how do I encounter the Divine?" I can hear you asking impa-

---

*The word "immanent," not to be confused with "imminent," comes from the Latin word *inmanere*, which meant to remain in place, and means: "remaining or operating within a domain of reality . . . inherent." "Immanentism" refers to the presence of deity or spirit as pervasive in the world.

tiently. If it were so easy, we'd all be doing it all the time. There's a reason why we don't realize how accessible the Divine really is.

GOD AS A POTTER

When I was doing publicity for *Book of Shadows*, I was on a very nice television show hosted by a rabbi and a priest. We were trying to find a common vocabulary and so the rabbi, with the priest's consent, explained the biblical idea of God and his relationship to the world: "In the biblical traditions, God is like a potter and the world is a pot. He created the world but he's not present in it."

"God isn't present in the world"—How tragic, I thought, as I felt the lightbulb over my head pop on. God exists outside of the world, he's transcendent, removed . . . He made it and then he left and so the world we live in is devoid of divinity. . . . What depressing thoughts! But it gets worse.

Every religion has its creation myth—I'm sure you've heard the one about the woman, the apple, and the talking snake. Most of us in the West were taught that because Adam defied God by eating from the Tree of Knowledge, brought about by Eve's susceptibility to the devil and her seductiveness, man is left alone, having been expelled from paradise and from the presence of God. He is born with the "stain of original sin" and condemned to a realm—the Earth—that, like man, has fallen from grace. Spirit and matter are eternally separated and the Divine is forever outside of us and our world.

The patriarchal religions teach us that the best we can hope for is to come to God's favor through living a "pure life," one that denies the earthly plane. We've been told that if we live in accordance with the teachings of the Bible, Koran, or Torah—or if we receive vicarious redemption via Jesus—then, and only then, God will hear us. But the assumptions beneath all of these "paths to salvation" are that we are devoid of divinity and in need of saving. True, many Christians subscribe to the belief that God *is* present in the world—through Jesus. But they also believe that the *only* way to God is through accepting Jesus as their "savior." The Earth itself, the creatures of the Earth, other human beings who subscribe to different faiths, are all excluded.

How endlessly and devastatingly lonely.

Most folks, whether religious or not, live under the influence of these dominant theological ideas. They feel disconnected from the Divine. And rationalism, which is wise and wonderful in many respects, pretty much keeps us disconnected as well. We have been trained not to perceive the magic and divinity that is all around, and within us. It's a blindness so ingrained, we're not even aware of what we're missing. But no one can deny there is an emptiness that all the fancy cars, designer clothes, alcohol, and parties just won't fill. Christianity, Judaism, and Islam teach us that faith is supposed to fill that void, but *as a Witch, you won't need "faith" in the Divine because you can actually experience the Divine.*

ENCOUNTERING THE DIVINE

The first thing you do to encounter the Divine is shift your perception, that is, alter your consciousness. Meditation is one way to clear away your mental debris, creating room for the Sacred to enter. A noisy and confused consciousness can't perceive the presence of the Divine, let alone participate in the making of magic and the cocreation of reality. As your mind becomes peaceful, your heart will begin to open, and your body and your life will become a temple in which the Divine dwells. What's more, you will come to realize that the Universe is not a machine; it's alive, and organic, and *you are the Universe's awakened self-consciousness.* Once that shift of consciousness and experience has been made, a world of endless possibilities opens to you. You can begin to make magic!

And as you open yourself up to the Sacred, you will begin to see that you *don't* have to be in an altered state of consciousness to have magical experiences and to know the Sacred is present. Everyone has magical encounters, regardless of how psychic you think you are or aren't. Unfortunately, in this cynical culture, such experiences are often scoffed at, and people don't cherish them as they should. And yet they are some of the most deeply spiritual and magical experiences you can have—like giving birth or watching your child being born, or standing on a mountaintop for the very first time, or recognizing the sacred power of human courage. Will you ever forget the sight of that one Chinese student facing down a tank?

You don't need to have a precognitive dream or hear the voice of the Goddess to have utterly magical experiences. One of my dearest friends had an epiphany one afternoon at the beach. A huge wave came up and crashed over her and her two-year-old niece. She said she never felt so maternal in her life as she did struggling underwater to hold on to the little girl. And just then, her mother-in-law, who was watching from the beach, had a premonition that my friend was pregnant. My friend has always felt that the ocean was telling her she was entering motherhood because, in fact, it turned out she *was* pregnant—and it's very likely that that was the day the egg implanted.

When you have one of these experiences, you have a powerful feeling that the Sacred is present. But it's easy to forget these magical moments and lapse back into unconsciousness instead of cultivating your awakened consciousness. The exercise that follows will help you remember that you *have* experienced the Divine.

BASIC EXERCISE: DIVINE PRESENCE

Begin with your quieting meditation. As your sense of peacefulness grows, focus on the memory of an occasion when you were aware of the presence of the Divine. What did it feel like? When did it happen? Bring the images clearly to your mind's eye— where were you? What were you doing when it happened? What did it feel like? Focus on the physical and the emotional feelings you had. Feel them again. Did you feel a tingling sensation rush through your body? Did you get "goose bumps?" Did you feel your heart race? Did you feel peaceful, serene, exhilarated? Remember the sense of presence, the joy, the awe, whatever it was that you felt. Did you begin to cry? To laugh? To sing? To pray? Allow yourself to feel as you did. Take your time. Ask the Divine, the Goddess or God, or both, to be with you and to guide you. Stay in the physical/emotional feelings, and when you are ready, say thanks.

ADVANCED EXERCISE: DIVINE PRESENCE

In my tradition, every skilled practitioner is able to experience his or her connection to deity by turning inward, or reaching outward. It's not necessary to wait for the experience of Drawing Down the Moon, or Sun, to make the connection.

I'd like you to close this book, and by whatever technique you prefer—but without relying upon a cast circle with a complete altar—just turn inward, or reach outward, and connect to divinity. Remain in that connection until you are filled with peace and joy.

Longtime practitioners know that as you cultivate your spiritual skills, your capacity to recognize divinity—to commune with it and transform yourself with its power—will grow. I have to warn you, even the smallest encounter with the Sacred has the power to transform your sense of reality, to break open the cages in which you have lived. And as you begin to experience the world in this new and genuinely magical way, it's natural to ask yourself: "Are my experiences and perceptions that the world is charged with divinity purely subjective? Is it magic or am I, well, just a little crazy?" I don't think there are any experienced practitioners out there who didn't ask themselves that question when they started. It's natural at first to discount your experiences as subjective. (Of course, psychologists say that the ability to ask that question proves that you are not crazy. So there you go—no need to worry!) But you soon receive objective validation—the dream comes true, the magic manifests, the Divine appears. And again, you don't need to experience dramatic, unexplainable things or have special psychic powers to be a skillful, sensitive Witch—for as you practice Wicca, you *will* start appreciating the divine magic in the world.

QUANTUM MAGIC

If magic's not supernatural, and it is real, why and how does it work? To some extent, because this new meaning of magic is based in the Divine, we'll probably never fully know. After all, we do call Wicca a Mystery Religion! Witches know that making magic does not defy Nature, but works in harmony with it. So, if we understand Her laws, which is the science of physics, we can make magic far more effectively. It's just that simple.

I don't think we need science to justify our spirituality, but personally, I'm much more comfortable with a religion that doesn't defy science. And the amazing fact is that science is now confirming what shamans and Witches have known for thousands of years: There is a hidden order or dimension of reality—the quantum level—and there are laws that order this reality. At its most fundamental or smallest level of organization, the Universe is a continuous energy field in which everything is interconnected. All the seemingly isolated, material objects we perceive—your body, the chair you're sitting upon, the dog that lies at your feet—appear to us to be distinct and separate objects. But it's a scientific fact that at the level of subatomic particles, which is the smallest building block of reality, they are all energy. (So much for dismissing Witchcraft, animism, or pantheism out of hand—it turns out that there *is* energy within the rocks and hills and water and air!)

And at that subatomic, quantum level, all the old rules about how things are "supposed" to work are called into question. But what's most fascinating of all, particularly for your practice of Wicca, is something called quantum superposition: According to this axiom, no particle has any particular property until you measure for it; for example, it does not have spin until you measure for spin. In fact, it doesn't become a particle until you measure it *as* a particle! (And as soon as you look at a particle, it can become a wave, and vice versa.) What seems to be happening is that all the properties of a quantum particle exist simultaneously, but at the moment of measuring, one feature emerges.

Why does this matter to magic? It seems to indicate that reality is not so easily divided between energy and matter, and that reality shifts according to your perception, participation, and expectation. It fits with our magical principle that we can alter our consciousness, and thereby alter reality. It also implies that we have a profound ability to interact with material objects—changing their very structure at the particle level. So, when a human being looks at a particle, it suddenly turns into a wave, and then back into a particle again.

There is also an observation in quantum physics that supports the Wiccan spiritual principle of interconnectedness. It's called the Einstein-Podolsky-Roisedan Paradox, which isn't really a paradox but a fascinating truth—namely, that things that are physically disconnected work in unison. A very powerful real-world example is what happens when you put separate living cells from a heart into a petri dish—they beat in the same pattern. At the quantum level what's happening is just as mind-boggling. Split a particle—say a photon of light—into two parts, creating two photons of light. Quantum theory says that when you do this the polarities of the two photons have to be opposite: If one is polarized horizontally, the other has to be polarized vertically. But remember, neither has a specific polarization until they are measured. So if you take the two photons, separate them by a billion light-years, and then measure one of them as vertical, the other will immediately become horizontal, even though it is one billion light-years away. How can this be? How could the information that the first photon is, suddenly, vertical, be passed along instantaneously to the second photon when supposedly nothing can travel faster than the speed of light? It should take a billion years for information to travel or be transmitted.*

The current thinking is that this instantaneous transmission of information happens because the particles are always entangled, or connected, in some sort of other dimension, subspace, or parallel universe, and so when measured you get instantaneous results. So here's the payoff for practicing Witchcraft—this new law of physics, explaining how reality works, supports our magical and spiritual principle that all life is in-

---

* This has actually been carried out experimentally at a fifty-mile distance of separation—it would take several nanoseconds to go that fifty miles, but in the experiments the information is "transmitted" instantaneously.

terconnected, for it literally is, at the quantum level. There are connections transcending our usual models of space and time and separation. And it is these connections that Witches and shamans work with as they make divine magic.

This law of physics also supports the idea of consciousness being able to affect the "material" world. More support comes from the many experiments that have shown that subparticles will move in the direction anticipated by the experimenter. In other words, the experimenter's expectation, his or her consciousness, affects the outcome of the experiment.

What does all this mean for you and for making magic? Just as Witches and shamans and mystics have also known, science is showing that the human mind has profound capacities to affect the outcome of events. As we've already begun to explore, the techniques that Witches use, many of them quite ancient and common to indigenous Earth religions all over the globe, literally alter your consciousness. With them, you will shift from daily survival consciousness—pick up the kids, pay the bills, don't get killed walking across the street—to an altered state of consciousness where you perceive the implicit order, the hidden reality, that exists at the level of subatomic particles.

What's more, neurophysicists, physicists, physicians, and consciousness experts are showing that by altering consciousness, shamans, mystics, and Witches can experience and more easily interact with the quantum level of reality, which core shamanism refers to as "nonordinary reality." In shamanic traditions, individuals enter into an altered state of consciousness and (among other goals) experience the ecstasy of divine communion. Fasting, prolonged chanting and dancing, drumming, using sacred substances, and other techniques enable the practitioner to enter the numinous reality that coexists with the "mundane" world. The shaman enters this reality and, by working with spirit guides and power animals, can see hidden causes of illness or ill fate, retrieve lost souls, commune with deity, and receive guidance for healing, practical matters, and spiritual change.

Some shamans enter into an altered or empowered state of being and consciousness so profound that spirits enter them, they sing or speak or act counseled by otherworld guides, and remember little upon returning. But most shamans are able to shift between aspects of consciousness quickly and easily, drumming and chanting while in an altered state, remembering precisely the divine counsel they received while in nonordinary, or sacred, reality. And most importantly, when they return to normal consciousness and the "mundane world," they are able to see the Sacred in the world in which they live. They read the signs and receive the messages and experience the magic that is everywhere around them.

Shamans live in an enchanted world that is charged with divinity, so it is easy and natural for them to attend to the presence of deity. They communicate with Nature, because they recognize that it is divinely alive, and so they learn about where to find sacred places of power, healing herbs, and food and shelter, and they receive the wise guidance of the animal and spirit world. And as you master shamanic techniques, you will apply them to your own practical concerns—discovering how to "hunt" for a job or "harvest" a healthy relationship. And most importantly, you will recognize the divine magic in your life.

REAL MAGIC

Where science leaves off, divine magic begins: As a very wise physicist remarked, it's like trying to explain music using math. And magic is the music of a Universe that is creative, conscious, and alive. Because it is organic, the Universe is unpredictable, and it has a wicked sense of humor!

People often criticize magic as irrational, as something we talk ourselves into believing. But anyone who has actually experienced magic knows that even though we can't easily explain our experiences in simple, rational terms—quantum physics is still pretty baffling even to the greatest human minds—our magic is *real*.

In fact, magic is as real as the cold, wet nose on my dog Webster, and he's experienced it also. It was the middle of summer and my husband, Bruce, and I had just adopted our Cairn terrier. That afternoon, a terrible phone call came to tell us Bruce's father had died.

I was sitting on the living-room floor with Webster as Bruce walked into the room to tell me the sad news. As I was looking at him, the air all around his upper body began to shimmer the way the horizon does during an intensely hot summer's day. And the space around him seemed to glow. Just as I noticed this, Webster began to growl. The hair on the back of his neck literally stood up as he took several steps toward Bruce. Webster stood staring, Bruce later told me, at a point just over Bruce's right shoulder.

"I can feel my father," Bruce said, a stunned look on his face. "He's here."

Although he was feeling shocked, he began to talk to his father, telling him he could feel his presence. He expressed his love and then, mentally, asked what his father wanted him to do about his mother, who was now alone and not well. He heard his father respond that he should take good care of her—that she would be with him very soon. (She died exactly one month later.) And then, Bruce told me later, he began to feel uncomfortable, wondering if what he was experiencing was real, and so he told his father that perhaps he should go visit his brother, who was grieving and could probably be comforted by his father's presence. And in the instant Bruce communicated that, he felt his father depart.

At that very moment, I saw the radiance disappear, and Webster finally sat down, relaxed. And then Bruce told us his father had left.

Any doubts I might have had about this experience disappeared when I realized that this little creature had experienced it too.

Many people who aren't even remotely interested in pursuing a spiritual practice have had similar experiences involving visitations from loved ones who've passed over. For example, a friend's mother described how a china cup "leapt" off a shelf and crashed to the floor the day after her sister, who had given her the cups, died, symbolizing the break in the family. I often suspect that overwhelming emotions such as grief open people to the magic that they are normally shut down to. While you may have yet to experience a similar event, by using Wiccan practices, discovering the signs and synchronicities in everyday life, and listening to the Sacred, you will open yourself up to them.

That said, you don't have to "believe" in the reality of magic or the

Divine to be a Witch. In fact, in Wicca, you don't have to "believe" any of the experiences that other people have, or have faith that the Goddess exists, or even that you can make magic that will manifest in your life. Wicca is not about *believing* in some invisible, transcendent deity; it's about feeling and experiencing and, therefore, *knowing* the Divine that dwells in all things. The Wiccan religion is a system of sacred, magical practices, and they work—if you work them. (Of course, I've certainly seen folks who don't practice but playact, getting all caught up in ego trips and politics—but interestingly, if they've come for the wrong reasons, or with the wrong attitude, their magic just doesn't work!)

Because the practices *do* work, you are going to encounter the Sacred and draw conclusions about reality—that it is divine, that everything is interconnected, that life is holy and to be lived with joyfulness and gratitude. And the reason that Wicca is a religion that people share is that they draw similar conclusions about divinity as a result of having similar experiences.

Wicca is also a path of personal spiritual exploration and growth. *It is a spirituality that respects the capacity of each of us to encounter the Divine.* No one else undertakes your quest for the Sacred. No prophet or saint, guru or master can replace your own direct encounter with divinity. And why would you want to leave the most extraordinary, profound, life-altering, empowering experience any human being can have to someone else?

Magic is as real as the Moon pulling the tides, and the first green shoots returning in the spring. It is as real as love—because that is what magic is made of. But you can't just passively wait for magic to happen. You must do your part. Crafting yourself as a Witch and making magic require taking responsibility for yourself and your spirituality. Take one small step at a time, and be sure to honor yourself and the Universe for each goal that you realize, each magic that manifests.

EXPERIENCING MAGIC IN A CONCRETE WAY

The sacred magic of immanent divinity is a direct, personal, and objective experience. Actively using Wiccan practices, not just thinking, or reading, or talking about them, helps you to see what is present but which you might otherwise not notice. A simple example is the house I now live in. The first time I saw it, I was looking at another house for sale. But as I looked across the creek at this lovely little house, the clouds parted, and the sun's rays fell precisely on it. I could feel my heart open and a sense of incredible happiness sweep through me.

"That's the house I want," I said to Bruce and the broker, pointing. But it wasn't for sale.

Two years had passed when a fax arrived about a house for sale. It sounded great and we quickly drove out to see it. As we turned up the road, I realized it was the house I'd fallen in love with those years before! As we turned up the driveway, I knew I was finally home.

Wicca's system of practices—our ways of making magic—enable you to take off the blindfold and see the Sacred in the world as clearly as I saw my house that day. You *know* the world is numinous and alive because you use your spiritual practices to sense it, engage in dialogue with it, listen to it, and most importantly, to learn from it—because you are awake to it! And magic, real magic, doesn't just take place in abstract or imagined realms, but right here in the midst of divine daily reality. You *know* it isn't just random coincidence that something is happening. Even though I had to wait two years for the magic to be fulfilled, that first time I saw the house I knew with complete certainty it was *my* house—and the Divine pointed me to it with that perfect ray of light.

To experience real magic, you have to understand that magic is not just extraordinary, it's divinely ordinary and anyone can experience it. The following basic practice will help you to connect to the Divine in a very visceral way.

BASIC PRACTICE
GROUNDING AND CENTERING

This is one of the most basic and powerful of all Wiccan techniques. It is the means by which we experience our connection to the divine life force that resides within the Earth. It is also a powerful way of energizing and healing yourself, or others.

Find a tree that you feel drawn to work with, one far enough from foot traffic that you won't be disturbed. Ask the tree for its help. You may do this silently—don't worry, the passers-by won't hear you, but the tree certainly will! If you don't receive a positive feeling in response to your question, find another spot. When you feel a tree's consent, sit down with your back against its trunk and close your eyes. (If you are working indoors, pick a spot with privacy where you can work undisturbed. Turn off the radio and the phone, and turn down the volume on your answering machine.)

Begin with the relaxation and meditation technique described previously, or any other method of meditation that you know works for you. Once you feel yourself relaxing, growing peaceful and still, take a long, deep breath, inhaling slowly and completely. Hold the breath for a count of three and as you do so, realize that you have just received a gift of life from the tree. Exhale slowly and completely and realize that you are giving a gift of life to the tree. Continue breathing slowly and fully, paying attention to the life flowing between you and the tree, you and all of the plants on this Earth. Feel the connection.

Now, sit up straight and feel your back becoming strong like the tree's trunk. Ask the tree to teach you what it is like to be a tree. (If you are working indoors, lean against a wall and imagine yourself sitting beneath a tree in a beautiful outdoor setting. You will need to work at the next step a bit more attentively since you'll need to penetrate carpets, floors, and foundations!)

Exhale and imagine that you are sending roots from the base of your spine down into the earth below you. *Feel* them pushing through the moist soil, sending out finer and finer tendrils into the nourishing Earth. Feel the minerals and water and life force flowing into the thousands of tiny root filaments, upwards into the base of your spine, up through your spine, and down through your muscles, your organs, your lungs. As you inhale, draw the energy of the Earth up into your body, feel it circulating through you, energizing and renewing you, healing any injuries or illnesses. You may feel tingling, or a sensation of warmth and light and energy—focus it in areas that need healing, and be sure to hold the energy in your heart.

As the Earth's power flows through you, feel branches growing from your upper torso, and from your head, feel your leaves spreading to catch the warmth of the Sun, the sweetness of the air. Feel the energy flowing through you and from you as it cascades out the top of your head and back into the Earth beneath you. Feel the circle of energy coursing through you, the energy of life empowering you. Breathe and feel the energy flow.

You will probably feel deeply energized, possibly a little light-headed, and very joyful. Let the power fill your heart, which you may literally feel opening like a flower. Hold the energy in your heart and gradually begin to withdraw your roots from the Earth. Feel them moving back up through the rich, life-generating Earth, curling neatly back into the base of your spine. Thank the Earth, and the tree, for their gifts to you.

When you are ready, slowly open your eyes. You will be dazzled by the beauty you see. You may see auras, or experience the world as particularly radiant.

It is always a good idea, especially when you begin working with these powerful energies, to ground yourself when you are done. Grounding after magic can work in either of two ways: First, if there are any excess energies running through you, you will return them to the Earth, instead of frying your circuits! Second, if you're depleted (because you've been using up your own energy), you can draw power back up to recharge yourself. To ground, simply place your hands, and forehead if you wish to, on the Earth and let the energies drain from you, or sit comfortably and bring the energies back up, holding them in your heart and belly.

If you are outside, you should leave some kind of offering as a thank you to the Earth and the tree—I like to leave birdseed, which the birds and the squirrels love!

You may wish to record your experience in your magical journal.

MAGIC AND DIVINITY

All magic flows from our connection to the Sacred, therefore all of our work must be guided by the divine nature of the energy with which we work. Because the physical world is an expression of the Divine, magic has always been used for practical purposes. But unless it is guided by the Sacred, practical magic based on the projection of will alone rapidly deteriorates

REAL MAGIC 43

into selfish ego gratification. You'll see that when magic is practiced only for this purpose it soon ceases to work, just as a car can't run on an empty gas tank. *All magic ultimately runs on your connection to the Divine.*

When you remain connected to the Divine, She will speak to you—in patterns and connections, signs and synchronicities, and all sorts of gifts. When magic rises to the surface of your awareness, and your life, you know you're blessed. It makes life a wild adventure. It's also a source of incredible strength, coming to you when you most need it—as I discovered when my father became ill.

Somehow, I had known since childhood that my father was going to die at the age of seventy. During his seventieth year, he fell and broke his hip. Because his health was already poor—too many years of smoking cigarettes, not exercising, not watching his diet—the trauma was life-threatening. Wanting desperately to help him, I journeyed for guidance. (Journeying is a shamanic technique for entering nonordinary reality; in this case, I used the common technique of listening to drumming to alter my consciousness.)

I called upon my power animals to help me, and soon found myself standing on the bow of a ship, surrounded by thick fog. Two seagulls flew out of the mist, startling me, then disappeared into the haze. I called my animals, asking for guidance, and was told that there was nothing I could do to help my father heal. It was his time to pass over.

The journey ended and I was left feeling frustrated and deeply disappointed. A few days later my mother called to tell me that she had spent the afternoon with my father. He had hallucinated that he and my mother were standing on the bridge of a ship in the midst of very heavy fog. As they were standing there, he saw two seagulls fly out of the mist toward them, and then disappear again. My father had gone to sea at the age of twelve, and until meeting my mother, had spent his life as a sailor. He was also a painter who signed all of his paintings with a seagull (his power animal, though he didn't know it consciously).

I went immediately to the hospital and spent as much time as I could with him until he passed away two days later. The journey had prepared me, in more ways than I realized at the time. Though I still grieve, the Universe showed me the reality that exists beyond the limitations of time and space and the human form.

Magic Is

Our practices are those of personal revelation and communion with the Divine, and with them you will discover that there is a divine energy within you that unites you with the divinity of the world. *Magic is everywhere.* It manifests in your life every day because of your connection to the Sacred. That connection is there for you, helping guide you, heal you, empower you, and make you wise.

Magic is not just something you do, or make. It isn't something one does *to* the Universe; magic is what a living Universe does *with* you once you have awakened to its divinity. It is the sacred dance we all share. It is joyous, it is erotic and ecstatic, and when it happens roses bloom in the December snow, butterflies fill the trees in Costa Rica, and lovers find each other across a river of time. . . . Most people know intuitively that when you fall in love, the world is full of magic. What they don't know is that when you discover the Universe is full of magic, you fall in love with the world.

And so let's explore an important Wiccan practice that will enable you to see the Divine within yourself and all around you.

Divination

Oh, to be able to see into the future! The delicious security of knowing you are making the right choice—that you should marry the man who just proposed, that your stock portfolio will guarantee your future security, that you should turn down the job offer. Seeing what lies ahead is one of the most magical blessings of divination.

Divination helps us to make practical decisions about everyday matters, such as whether to take a new job or end a relationship. It is a valuable tool for personal growth, not only because it offers you a view of the future, but because it explains the past and clarifies the present. Divination is also a rarely used yet invaluable part of spellcasting. But it is much more than just a telescope to peer into tomorrow, offering you even more startling and profound gifts.

Witches have always been skilled at the art of divination, but its most important role in the spirituality of Witchcraft is hidden within the word itself. The word "divination" comes from the Latin word *divi*, which means "deity." *Divination is the means by which you engage in dialogue with the Divine.* Communicating with deity provides proof that you are not alone, that the Universe *is* alive, and that it is aware of your presence, your longings, fears, needs, wounds, gifts, and truest self. As you craft yourself as a Witch, you will find that divination provides divine guidance when you most need it.

Divination has often been treated as a supplemental or secondary subject in the story of Witchcraft, but I want to address it right away in this book because it is one of the most accessible techniques you have to experience the reality of immanent divinity in powerful and personally meaningful ways.

One of the first ways you discover that the Divine is present, conscious, alive, and aware of you is through divination. How amazing it is to see the Universe responding to you! It boosts your confidence that you can indeed make magic. What's more, the shock and the joy you experience when the Universe engages you in dialogue is so powerful, so magical it can change your entire life.

How and why does divination work? We don't know exactly. Jung was fascinated by the I Ching as an illustration of synchronicity—the a-causal relationship that exists in the world and that expresses profound patterns of personal and spiritual meaning to those who experience them. How do they occur? Since energy and matter change form, it may be that your consciousness is translated into the form of the symbol that comes to you when you use a divination tool. Or perhaps your life is simply the translation, the symbol, of a greater consciousness—that of the Divine expressing itself in the world through you.

If the Divine is the creative force behind the Universe, it can certainly be the force animating the movement of symbols for sacred messages. It could be that, as we know, your mind has the power to affect events at the quantum level—and so, perhaps, your mind is directing the movement of matter to provide you with an answer. And there's another interesting possibility: There is apparently an organizing principle within the quantum reality that I think of as "birds of a feather"—or why some people look like their pets! This principle states that similar energies, events, and materializations seem to exist together in the field of all possibilities because of their similarities. Pythagoras described this organization of the

Universe as harmonically resonating strings of energy, and this has now become the title of the most fascinating new development in quantum physics—"String Theory." Events are not isolated, they are connected, and furthermore, they are organized so that a joyful event—like falling in love—and your joy as a response to that event, and various divinatory symbols for joy are actually all connected in the quantum field. So if you are feeling joyous when you throw a hexagram, you will throw the hexagram called "the Lake," which symbolizes joy.

❋ *Know Thyself* ❋

Written over the doorway to the temple at Delphi, the most famous center for prophecy in the Western world, was the challenge "Know Thyself." Before entering the inner sanctum to receive the priestess's vision of their future, every visitor was required to find a vision of him/herself. In order to know the future, you too have to know yourself. Self-awareness is the greatest wisdom and Wicca is, after all, the Craft of the Wise.

Divination is a magical mirror of brilliant clarity. Stare into a rune stone drawn from a bag and you are not looking at some random, alphabetical symbol from ancient Scandinavia. You are looking at an image of yourself—your hopes, fears, longings, conflicts, motivations—brought to the surface of your recognition at the very moment of consulting the oracle.

The more you work with methods of divination, particularly those such as the I Ching and runes, the more you will come to realize that the future is not fated. Divination reflects probabilities, not inevitabilities. Your current state of mind and feelings have you on a trajectory that will, most probably, lead to a particular destination. Methods of divination will show you your role in creating the future, reveal your hidden motives and emotions, and recommend right action for your best interest, but you are always free to choose which road to travel. And with divination, you can make that choice, confident you are not traveling alone but with a sacred presence that you can consult and confide in.

Like the wisdom we garnered from quantum physics—that the emo-

COMMON TOOLS FOR DIVINATION

Runes or Rune Stones

The word "rune" is derived from an early Anglo-Saxon word meaning "secret" or "mystery." Though some scholars believe their origins may be Greek-Italian, the runes are primarily an ancient Scandinavian oracular alphabet, said to have been given to the God Odin after he made the sacrifice of hanging, upside down, for nine days on the Ygdrissil tree. Each letter has a magical and prophetic meaning, a name, and sound. The most common system is comprised of twenty-four runes, and was used throughout Scandinavia, Iceland, Scotland, England, and Ireland. Today, for divination, each rune is usually marked on a stone (or other natural surface such as circular pieces of a tree branch), and then one or several are drawn from a bag, in a manner similar to drawing lots, to answer a question, and provide spiritual insight and practical guidance. A common practice is to draw three stones—the first to explain the past, the second the present, and the third the future—but the greatest gift runes provide is their insight into the dynamics of the present moment. I recommend making your own set of runes to work with.

I Ching or Book of Changes

The I Ching is a four thousand-year-old Chinese system of divination. It provides insight and guidance based on the spiritual wisdom of Nature as interpreted by Lao Tzu (a spirituality with many similarities to Wicca referred to as Taoism). Using the binary logic of yin/yang, the I Ching is most commonly worked with in the form of a book of interpretations of sixty-four different hexagrams. The hexagram is created by tossing three coins six times—or more traditionally, by tossing two-sided yarrow stalks. Each toss of the coins or stalks creates one of the six lines in the hexagram. The hexagrams are explained using a nature metaphor, such as "the Lake," which is the hexagram of joy, or "the wind over the Earth," the hexagram that symbolizes contemplation. The I Ching is a perceptive oracle for discerning the meaning of the moment, and for providing insight into the longer-term effects of these immediate emotions or actions.

Tarot Cards

These cards—which have ancient, sacred, and magical meanings— appeared for the first time in Italy and France in the fourteenth century. Originally they were used for card games as well as for divination. Now, however, they are one of the most popular divination tools. The Tarot provides psychological, spiritual, and practical insight using a symbol system composed of seventy-eight cards. The Major Arcana (twenty-two cards) includes cards like the Empress and the Wheel of Fortune, and the Minor Arcana is comprised of four suits (Disks or Pentacles, Cups, Swords, and Wands) with each suit containing four court cards (King, Queen, Knight, and Page) and ten number cards. Today, someone seeking a "reading" asks a question and shuffles the cards. Then the cards are arranged (by the seeker herself or by someone else who is reading the cards) in any one of a variety of patterns, or spreads (the most common is the Celtic Cross). The cards and their symbols are then interpreted. Tarot cards can help you discern the immediate past and its influences on the present and future, but they generally do not predict the probability of events more than six months ahead. Many Tarot decks are available today, drawn by dozens of artists. I recommend the Rider-Waite deck, which is the best known, or the Robin Wood deck, which is my favorite.

Astrology

One of the most ancient, and popular, forms of divination, astrology is based upon the position of the planets, Sun, and Moon, and the forces they represent. Your horoscope, or natal chart, shows the position of these heavenly bodies at the moment of your birth, and describes their influences on your character. An interpretation of your natal chart is not a map of destiny—it is a map of disposition, providing insight into your issues, problems, talents, and inclinations. How you work with the energies that are contributing to your personality and the events of your life is up to you.

As the Sun moves throughout the year, it takes about one month to pass through each of twelve different houses of the Zodiac (the complete circle of travel through the sky and constellations divided into twelve units). The planets and the houses each have specific elemental properties—air, fire, water, earth. And each of the twelve Zodiac signs is "ruled" by one of the planets. Astrology is a method of divination that reaches far into the future, so charts may be drawn up for all sorts of purposes—to show the influences and possibilities for an upcoming year or an event, such as a wedding or business venture. Lunar horoscopes show what forces will be in play in a given month.

Aries—March 21–April 19 (fire), ruled by Mars

Taurus—April 20–May 19 (earth), ruled by Venus

Gemini—May 20–June 20 (air), ruled by Mercury

Cancer—June 21–July 22 (water), ruled by the Moon

Leo—July 23–August 21 (fire), ruled by the Sun

Virgo—August 22–September 22 (earth), ruled by Mercury

Libra—September 23–October 22 (air), ruled by Venus

Scorpio—October 23–November 21 (water), ruled by Mars

Sagittarius—November 22–December 21 (fire), ruled by Jupiter

Capricorn—December 22–January 20 (earth), ruled by Saturn

Aquarius—January 21–February 19 (air), ruled by Uranus

Pisces—February 20–March 20 (water), ruled by Neptune

tions and expectations we bring to the experiment will affect its out-come—divination teaches us that our attitudes and emotions have an enormous impact on the lives we are living. As you learn to make magic, you come to realize that feelings aren't facts. You have the power to change them, to make the magic of changing consciousness at will, and so change events.

This was one of the greatest gifts I received from the I Ching when I was just beginning to study the magical arts. I spent an afternoon con-sulting the oracle and it taught me how to work with it to change myself. I was feeling deeply discouraged: I had just left my job, didn't know what to do, and I questioned my judgment. I was very worried and the first hexagram showed that: It reflected and described my feelings precisely, but as I meditated on its natural imagery and the wisdom of its counsel, I began to feel a little less despairing. A half an hour later, I asked "Teach me," and I drew again. This time the hexagram reflected the improvement in my perspective. I meditated on it, and when I felt myself truly embrac-ing its wisdom, I drew again, asking, "What more do I need to under-stand?" I continued throwing hexagrams, and meditating on their meanings until I could feel my emotions had shifted positively.

Divination helps you to ask the tough questions that you must face if you wish to craft yourself as a Witch: "What am I afraid of? What are the fears that are holding me back?" It will also help you to find the an-swers and face your fears, to penetrate them and to emerge on the other side with new insight, strength, and courage. Divination provides sacred counsel as you change yourself on the inside—which will change your life on the outside. Seeing yourself and really knowing who you are—what drives you, what impedes you, what makes you uniquely you—is pro-foundly empowering. You can confront your weaknesses and transform them into strengths. And you can acknowledge your gifts and transform your life with them. Then you can truly begin to make real magic and manifest what is best for you—and what is best for others. This is what used to be called the magic of alchemy—turning the dross of uncon-sciousness into the shining golden light of self-knowledge and divine in-spiration.

❋   *Consulting the Oracle*   ❋

You don't have to be psychic to work with divination. In a sense, the oracles do it for you; they provide you with "second sight." If you are "psychically nearsighted," using an oracle is like putting on a pair of glasses, or using a telescope, or even a microscope. They help you to see what you can't see without them.

So, what exactly is an oracle? Any method of divination can be an oracle. The *Oxford English Dictionary* (one of my favorite oracular devices! See the Library Angel exercise on page 57) defines an oracle as "the instrumentality or medium by which a deity makes known its will." Its root is the Latin *orare*, which means "to speak." So, by definition, *an oracle is a means by which we talk to the Divine within ourselves and in the world, and by which the Divine talks to us.*

BASIC PRACTICE
CONSULTING THE ORACLE

You can use any method of divination to see yourself. For this exercise I suggest working with a single rune stone, tarot card, or I Ching hexagram.

Begin by grounding and centering, or meditating.

Honor your method of divination by acknowledging its power to help you see clearly, and then, holding your oracle to your heart, state your purpose for consulting it. For example, *"I am seeking a clear and helpful vision of myself. What do I need to know about myself to* (fill in your intent or goal such as: be happy, or to make the decision that will bring about what is best for me, or to live a more fulfilled life, or to stop smoking, or to find the work that will give me satisfaction)?

Then consult the oracle. (Throw your I Ching coins to get a hexagram, or draw a single rune from your rune bag, or Tarot card from your deck.)

Look at the oracle and allow yourself to freely associate. Note the images and ideas that come to mind in your magical journal.

When you feel you've received as much as you can intuitively, look up the symbols in whatever book of interpretive text you prefer to use. Then meditate on the practical and spiritual meaning of the vision you have received. Allow it to move from your head into your heart. If the answer seems cryptic or confusing, you may ask for further clarification with one, but only one, additional question, such as, *"Will you please provide further clarification for me about* (and restate what you need to understand about yourself or the situation)?" Consult the oracle again, following the steps above. If you have integrated the oracle's advice, you can continue to work with it as described above.

Be sure to write down your reaction to the guidance you've been given, and the self-awareness you've gained, and thank the oracle.

You may wish to place the symbol, or a drawing of it, on your altar. You may create a personal sigil (an object with the symbol) that you can carry or keep in a place of power or visibility.

If the oracle helps you to see a personality flaw (or challenge), you may initially respond with anger or denial. Allow your defensive reaction to be, and to subside. Notice how you feel physically and emotionally. Remember, seeing your shadows, and acknowledging them, is a critical first step in integrating and transforming them. Shadows are a precise reverse image—if you see that you are frightened, comfort and reassure yourself. If you are lonely, seek companionship. If you are angry, find ways to make peace. If you have been shown a shadow side of yourself, ask the oracle what you need to understand and what you need to do to transform the negative you have been living with into what is positive and best for you.

And always remember to thank the oracle, and to follow its advice. (An oracle will cease advising if you ignore it.)

Changing yourself takes courage—it also requires you to be honest, generous, compassionate, and patient with yourself. And in learning to give yourself understanding and sympathy, you learn to give it to others. As you work with divination, and the Divine, you also begin to sense patterns of meaning and a deeper purpose in events that might otherwise seem chaotic and meaningless. You start to see your life as a journey filled with magic, because events begin to take on their real and sacred meaning. *Divination is a mirror that enables you to see your sacred self, the one who has the power to make magic.* And with the magic mirror of divination, you are now preparing the temple of yourself to receive a very important guest—the Divine.

✳ *Using Divinatory Tools* ✳

Finding methods of divination that work for you can be an exciting adventure—you should feel free to experiment and explore, and to create your own divinatory tools. By studying a variety of divinatory techniques and learning the symbols and metaphors of sacred communication, you will greatly enhance your ability to dialogue with deity.

There are so many divinatory tools available now it can be absolutely overwhelming to choose. There are Goddess cards and animal power cards, countless kinds of Tarot decks from Egyptian to Native American, I Ching coins, pendulums, rune stones, and the famous crystal ball, to name just a few. The best advice I can give for choosing your first method of divining is to follow your instincts. Literally let them guide you— spend time looking at the various divination tools, handling them, allowing them to speak to you, and you will know which one to begin using. You may be drawn to rune stones because of your Scandinavian background or because you respond to the tactile quality of the stones, or you may want to work with Tarot cards because you have been deeply affected by a Tarot reading in the past. You may start with a method, and then find it just doesn't work for you—it feels dull or flat when you use it. You'll know that the system is working for you if you enjoy using it, are interested in learning about it, find your communication with it meaningful, and feel the energy flowing. Once you are comfortably working with a system, images and impressions will begin to appear in your mind.

ADVANCED PRACTICE
SCRYING

Scrying, which involves staring into a shiny surface until a vision appears, is an ancient method of divination of unknown origin, but it has long been associated with Witches. It is not an easy method of divination to use, and many give up in frustration. Scrying comes from the English word "descry," which means "to make out dimly" or "to reveal." It is a method of "seeing" the unseen, whether that is the future, past, or hidden aspects of the present. The very best time to scry is at night during the dark of the Moon, and at Samhain, when the veil between the worlds is the thinnest.

The most common object used for scrying is the crystal ball, but the Egyptians used ink and other dark liquids in a bowl, and the Romans used mirrors and shiny stones. You can use a dark bowl filled with water (preferably charged by moonlight), or a mirror that has been painted black on its back surface. These will work as well as a crystal ball, and will cost far less!

Your scrying tool should be used in a darkened room that has a small amount of illumination, such as a candle positioned so that it will not reflect into the surface of the water or mirror. If you are working with a crystal ball, be sure to place it on a black, nonreflective surface. You may cast a circle if you wish, then use your meditation to clear your mind. Do not visualize! Allow your mind to remain open and clear of images as you focus on the scrying surface. You may have a question or purpose in your mind, however.

As you stare at the scrying tool, it's all right to blink. The surface should appear to cloud or become misty, and then clear. When the fog disperses, there should be an image in the scrying surface—it may be still or moving, black and white or in color. It may be realistic or symbolic. It may last for a moment, or longer. It may require interpretation or be clear in its meaning. Or it may not appear at all.

Give yourself about fifteen minutes and if nothing appears, thank your scrying surface, and rest. You can try again another time.

Do not expose your scrying surfaces to the Sun, and charge it once a month, or as needed, under the light of a full Moon. Do not use salt to clean and purify a crystal ball or scrying mirror as the salt will pock the surface. Instead, use a bath of warm water and mugwort. Keep your scrying tool wrapped in black silk, out of the Sun's light, and be sure to purify and consecrate it when you first work with it.

ADDRESSING THE DIVINE

As with all magical work, the attitude with which you approach divination will affect the experiences you have. Always choose a quiet place to work, and empty your mind of distractions. I like to begin all divinatory work with an acknowledgment of the Divine in divination, and I suggest you create a similar practice for yourself.

Step 1: Request respectfully that the sacred Presence(s) join you. For example, you could say, "*Great Goddess who dwells in all things, please bless this divination.*"

Step 2: State your purpose, such as, "*I ask your guidance, your wisdom and inspiration.*" If you are working on behalf of someone else who has come to you for assistance, you may wish to add: "*Grant me clarity to present your message for*———(state the person's

WORKING WITH YOUR TOOLS

You should establish a personal bond with the tools of your divinatory art. Begin by purifying and consecrating them (see page 232 in Chapter 9, Potions, Notions, and Tools). Then sleep with them beneath your pillow or beside your bed for at least one full lunar cycle. This gives them the opportunity to tune into your psychic energy field, which is highly activated and uninhibited by conscious thought while you are in the dream state. When you do this there is also, on the quantum level, a mutual exchange of information, symbols, and teaching between you and the divinatory tools. And soon you will find yourself dreaming about the symbols. A friend of mine dreamed of the XX rune stone, which means the Goddess or the womb, and is the secret sign for a covenstead and the home of a Witch. She had placed this stone under her pillow and had also used it in her spells to find her new home, which would be the home for her coven. The day after the dream in which the rune stone appeared to her, she found the home she wanted!

name) *so that s/he will be aided for her/his greatest blessing.*"

In this way you've addressed the three important points of focus: a request for *divine guidance, clarity* in receiving the guidance, and *the recipient's greatest good.*

Step 3: Express aloud your feelings of reverence, respect, and appreciation, such as: "*My heart is open to your counsel. Thank you for your presence.*" Speaking this request out loud will immediately begin to alter your consciousness, particularly if you do divinatory work on a regular basis. It also charges the hearer, and the space, with sacred purpose.

Step 4: When you complete your divinatory inquiry, take up the tool, once again hold it to your heart, and thank it. You should say, out loud, something like, "*I thank you for your insight and inspiration, your wisdom, and guidance. I honor the gift you have given me.*"

ASKING YOUR QUESTION

In divination, to get the right answer you've got to ask the right question. Often I break my query into two parts. First I ask: "*Which way should I proceed in this situation that will provide for my greatest good and happiness?*" And then I ask, "*What frame of mind or understanding should I have in order to achieve my greatest good and happiness?*"

The following exercise is a fun and easy way to practice the art of centering one's self, framing a question, and consulting your oracle.

BASIC TO ADVANCED PRACTICE
THE LIBRARY ANGEL

I've consulted the "library angel" at home, in libraries all over the world, in bookstores, and with friends' books for many years. I suggest you begin at home next to your own bookshelf, where you'll have the most privacy.

Begin by relaxing, and then quieting your mind. Focus on your intent and address the magical portals into divine wisdom that are before you by acknowledging their power and their role, for example: *"I invite the numinous spirit that resides within these volumes to guide my hand, and my inquiry. Please help me find wisdom."*

Close your eyes. Allow your hand to move freely back and forth, up and down in front of the books. Allow your hand to move freely, while keeping your eyes closed. When the moment is right, you will feel a gentle pull toward the bookcase. You may feel a sudden sense of certainty as your hand is guided to the volume you are meant to work with. Pull it from the shelf. Hold it to your heart and say: *"I acknowledge you as my guide."*

Now recite your question aloud.

Allow the book to open in your hands. Open your eyes and let them light upon the page. Read what is before you.

It may take time to meditate upon the answer you have received, or the message may be absolutely clear immediately. You may ask for clarification if you need to, but don't ask the same question twice.

Write down the passage you received and even if it does not seem immediately meaningful, let it evoke feelings. And end the divination by giving thanks to the book, the library angel, and the Divine for their assistance.

ASKING FOR CLARIFICATION

An old rule of divination says you should not ask the same question twice. There's always a temptation to ask again because you want a different answer, or because you really don't want to confront what the oracle has shown you and examine yourself and the road you're on. You may, however, ask for clarification to help you to understand and work with the oracle's advice.

Of course, it's important not to become a divination junkie, relying on the oracle to guide your every decision, but I've found that these ancient tools are wise counselors who resist the pokings and proddings of impatient young students who want constant reassurance and guidance. The I Ching even has a hexagram that basically says: "Go away, you've asked that question already and I've given you your answer." Gotta love it!

Remember, you can't have the adventures that come from getting lost if you're always checking the road map!

SYMBOLS AND INTERPRETATION

Beginning to work with any system of divination is like traveling in a foreign country: You'll need to learn the language in order to communicate effectively. Symbols, as Jung pointed out, are the vocabulary the Divine uses to communicate with us—just as your subconscious speaks to you in dreams with images and symbols. In fact, many consciousness experts say that the Divine dwells in the realm of your subconscious. Symbols allow the communication to go both ways—from the Divine to you and from you to the Divine—so Witches use symbols and tools in magical rituals to help them to communicate with the Sacred. And symbols and tools remind you not to think or analyze too much but instead to use your intuition in interpreting signs and messages.

At first, if you use a method like the I Ching, the Tarot, or runes, you're going to constantly refer to books to help you interpret what the oracle says. Each method of divination has its own unique vocabulary of symbols and metaphors, its own set of meanings. Each Tarot card has a myriad of meanings, and more depending upon its placement in a spread of cards, and still more depending upon the cards that surround it. And if the card is turned upside down it has an entirely opposite or different significance! In addition to traditional interpretations, the pictures themselves can and will trigger all sorts of images and impressions that you should pay attention to. With practice, you'll begin to develop your own set of interpretations. But when you start, it can be absolutely overwhelming to stare at a sea of unfamiliar pictures.

One way around this problem is to use a simpler divinatory method—a rock that has "no" painted on one side and "yes" on the other, or a pendulum that swings one way for "yes," another for "no." Simple yes/no systems are a wonderful way to begin your communication with the Divine.

However, when you are working with a system filled with nuance and intricacy, like Tarot cards or astrology, you should consult a book to help you interpret them. Personally I prefer to work with one book, usually the one written by the creator of the system. Once you have mastered the creator's interpretation, you can add the perspectives of others.

One of the best ways to master the vocabulary of a divination system is to work with it every day. You don't need to do an entire spread of Tarot cards, or throw the I Ching six times. Start by simply picking one symbol to be your message of the day. Adept practitioners who have long ago memorized the symbols often use this method as a daily magical practice, so it is more than just a beginner's exercise.

BASIC TO ADVANCED DAILY EXERCISE: TODAY'S ORACLE

First, take a moment to relax, breathe, and shift your focus to receiving your divine message. Quiet your mind, and open yourself.

Hold the oracle—the deck of cards, bag of runes, I Ching coins, a book that interprets divination symbols, or whatever method you have chosen—to your heart. Acknowledge the oracle as your teacher, ask for its guidance, and thank it for its help. Affirming its power literally changes the energetic field between you and the divinatory tool.

Ask your question. It can be as simple as "What do I need to know to have the best day possible?"

Now, reach into the bag and pull a rune, or into the deck to pull a card, or allow the pages of the book to fall open to a particular hexagram or symbol.

Read the interpretation of the symbol. Take a moment to reflect on its meaning to you—and how the symbol answers your question. If you have time, you should draw the symbol on a piece of paper, or write down what it is-——such as "the Empress," and write down key words that interpret the symbol's meaning.

Take the drawing of the symbol and the key interpretive words with you into the world. Keep it in a place where you can see it so you can refer to it during the day. Then, at the end of the day, enter your question, the symbol, its meaning, and any reflections or significant experiences you had during the day into your magical journal. You may also wish to repeat this exercise at the end of the day, asking for guidance in understanding the day's events.

Don't forget that your intuitive impressions, not just the literal image or interpretation of a divinatory image, are a critical part of understanding the real meaning of the message. Working regularly with divination as part of your spiritual practice, you'll be amazed at how quickly you master a symbol system, how much guidance you receive, how much better each day goes, and how sensitized you will become to the presence of the Sacred in your daily life. As you memorize and integrate the symbols into your field of heightened awareness, you will discover that symbols increasingly work in a new and wonderful way—appearing just when you need them, in unexpected places and at unexpected times.

From the very beginning of my Wiccan odyssey, I've been accompanied by the energy of Dionysus. For me, this energy was captured by the actor James Dean, by the poet/singer Jim Morrison, and musician Bruce Springsteen. Whether it's a movie, or a song, or a reference, they pop up in my life at very big moments, in very big ways: As I was writing *this* section, the phone rang and it was my friend Patricia Kennealy Morrison—Jim's wife—calling to figure out when we were going to celebrate finishing my book. She also mentioned that when I visit the publisher, whose office is right in the middle of Times Square, to deliver it tomorrow, I'm going to find two enormous billboards: one of James Dean, and the other of the Boss. I couldn't have a bigger or more magical reminder to really enjoy and celebrate—something I don't give myself enough of, since I'm always looking to the next responsibility.

Whenever you consult an oracle, be sure to write down your question and the answer you received in your divination journal or magical diary. I have found many divinations that did not make sense when first given had the most profound meaning months or even years later. In fact, some of the most significant messages are those that arc far forward into our destiny. It may even take years before the message's full meaning is made clear to you. A combination of an I Ching reading and a dream I had fifteen years ago only recently manifested: In the dream, I saw a symbol, somewhat like an elaborate Y, written on a blackboard in front of me. A white line cut through the symbol so that half was above, and half below. When I woke up, I threw a hexagram and was told it meant a journey leading to rebirth. But what did that mean? Nothing, I thought at the time. In fact, I was beginning to develop symptoms, though I didn't realize it, of a parasitical infection that lasted many years, and that almost killed me. Years later, after the diagnosis had finally been made and I was healthy again, I was stunned to find the symbol—a Chinese figure representing rebirth— in a book on Taoism. I finally realized the meaning of the long-ago signs, patiently waiting for me to find them in my magical journal!

It's important to honor your tools for sacred communication and the messages they give you. An oracle will cease advising you if you ignore its advice. You may want to further honor the oracle by creating a work of art—ritual tools, an altar, sacred songs and poetry, or invocations and decorations that include the symbol. I was recently at a book party for a dear friend and was dazzled by a magnificently colored coat of embroidered and appliqued magical symbols and images from Tarot cards worn by a woman who is a Tarot designer—the coat was filled with images of profound personal meaning for her. Much of shamanic art—masks and rattles, statues and robes—is based upon the guidance received from divination. Whenever I see these magical creations, I am awestruck by the sense of spiritual presence that radiates from them.

CARING FOR YOUR DIVINATORY TOOLS

Whatever divinatory tools you choose to work with—runes, Tarot cards, books, etc. —they are the embodiment of divine energy. They are a sacred voice, so you should treat them with respect. I was taught to wrap my Tarot cards in silk, and over the years I have also developed a beautiful collection of carved boxes to keep them in. I have a deck I use for reading other people, and I periodically purify and cleanse that deck. A dear friend of mine who reads cards professionally has more than a dozen decks, which people may choose from for their readings. Some people keep their divination tools on their altars, or in a chest with other magical tools.

But while the divinatory messenger is something you will treasure, what is most precious is the divine spirit animating the messenger. You don't need an original Tang dynasty set of I Ching coins for the divination to work. The Divine will work with whatever is at hand if you are open to receiving its message.

As you master one method of divination, start exploring others. You will be cultivating an extraordinary vocabulary with which to engage in your dialogue with the Divine.

❋ *Other Forms of Divination* ❋

A vision in a dream, the cry of a crow, a sudden rush of wind that rustles the leaves—the Divine speaks to us through countless signs that accompany daily life. These signs offer guidance and a glimpse of the future, healing and consolation, understanding and direction, and most importantly, proof of divine presence. But with rare exception, we do not recognize these magical messages. At night, the Moon rises and the crickets call, and each of us enters the enchanted realm of dreams. But as the Sun rises, we are blinded by the rational, analytical, goal-directed thinking that our culture treasures above all other ways of knowing.

Yet the world is alive with holy wisdom, and there are countless ways to seek and to be given the guidance of that universal intelligence. Cultivate the ancient and accessible art of divination that opens all of your senses, including your "sixth sense," to the Sacred and you will tap into tremendous power when you make magic.

There are countless kinds of divination beyond those available from your local Wiccan or New Age store. Dreams, trance, and other altered states, oracular wisdom, interpretations of natural signs, augury, astrology, the guidance of spirits and *genius loci* (the spirits or soul of a place), numerology, animal guidance, drawing of lots—thousands of means have been discovered and devised in every culture and every century. It's impossible to do them all justice in this chapter, but here are a few that are as easy and natural to use as any of your five senses.

DREAMS

Each night we step into the sacred cave of dreams where the Numinous rules. Symbols come to life, counsel is given, and visions are granted. Some dreams can show us the road to take by giving us signs to watch for—my introduction to Wicca came in the form of the Libyan Sibyl who appeared repeatedly in my dreams. Other dreams open a window into the deepest part of ourselves. A friend of mine regularly dreams about the house she grew up in, and when she does she is careful to remember it because she knows it is a dream about herself. And sometimes we are blessed with the gift of a prophetic dream of events that come true.

A practice for receiving a dream that provides a vision or sign of the future, or contains information that is healing or transformative, is called incubating a dream. It is one of the most ancient practices of divination, and was widely used throughout ancient Greece and Rome. Temples were created where people would go to seek sacred dreams. "Incubate" comes from the Latin *incubare*, which meant "to sleep in the sacred precinct." Another ideal place to have a sacred dream is in the wilderness, where you will be aided by the spirits of the land. But you can certainly seek such a dream right in your own bed. It's best to sleep alone when you are seeking a divination dream so that you can sleep undisturbed, physically and psychically.

BASIC TO ADVANCED PRACTICE
INCUBATING A DREAM

Begin by taking a purification bath and then head straight to bed immediately afterwards. You may wish to drink a cup of mugwort tea (three tablespoons steeped for five minutes in a cup of boiling water) because the herb mugwort enhances psychic dreaming. Scatter mugwort under your pillowcase, or place some in a dish by your bedside. Also, place your magical journal by your bedside, with a pen.

Acknowledge your dream as a state of empowered being. Ask, aloud, to be given a dream of insight, or prophecy, or healing. Then climb into bed and turn out the lights. Use your relaxation techniques to ease any tensions and allow yourself to drift off to sleep.

In the morning, before you get out of bed and before you do anything else, write down whatever you dreamed. As you are writing, the dream may begin to evaporate, though big dreams have a way of remaining vivid for many years. You may awaken with only a faint memory, or scattered images—write down whatever you recall. As you write, details may return. Be sure to note how you felt in the dream, and how you felt upon waking. Note any objects, symbols, advice, or other information.

Some dreams may be extremely vivid, and you may feel as if you are awake in the dream. You may awaken with strong and clear images, and a coherent sense of what they mean. Then again, even if the vision was powerful and vivid, you may not know its meaning right away. However, these dreams don't happen every night—once or twice a year is remarkable! And it may take time for you to cultivate the ability to have lucid (meaning you're aware in the dream) or prophetic dreams. Paying attention to your normal, nightly dreams by writing down whatever you remember *before* getting out of bed will help you. As with other divination techniques, the more you practice, the better you'll get.

CLEDONS

One of the most ancient forms of divine guidance is called a cledon. A cledon is a voice in the crowd. They are words or phrases seemingly heard at random or out of context, spoken by a stranger or passerby, but their precise timing delivers a message of profound personal meaning to the hearer. In the modern world we are likely to hear cledons coming from a radio as we are walking down the street, or see them on a television screen as we channel surf, or even read them on a billboard or bus ad. There's a cledon story about John Lennon that I find very moving. In December 1980, right after John had been shot, a man ridiculed the grieving kids at the Dakota, ending his diatribe with "I fought the war for your sort!" —a line from *A Hard Day's Night*, obviously unbeknownst to him. The crowd, recognizing their cue, spontaneously shouted in unison John Lennon's comeback from the movie: "Bet you're sorry you won!" The man, shocked, muttered and walked away and the kids found themselves laughing, certain that this was John's way of cheering them up.

Cledons are one of my favorite methods of divinatory guidance because they catch me by surprise, often make me laugh, and always make me marvel at the ingenuity and genius of the universal consciousness. You can't really create a cledon, or practice a cledon, as you would practice other forms of divination. It is, by its very nature, spontaneous. But we can pay attention so we don't miss them!

FAMILIARS AND ANIMAL ORACLES

Animals as spirit guides direct and counsel a shaman while s/he is in nonordinary reality, and they watch over and guide us in the "mundane" world. They see and sense things that we cannot, but if we honor them, and ask them, animals can show us how to live connected to the web of life. Those interconnections are where magic is to be found.

Witches have always had animal guides—most famous, of course, is the Witch's familiar, which acts as a spiritual aide and as messenger between you and the Sacred. People always think of a familiar as a cat (cats are renowned for their sensitivity to human emotions), but a familiar can be any animal with whom you develop a deep and intimate bond. I've learned many things from my terrier, Webster, who is my familiar. In fact, he helped me receive a powerful lesson just moments ago, motivating me to add this section about animals, who are an overlooked tool of divination.

As I was working, Webster, who was outside, sat staring at me through the glass door, urging me to come out for our customary walk at dusk, but I ignored him because I had too much work to do. But he would not be ignored! He scratched at the door and moaned until I relented. Annoyed and frustrated at being distracted from my responsibilities, I opened the door, urging him to come in. He darted away, looking back over his shoulder, so I wrapped my sweater around myself and stepped into the freezing cold. He shot down the path and grumpily I followed him, but instead of the walk he usually led me on, he stood dead still in the middle of the sloping front lawn.

"What's up?" I asked him, and then I heard what he wanted me to experience—from far away, almost imperceptibly, the sound of geese. Suddenly, there were hundreds and hundreds of geese, more than I'd ever seen at one time. They flew right over the house in dozens of elongated Vs, some of them so low I could hear their wings beating. I was stunned and breathless from the percussive rush of wind they created, and the sound was so mysterious and powerful—it was a visitation by the ancient powers of air. My mind was clear, my energy renewed, and the inspiration they brought me carried me lightly back into writing with a sense of complete joy and gratitude. Webster was paying attention and he knew a message was on its way.

Your pets have a strong ability to pick up your thoughts and feelings, and to guide you to important lessons. Animals live guided by their instincts and if you let them, they can teach you how to retrieve and trust yours. Your instincts are one of your most organic methods of divination.

BASIC TO ADVANCED PRACTICE
LEARNING MAGIC FROM YOUR FAMILIAR

The best way to learn from your pet is to just start spending time everyday with her/him, treating your pet as an equal, following her/his lead, paying attention to what she/he pays attention to. If your animal is accustomed to being indoors, spend time observing her or him, just watching. If she/he sits, you sit, if she/he looks out the window, you look out the window.

Observe the world through your animal's eyes. What does she/he see, hear, react to? How does she/he react? Let your pet teach you. What you'll begin to see are expressions of divinity—and magic.

Express your love and appreciation to your pet. Do it out loud, then silently. Your animal can hear you and can transmit images and ideas to you telepathically. Remain quiet and pay attention.

As you and your animal become increasingly attuned to each other, your consciousness and your ground of being, and that of your animal companion, will increasingly merge and you will be able to communicate more and more effortlessly with each other. Often, you'll find your animal companion will have skills and wisdom superior to yours, which will be invaluable to you. Make sure you take his or her advice, and express your gratitude and love.

BECOMING THE ORACLE YOURSELF

Divination triggers your innate intuitive abilities. Even folks who don't consider themselves psychic find that working with divination seems to increase their psychic sensitivity. As you work, it's important to embrace the images, emotions, and associations that enter your mind or the sensations that come to your body. Recently I met a young Finnish woman who comes from a family of shamans who can tell when someone in the family is ill or dying because their teeth ache. And I'll never forget how mysteriously ill I became as Chernobyl occurred, before we had any news of it. (See page 263 in Chapter 11, Solitary Practice, for exercises to help you cultivate your intuition.)

As you work with methods of divination, you will find that *you* are increasingly *becoming* the oracle, the speaker, or interpreter of divine meaning. You will read the signs and receive the messages that are everywhere around you because you live in a world that is numinously alive. You will also realize that divination is not just a method of communication, it's also one of communion. Like the Priestesses who served as the Oracles of Delphi, and the countless village shamans, you, as a practicing Witch, will become a voice of the Sacred. Learning to trust the holy voice within takes time, and as this wonderful change occurs, there is another source you can always turn to if you need to connect with the Divine: Nature.

Nature

Dancing wildly around a huge bonfire as thousands of sparks shoot into the star-filled sky above, or sitting silently beneath a brilliant full Moon, or floating weightless in a warm, salty ocean, or drumming deep within a dark and mysterious cave—any one of these magical experiences can change your life forever. While divination helps us to find the Divine within ourselves, and at play in our lives, getting in touch with Nature is a powerful way to connect to the Sacred in the world around us. It's a vital force in crafting yourself as a Witch, and for making magic.

A PHYSICAL CONNECTION WITH DIVINITY

Nature is the embodiment of divinity. Indigenous peoples lived close to the land and therefore knew the natural world was holy. If you're like me, you live much of your life largely separated from Nature, and so you and I must work harder to reestablish this sacred and magical relationship. But the rewards are well worth the effort.

One of the old definitions of a Witch was someone who worked with hidden or unseen forces. In a sense that's true—you can't see subatomic particles, nor can you see the waves of energy at the heart of those particles. But you *do* see the material expression of that energy. Just as seeing someone smile is seeing the outer or physical expression of her/his inner emotional (or energetic) life, when you see the Earth in all of its perfect and balanced beauty, you are looking at the outer expression of an inner divinity.

In fact, I have a new definition of a Witch: A Witch is someone who is paying attention, who is aware of the Divine Presence in all things. And if you are seeking the Sacred, you will find it by immersing yourself in Nature.

Nature makes the Divine tangible. Nature is the gown the Goddess wears to make herself visible, and the dance the God dances to express his joy. Looking at Nature, we see living, incarnate divinity.

Yet so much of our magic is made indoors—in our houses, our apartments, and in our imaginations on transcendental or akashic planes. We visualize being in a spring meadow, or sitting beneath a towering oak, or circling in a sacred forest glade. We imagine traveling to power places on the astral plane. Much of this mental work is an inheritance from our ceremonial forebears, whose magic was deeply influenced by biblical theology and patriarchal culture. Though they were certainly amongst their culture's avant-garde, and strongly influenced by the Romantic era that embraced Nature, they were also products of their own Victorian culture where the desires of the body were largely suppressed and denied, and they confined most of their magic to the head.

The common approach to Witchcraft, and to making magic, is to imagine the air, the water, the Sun, the Earth. But magic can't just be imagined—it has to be felt, and lived, and embodied. You don't need to *imagine* divinity when you are standing in the midst of a redwood forest, or diving with ancient tortoises near the Great Barrier Reef, or helping to harvest a field of golden corn, or dancing naked beneath a full Moon. You can *feel* it with every fiber of your being. And so, whenever possible, you should perform your magic and your rituals and the exercises and practices in this book outdoors—cast a circle under the Moon's light, ground and center in a forest clearing, purify in the sea.

We make the best magic in Nature because Nature makes the best magic. Nature *is* magic, because it is the body of the Divine. And Nature's magic doesn't have to be imagined, it just has to be experienced.

I'll never forget one of my earliest lessons on getting out of my head and into Nature. It was March, just a few days before the Spring Equinox, and I decided to do some spring cleaning—with magic. I cleaned out my closets and scrubbed my apartment until it shone. I even did my taxes! I took sage and salt water and moved widdershins (counterclockwise—the direction of banishing) all around the edge of the apartment. I opened the windows and the front door and I swept out all the stale energy of winter.

But there were still some cobwebs—in me! So, I got in my car and drove to one of my favorite natural spots, the Delaware Water Gap. I hiked into the still-barren woods, astonished at how soft and soggy the land was. Every time I saw a tiny shoot of green poking through the ground I felt happier and more optimistic. The snows had melted and the runoff from the ridges had filled the streams with rushing water. My plan was to wash my hair under a tiny waterfall in one of the streams I often visited.

The air was crisp and exhilarating as I scrambled along the bank of the stream. I carefully worked my way up to a small "waterfall" about eighteen inches wide. The sound of the water was wonderful and hypnotic as I stared into the tumbling cascade. I took off my coat, pulled off my sweater, and carefully leaned forward, sticking my head into the water. I was stunned: The water was freezing cold and hit me with the force of a sledgehammer! I gasped for breath as it ripped all thought, all worry, all intention from my mind. I pulled myself from the stream, grabbing for my towel and collapsing against the damp Earth. I have never in my life been so utterly, ecstatically clear.

It sure beat politely dipping my fingers in a dainty bowl of salt water back in my newly cleaned apartment. Nature knows how to make magic, and She's more than willing to teach us.

How Nature Crafts Her Witches

Because it is the embodiment of the Divine, Nature is our greatest spiritual teacher. When the student is ready, the teacher will appear. Practitioners of Earth religions, such as modern Witchcraft, are students of Nature's wisdom, and your teacher—Nature—is always available. Though we may not have ancient books of wisdom, or an unbroken line of traditions, we have the same teacher that our forebears learned from. And even if all you have is a small city park to walk in, or a plant on your windowsill, Nature is present, if you'll just pay attention. What will it teach you?

The answer depends upon how you approach being taught. What mind-set, emotional framework, and posture will you take? The old relationship of imposing our will on Nature, whether with magic or technology, doesn't serve anyone; in fact, it only separates us from Nature, and from the Divine. Most of our problems come from this separation, for to be cut off from Nature is to be cut off from divinity. Just as we need the Earth in order to live physically—for food, air, water, and countless other blessings—we need the Earth if we are to live spiritually.

Physics has taught us that what you bring to the experiment affects the outcome. So when you approach Nature as your spiritual teacher, you need to be open, receptive, attentive, respectful, and grateful. This is the "right relationship" Native Americans and Buddhists refer to—it is based on attentiveness to the divinity of Nature, respect, and gratitude.

Below is an innovative magical practice that is not just for beginners, but is especially for veteran practitioners who have mastered the arts of changing consciousness at will with mental skills. This is a practice that will ground your magic in your body and the Earth, and greatly enhance your experience and your results wherever you work, indoors or out.

BASIC TO ADVANCED EXERCISE:
SENSITIVITY TRAINING

We're a very busy culture, and making a quick transition to a meditative state in a natural environment is not always easy. Physical activity—such as hiking, working in your garden, or cleaning up the natural area you are going to work in—can help you relax and focus. It will also help you reap the magic that paying attention provides. You may wish to tape this exercise to listen to it.

After you have done some moderate, comfortable physical exercise, such as walking or stretching, find an attractive, natural setting that appeals to you. It can be your backyard, a local park, a wilderness trail, or other outdoor location. Find a "power spot" —a place that gives you a positive feeling, or where you receive a visible sign, such as an animal appearing and not being disturbed by your presence. Ask the spot's permission to work with it. It's good to pick a place that you can come back to because each time you work with it, the place will become more powerful for you, and you in turn will contribute to its well-being.

How long you practice the exercise is up to you—it depends on your attention span and your feelings as you remain in the spot, but ten minutes is a good length of time. The goal is to isolate one of your senses, and then to concentrate on it, paying attention to your experience of the natural environment you have chosen.

Sit down, close your eyes, breathe deeply, and clear your mind of wandering thoughts. Now bring your attention back to your body. Notice how you are feeling—are you cold, hot, uncomfortable sitting on the ground? And now bring your attention to one of your senses and what it is experiencing.

Begin by listening to the sounds carried by the air. Remain still and really listen. What do you hear? Are you hearing distracting sounds such as traffic, machinery, airplanes, or the voices of other people? I live in the country, but there is almost always a background hum of human sounds, even late at night. You may have difficulty finding a place that is free from noise pollution, but we can even learn from that.

If there is indeed a background hum of humanity, listen to that first. Notice what the sounds are, where they come from, and most importantly, how they make you feel. Now open your eyes and look around you. Enjoy the beauty of the spot.

When you feel ready, close your eyes again, and this time focus on the natural sounds of the setting you have chosen. Let go of any distracting noise pollution, just as you learned to let distracting thoughts float by when you meditate. Focus on the natural sounds, and keep your eyes closed while you listen carefully.

What do you hear? A bird? Several birds? A flock? Where are they? Are they talking to each other, as crows do? Are they singing? How do their songs make you feel? Do you hear the wind blowing, leaves rustling, trees whispering? Do you hear dogs barking? Do you hear insects, bees, frogs? Are you hearing sounds you never noticed before? How do you feel?

Listen to the silence between sounds.

If your mind starts to wander, you can return to being present in the moment by again focusing on the sounds of Nature. When you're ready, open your eyes. See if you can spot the sources of your sounds. Do you know what made the sounds? How does listening to Nature make you feel? You may wish to write down how you felt and what you experienced in your magical journal.

Try to return to this spot at different times of the day, and night (if it is safe to do so), and during different seasons. Pay attention to the differences in what you hear, and feel.

In the future, when you return to this spot, or repeat this exercise of attentive listening, you may hear a song or poem within you. When you do this exercise again, you may wish to begin by singing or reciting your inspiration.

Be sure to thank the place, and your companions.

The Sensitivity Training exercise can, and should, be used to develop your other senses as well. For sight, notice all the details you can; for smell, concentrate on what you smell, etc. Try this exercise again at a different time of day, or in a different season and notice what changes.

As you learn to focus your attention, your senses—sight, sound, taste, touch, smell, intuition, and other natural senses that we have all neglected, living in an overcivilized world—will become keener and more sensitive. By paying careful attention to our teacher, Nature, you are beginning to attune yourself to Her rhythm, to the sacred wisdom in Her flow of energy. She is crafting you as a Witch. It's so delightful to live in a magical world! As I am writing this, I hear an unfamiliar bird in the still, winter afternoon air. I just opened my door to see two wood-peckers exploring one of the weeping birch trees in the front yard. They are rare and wonderful visitors—so I send you their greetings and en-couragement!

❋ *The Enchanted World* ❋

Spending time outdoors is important for the spiritual rhythm of your life. The animals, the plants, and the Earth itself are all voices of the Divine that will sing to you; indeed, the word "enchantment" means "to sing over." The world is an enchanted place. It's time to rediscover it.

As I said before, when we are cut off from Nature, we are cut off from divinity. So, set aside some time at least once a week, preferably once a day, to spend outside in your backyard, a local park, or the beach or coun-tryside, preferably in your place of power. What do you see around you that gives you pleasure, a feeling of well-being and connection? What do you see, smell, hear, touch, intuit?

You should also make a point of learning about the natural environ-ment of the place where you live. You can begin at the library, the local col-lege, or even online. Learn about the local indigenous plants, animals, and insects. Find out what native peoples once lived in the area, how they lived, and whether they fished, hunted, or farmed. Everyone comments upon the wonderful, healing, recuperative energies of my little country house, so I was not surprised to learn that it had been the site where long ago the native tribe had not only hauled in their oyster catch, but celebrated their harvests from the sea. Learning that wonderful fact also explained why I kept finding so many oyster shells in the deep soil of my garden!

Study the geology of the land, or the healing properties of the indigenous plants. And if you can, try to find the history of the spirits of the place in which you live. All places have spirits. The Greeks called them *genius loci*, and they are your allies in making magic in Nature. Watch for them, bring offerings to them, and thank them for showing themselves to you.

I'll never forget one of the most magical meetings I've ever had with a spirit of place—I was walking in the winter woods of a beautiful state forest with my fiancé. We were up to our knees in snow and it was slow going but incredibly exhilarating. Suddenly, I felt the oddest sensation, as if something on the side of the path were tugging at me. I turned and saw a very small oak tree with huge brown leaves waving in the wind. As I stared at it, I felt this incredible charge of energy coming from the little tree to me. I asked my fiancé, a professional photographer, to photograph the tree for me. I spent the rest of the day feeling happier and more blessed than I could remember. Later when the film was developed, we were astonished to see a shining arc of light coming from the tree to me! A careful examination of the print and the negative proved that it wasn't a result of damage or anything in the developing process but was in the photo itself. I had met a *genius loci*!

There are many of these spirits of the Earth, including the Green Man, and in a sense the greatest of them is the Great Mother Earth Goddess, who gives life to all of Her children. You will meet them as your familiarity with Nature grows, and you'll find your appreciation, joyfulness, and sense of reverence growing as well.

BASIC EXERCISE:
MAKING MAGIC WITH AN OFFERING

One of the finest offerings is to help clean up a park, or to create a garden. Getting active with your local green community is another wonderful way to learn from Nature, and to give something back. Get your hands in the dirt, even if it's just a flower-pot on your windowsill. You're making magic by participating in, and contributing to, the natural flow of energy. You'll also be making magic by attuning yourself to Nature's wise rhythm.

Elemental Magic

Elemental magic is a wonderful, and very immediate, way of working with the living divinity of Nature, and is a very important part of Wiccan practice. Each of the natural elements—air, fire, water, and earth—is always present in magical circles (as you will see on page 103 in Chapter 4, Casting Circle) and when you invite them to work with you, you are engaging in active meditations that attune you to the sacred wisdom and power of Nature. You are discovering how you and the Earth are interconnected, and when you make magic with the elements, their energies help you to transform yourself. They enrich your humanity and show you how magnificently present deity is in the world, and how these very special aspects of divinity are present in *you*. Each element, and its corresponding direction, represents a part of yourself—your mind, will, emotions, and body. As you move around the circle and through the four elements, you move through yourself, learning how to balance your inner and outer nature, discovering your challenges and your strengths, and creating a magical life.

Modern Witchcraft organizes these interconnections as "correspondences": Each of the four elements corresponds to human qualities and aspects of Nature, to animals, plants, colors, times of day and of year, as well as seasons of life. Elemental magic is an important technique for Witch crafting. By working with each of these elements, and the energy forces they embody, you are going to attune your psyche to a profound and important aspect of the natural world, and therefore the sacred reality in which you live. Air magic helps attune your mind (both aspects of intellect and intuition), fire magic the will, water magic your emotions, and earth magic grounds your magic in your body and your life.

THE TABLE OF CORRESPONDENCES

	EAST	SOUTH	WEST	NORTH
Element:	Air	Fire	Water	Earth
Nature:	Wind	Sun	Oceans, Rivers Rain	Mountains, Fields
Aspects:	Mind	Will/Energy	Emotions/ Womb	Body
Qualities:	Imagination, Intelligence, Intuition, Inspiration Music Communication	Passion, Courage, Determination, Drive, Desire, Power	Love, Compassion, Dreams, Playfulness	Creativity, Fertility, Strength, Groundedness
Goddesses:	Nike, Arianrod, Isis, Aurora	Amaterasu, Brigid, Pele	Aphrodite, Yemanja, Tiamat	Demeter, Parvati, Freya
Gods:	Hermes, Thoth, Quetzalcoatl	Horus, Surya, Lugh, Sol	Poseidon, Njord, Agwe	Dionysus, Cernunnos, Osiris, Green Man
Animals:	Winged creatures, such as: Birds, Butterflies, Dragonflies	Clawed creatures, such as: Lions, Dragons, the Phoenix	Finned creatures, such as: Dolphins, Porpoises, Whales	Paw and Hoofed creatures, like: Bear, Wolf, Bison, Horse
Time:	Dawn	Midday	Sunset	Night
Colors:	White, Lavender, Pale Blue	Red, Orange, Yellow	Blue, Sea Green	Green, Brown, Gold, Purple
Tool:	Sword	Wand	Cup	Pentacle
Zodiacal Signs:	Aquarius, Gemini, Libra	Leo, Aries, Sagittarius	Scorpio, Pisces, Cancer	Taurus, Virgo, Capricorn
Plants/Herbs:	Lavender, Bodhi Tree	Myrrh, Olive Tree	St. John's Wort Willow	Patchouli Oak
Spirit Form:	Sylph	Salamander	Undine	Gnome

As you invoke the elements, learn from them, work with them to make magic, and encounter their spiritual forms—called elementals—you will become more attentive and therefore more sensitive to the presence of divinity in the world. You will attune your mind, body, heart, and soul to Nature's divine wisdom as you become one with Nature, and the Divine. *This oneness is the source of the power with which Witches make magic.*

Let's make magic with each of the elements in the order in which they are invited to join you in your magical circle. Although the elemental practices may seem quite basic, they are equally important to experienced practitioners because, like the sensitivity training, they will help you to ground your magic in your body and in Nature, allowing you to tap into much more power—the power of the Divine.

Air Magic

Air is the element of inspiration. It is the element of vital energy that Hindus call *prana*, Taoists call it *chi*, and Witches recognize it as part of the life force. The element of air corresponds to all the gifts of the mind such as imagination, laughter, music, writing and poetry, intelligence—both intuitive and intellectual—and our capacity to focus our attention. Like a summer breeze, divine inspiration can come to us spontaneously, once we have begun to pay attention. Use air magic whenever you are seeking inspiration, communicating, or need to do work involving your mind—such as learning, writing, lecturing, or taking an exam—or you are cultivating your intuition, or making a new beginning in your life. Breathing and chanting are important meditation tools for clearing and quieting the mind, and they are also wonderful forms of making air magic. See the Table of Correspondences (on page 78) for more information when you want to make air magic, but for now remember that all the creatures of the air—birds, butterflies, dragonflies—will help you learn about this magical element.

A member of the Ara community had a magical learning experience with the creatures of air: She has a power spot—a huge granite rock in the middle of a park that she always goes to when she needs to "figure things out" or just "to clear her head." One day, when she needed to write a ritual and couldn't get started, she went to her spot and just opened herself up to the surroundings. All of a sudden a little female bird came and sat on the fence in front of her and looked at her. The woman waited quietly, and soon the little bird's male partner joined her. Seeing this, the woman realized that her ritual needed to be about bringing balance to her path. She returned home and easily wrote her ritual.

BASIC TO ADVANCED PRACTICE
AIR MAGIC—BREATHING THE CYCLE OF LIFE

One of the simplest and most enjoyable ways of making air magic is to breathe. It is also a profound way to meditate and to alter your consciousness.

Go outside on a breezy day. Breathe deeply. Close your eyes. Feel the wind on your skin, feel it lift your heart. Inhale the perfume of flowers. Notice how the gifts of air make you feel—happy, free, like singing or laughing. Listen to the sound of the wind in the trees. Open your eyes and see how the wind makes the trees dance and sing, how the birds coast on thermal currents, and the clouds fly past above you.

Invite the air to be with you and to teach you. You might say: *"Spirits of air, bless me with your inspiration and wonder. Bring me a clear and open mind, help me hear the birds singing, the children laughing. Help me to spread my wings and fly forth into life."*

Don't be surprised if you are given a gift—a poem, a song, a joyful thought. Be sure to say thanks, and make more magic by writing about your experience, your feelings, and your gift in your magical journal. And don't forget that one of the best ways you can make air magic is to write a poem, a song, or anything else that expresses your feelings.

Other forms of air magic include writing in your journal, whispering in the ear of someone you love, writing a spell, flying a kite with your spell attached to it, or attaching a spell to a feather that you place in a windy spot for the spirits of air to carry off, going for a ride in a glider, parasailing (riding in a parachute that's pulled by a speedboat) while shouting out your heart's desire, following your intuition, and creating and using an incense—since it burns and perfumes the air, this is one of our favorite forms of air magic and is always included in casting circle. And birds teach us that playing music is an exquisite and sublime way of making air magic!

Your sense of smell can reveal divine magic too. Many people can tell when the spring is coming—in fact, we say, "Spring is in the air!" A member of the Ara community in Toronto recently wrote to say how this year, toward the end of January and just before Imbolc, the air smelled of life returning to the Earth. She knew that even if they got more snow and cold weather, the shift had happened and she was filled with expectation, optimism, and happiness.

FIRE MAGIC

Fire is the element of transformation, and in many ancient cultures is considered the element of spiritual power, rebirth, and the immortality of spirit. Fire is associated with the direction of the south (that is, in the Northern Hemisphere, and the direction of north in the Southern Hemisphere), with dragons, lions, salamanders, the phoenix, and other creatures with claws who live where the Sun's heat is most intense. It is also associated with the human qualities of courage, passion, independence, determination, and the power to transform our lives with divine magic. We make fire magic whenever we need these qualities, and when we want to make magic that will manifest quickly! And fire is often used for banishings because of its unique energy that transforms by consuming. While something is destroyed by the fire, that process also creates heat and light and is the means by which we cook food—another process of transformation. The following exercise will help you make fire magic.

FIRE MAGIC—GREETING THE SUN

This exercise should be done every day for at least a week.

Begin every day at sunrise, just as our ancestors did, before electric lights allowed us to reprogram ourselves. Let the Sun recondition your body, and your soul, to a natural rhythm. Rising with the Sun everyday requires a great deal of determination, and will also reward you with tremendous passion and magical power.

If possible, greet the Sun by going outside. Reach your arms out and watch the sky change colors. Focus your attention on the transformation that the Sun and its fire brings about. Feel the warmth of the Sun on your skin. Listen to the birds singing to greet the new day.

"Cup" the Sun between your hands. Bring your hands, and the Sun, into your heart. Feel it open, and glow, and radiate power and passion through your body. Feel the optimism and empowerment the Sun gives you to do anything you commit yourself to. You might say: *"Blazing spirits of fire, bless me with your passion and powers of transformation."*

Give thanks for this new day of life. By the end of the week, meditate on how your courage, passion, and determination can transform your life.

My doctor recommended beginning each day with ten minutes in the Sun—something I've been doing for years. The light stimulates your brain, which releases all sorts of happy chemicals into your bloodstream to make you feel awake and glad to be alive! Even in the middle of the night, or on a rainy day, the power of the Sun is present in the fire we so easily take for granted. Other forms of fire magic include the life returning to the Earth in the spring and growing in the summer, cooking (one of my students is a chef and this is her favorite form of magic), burning a piece of paper on which you have written something you want to banish, spending an evening with no illumination but the light of burning candles, making love in front of a fire, and building, tending, and watching an outdoor fire—and dancing around one is even better! A friend remembers fondly a night spent camping with her Girl Scout troop. Each girl spent one hour alone sitting in silence and watching the fire, and writing about her experiences. She laughs when she tells the story, ending by asking, "Who knew we were making fire magic?"

WATER MAGIC

Water is the element of life, love, and the Goddess. It is the life source, the womb from which we are all born. Water is associated with the west, and with creatures who live in the sea, like whales, dolphins, seals, and sea otters, and all the wonderful fish, most especially the mystical salmon. Water is also associated with dreams, memories, the womb, and the heart. Water is the element of our intuitive and feeling capacities. Water melts the walls we have created that block the flow of our emotions which, like the rains from heaven, nourish the landscape of our lives so that our dreams can grow wild and fruitful. It's also an element most often used for purification, so it's appropriate to do water magic to remove emotional clogs and congestion, to cleanse away cares, heal wounds, soothe your soul, and reconnect to your feelings. You'll be surprised how many problems are water soluble!

> **BASIC TO ADVANCED PRACTICE**
> ## WATER MAGIC—BATHING IN THE WATERS OF LIFE

If you can, visit a natural body of water. Sit and pay attention to the water, to the way it moves and sounds. Pay attention to the way light plays on its surface, to the creatures that swim in it, and float on it. Listen to what it says, look at what it shows you.

When you are ready, ask if you may immerse yourself in the water to cleanse and to purify yourself.

If there is something in particular that you want to wash away—such as the pain of losing someone you love through a breakup or a death—state it out loud, for example: *"Mighty and gentle waters, spirits of dreaming and the womb of becoming, spirits of love and compassion, cleanse and purify me, cleanse my heart, my body, my mind, my soul."*

Enter and bathe. Feel the temperature of the water, feel its texture. Feel how your body moves in the water, the drag on your limbs, the buoyancy that keeps you afloat. If you can, float. Allow your feelings to flow freely.

When you are done, say thanks and return to shore. Then cast your offering into the water.

If you're unable to work with a natural body of water, you can work at home. Take a purification bath with sea salt and cleansing herbs such as eucalyptus, calendula, lavender, and peppermint.

I have always loved the ocean and spent all of my summers by the seaside. My mother taught me to swim and many of my happiest memories are of spending time with her at the beach. When she died, I went to the beautiful bay near my home in the country. I waded into the water, and cried. Until the summer ended, I made this pilgrimage of grieving and healing almost every day, at the end of the day as the Sun was setting in the west—the direction that is also associated with the spirits of our ancestors. I still miss my mother and find myself crying at the most unexpected times, but the tides of the waters I wept in have carried the worst of the pain away. Now when I float on the waves, I am filled with perfect memories, gratitude, and endless, flowing love.

Before casting a circle, performing a ritual, or making any kind of magic, water will help you to purify and cleanse yourself. And there are lots of ways to make magic with water: Swim naked, dance in a summer shower, take a walk in the fog, go rafting in white water, go sailing, float in a pond, watch the creatures that live in a creek, jump from a diving board or into a swimming hole or lake, water your garden, wash your face in the snow, bathe in a natural hot spring.

EARTH MAGIC

The Earth is the body of the Divine. It is Goddess, God, and the gender-less Sacred. The element of earth is associated, in the Northern Hemisphere, with the direction of north (it's associated with south in the Southern Hemisphere), and with animals such as bears, wolves, stags, and horses. It's also associated with forests and fields and the powers of growth, fertility, mystery, and rebirth. With earth magic you can attune yourself to Nature's rhythms, her cycles of growth, death, and rebirth, and so understand the rhythms of your own body as you age and mature, and the events of your life as you grow, create, outgrow things, and begin again. Earth magic helps you manifest your ideas and desires, tap into your creativity, create prosperity, and give birth to the life you want.

BEGINNING TO ADVANCED PRACTICE
EARTH MAGIC—TOUCHING THE EARTH

Find some way of working with earth. Start a garden, join a city garden group (there are many such groups all over the country converting littered lots into beautiful, food-creating gardens). Work with a local environmental group on a project that gets you outside and working with the land. Begin slowly, gradually increasing your commitment.

As you work, pay attention to the Earth, and to your body. Feel your heart beating, your muscles stretching and aching, your bones supporting you as you work in the earth. Feel the strength and stamina and health of your body increasing.

Plant something and see how the Earth responds to your care. Share what you grow with others, especially those who are housebound or in need.

Integrate the Sensitivity exercise on page 72 with your earth work and you will begin attuning yourself to Nature's wise rhythm of life. Ask the Earth for its blessing and thank it. Write about your experiences and feelings in your magical journal. Share them with others.

ELEMENTAL MAGIC

Air Magic: Mental Concentration Incense

Call upon the element of air to help you. Using a mortar and pestle, grind together these herbs in equal parts: mastic, cinnamon, myrrh, lavender, sandalwood. Place the mixture on a piece of burning charcoal (this is a special charcoal just for incense, available at Wiccan, herbal, and religious supply stores) on a heat-resistant surface, such as a brazier or a cauldron filled with sand. Meditate and breathe, speaking and sending the vision of your goal upward with the smoke of the incense. Give thanks, close your circle, and act in accord.

Fire Magic: Candle Ritual

Get a candle of the appropriate color for your goal (see the Table of Correspondences on page 78). For example, if you wish to create greater prosperity, choose a green candle; for love, use a red candle; for peace and healing, use blue; for success or empowerment, use orange, etc. With a pin or knife, carefully carve into the candle your name and a symbol for your goal (a dollar sign for prosperity, a heart for love, etc.), and as you carve, meditate on the power that you have to make your dream come true.

Hold the candle to your heart, charging it with the power of your desire. Invoke the power of fire to help you achieve your goal. Light the candle. Then sit and meditate on the flame, and your goal. Cup your hands near the flame and feel the tremendous heat that even a tiny flame gives off. Realize how much power the flame of your passion and courage gives you. Feel the fire of the candle burning within you. Focus your attention on the feeling of fire in your stomach (this is traditionally the area of fire power in the body).

When you are finished, thank the fire. Place the candle somewhere absolutely safe, such as the bathtub, and allow it to burn until it goes out by itself. If this is not possible, let it burn for as long as possible before blowing it out. Each time you relight it, repeat your invocation.

Water Magic: A Venus Love Bath

Water is the element of the heart, love, and our feelings, so one of my favorite love spells is a love bath. You can add a little fire magic to this, since love should be passionate, by also using a red candle carved with your name, a heart, and the words "my true love and soul mate," which you'll burn as you're bathing in the love potion. Venus/Aphrodite is the Goddess of love, so ask Her to help you. Use pure, essential oils and feel free to vary the amounts below depending upon your personal reaction to the scent as you are blending.

Mix together one teaspoon each of the following oils: rose, almond, jojoba oil, musk, ambergris. Pour two tablespoons of your Venus oil into a warm bath, light the candle, bathe, let yourself feel love, and send out waves of love to your beloved. Keep the rest of the oil for anointing yourself or for use in future love spells.

Earth Magic—Herne's Talisman for Empowerment

Herne is a God of the Forest and the Hunt. He is a force of great power and protection and His talisman is made of plants of the wood. Carry it with you, rub it between your hands, breathe in its scent, and let the power of the Earth course through you.

Using a mortar and pestle, grind together one tablespoon each of pine, deer's tongue leaves, vetivert, cedar, and rue, plus three crushed oak leaves and nine drops of High John the Conqueror oil.

Take a four-inch square of brown cotton or silk cloth and stitch or draw your name, initials, or personal symbol on one side of the cloth, and on the other draw a pair of deer antlers. Wrap the ground herbs in the cloth, tying the bundle with a green or brown cord. Hold it to your heart, ground, center, and run the Earth's energy into yourself and into the talisman. Say: *"Might Herne, Great God*

> *of the Forest, God of the Wild Things, God of the Earth, charge and*
> *bless this talisman with your power and protection. Strengthen and*
> *empower me. So mote it be."*
>
> Feel the energy filling you, feel yourself secure and empowered.
> Carry the amulet with you, and when your need for it has passed, bury
> the herbs in the Earth and give thanks by helping someone in need.

There are many ways to make earth magic: Plant a garden, grow
houseplants, plant a tree, go hiking, go camping, build a stone fence, recycle your garbage, learn to ride a horse, get a dog, take care of and enjoy
your body. Just as the Earth is the embodiment of the Divine, your body
is the embodiment of your divinity. Working physically with the earth element grounds your magic in your body, and helps you to tap into the
powers of your body when you make magic. Just as we treat the Earth
with care and respect because it is sacred, you must take care of your body
with exercise, proper diet, medical checkups, etc., so that it will become a
healthy, joyful, creative expression of divine energy. As a member of the
Ara community wisely pointed out, we often don't think of ourselves as a
part of Nature, as if we're not a part of the ongoing creation of the Divine. But everything is a part of Nature, and therefore divinity, including
the human race—and you! And by making earth magic, you'll find that
your relationship with the Earth will also begin to change from one of
separation to one of intimacy and affinity.

BASIC TO ADVANCED PRACTICE
A LUNAR CYCLE OF ELEMENTAL MAGIC

Spend a week working with each element. Wear the colors of the element,
and come up with a different way to make magic with the element every
day. For example, with air, the first day you could do breathing meditation;
the next day you could chant; the third you could next create an incense.
On the fourth day work with music, the next day write a poem, spell, or in-

vocation; the sixth spend the day watching and listening to, feeding, and learning about and from birds; and then make magic combining all of these! Create an altar devoted to the element placed in the correct direction. Use an altar cloth and items of the appropriate color. Place on the altar the element or objects that symbolize the element (you can use incense or a feather for air). Include images of the animals and deities associated with the element.

Work with the magical tool associated with the element. Use divination and reflect on the meaning of each element's qualities to you and your life. Do you need more of the element and its qualities, or less? In what ways can you bring an element's qualities into your life and your psychology? And use your creativity!

More Earth Magic:
✳ *The Magical Power of Unnaming* ✳

In my tradition of Witch crafting, rather than imposing our will on a divine Universe, we open ourselves to receive its presence and all of its blessings. The magical practice of "unnaming"—which I have borrowed from eco-psychologist and environmental educator Dr. Michael Cohen—helps us to make this shift.

There is an old belief that if you can name something, you have power over it—think of how the princess gained power over Rumpelstiltskin when she discovered his name; or how Adam was given dominion over the animals and the power to name the birds and the beasts; or how in ceremonial magical traditions it is believed that if you can name a demon, you can exorcise or banish it, and if you can name a spirit you can command it to do your bidding. This idea reflects patriarchal, biblical attitudes about power and the Divine as being outside of oneself: Naming gives you control over what you are naming.

But Witches reject the premise of magic as a way of having power over something or someone, because it contradicts the spiritual principle of immanent divinity. And labels become a way of distancing ourselves from that which we label. We see a river and it is only a "river," something we can pollute or dam up and redirect or use for transportation or drinking water or whatever else we choose. It is something we have power over. When we label, we have created an illusion of understanding and control.

"Unnaming" enables us to discover the real identity of whatever we are interacting with, whether it is an aspect of Nature, another person, or even a part of ourselves. It also enables us to relinquish the old definition of power as having and using control over someone or something else.

ADVANCED PRACTICE

UNNAMING, OR LETTING NATURE TEACH YOU

How does unnaming work? By lifting the label and seeing what you discover underneath. When you call something a "tree," you distance yourself in a superior way: "Oh, I know what a tree is." But do you really?

Go outside. Take along a paper and pencil. Sit in front of a tree, or a flower, a rock, a lake, a stream—anything that calls to you and that agrees to work with you.

You are now going to remove its label. For example, let's say you're working with a "tree." Describe what the tree is without using the word "tree," or "branch," or "leaf," or "root," or "forest," or any other label. In order to describe it, you must ask the tree to show itself to you, to explain itself to you. You must pay careful attention.

Write down the things that you observe about this unnamed mystery, such as, "It's a place where birds and squirrels live. It's a living being that creates oxygen and uses carbon dioxide. It's a being that is strong, but which bends in storms," etc.

When you are finished, thank whatever teacher you have worked with—the tree, or flower, or stream, for working with you and teaching you about itself.

As John Muir, one of America's greatest naturalists observed, "Every natural object is a conductor of divinity." Next time you go for a walk, silently repeat this wise way of knowing the world. And when a tree or plant, an animal or rock, a stream or butterfly captures your attention, stop. Unname it—discover the deep and true nature of what you are looking at, and interacting with.

As you begin to unname, you'll start to discern energy within all of the aspects of Nature. You'll begin to see the relationships between the parts of Nature, so when a tree is described as making oxygen and using carbon dioxide, you understand and experience and appreciate it as the lungs of the Earth. With the practice of unnaming, you can begin to see and to experience the interconnectedness and interdependence of all life. And it is through these interconnections that you can make magic and discover your true self.

Nature also shows you that the Divine is not just masculine and feminine but beyond gender. The grass, the air, the water, and the rocks are neither male nor female, but all are sacred. This is an important lesson, because many Witches confine themselves to thinking of divinity just in terms of Goddess and God and thereby place an unnecessary limitation upon their experience of the Sacred.

We can always find a source of divine inspiration in Nature, even if it is just a dandelion growing between the cracks in a city sidewalk. In fact, that single flower can be more hope-inspiring than a view of the Grand Canyon. You can have the most profound encounter with the divinity of Nature in the center of a teeming city because you are now able to see that little flower in an entirely new and empowering way.

Let Nature teach you, and you will discover divine magic and profound lessons about how we should be living: Everything in Nature lives together in relationships based on affinity, diversity, mutual dependence, and balance. A healthy environment is composed of a varied community (not all pine trees or all chipmunks) whose members are bonded in a harmonious kinship of attraction, mutual support, and assistance in sustaining life. *Nature reveals the wise perfection of divine order. And by living in harmony with*

Nature, you are living in harmony with the Divine. You are also living a magical life. You can see the entire world differently—as the body of the Sacred—because, perhaps for the first time, you are seeing the world clearly.

Thank your teacher for the beauty you've been shown, the wisdom you've been given, and the joy you feel. With these gifts you are ready to work with another important Wiccan technique for seeing the Divine and crafting a Witch: casting a circle and creating sacred space.

Sacred Space

I am still wrapped in a circle of joy and fulfillment, having just returned from teaching an all-day workshop on Wicca and the Goddess for a group of fifty women ranging in age from late teens to early seventies.

As they stood in a circle, each woman took the hands of the women on either side of her, making eye contact, smiling, and speaking the magical words that express our readiness to take responsibility for our spiritual journeys, that join us in community, and that summon the Sacred into the world: *"Hand to hand I cast this circle."* The energy of sisterhood, and the Goddess, moved visibly around the room, flowing into a soul-stirring chorus of women's voices chanting, "Om."

We grounded and felt the power of the Great Mother Earth rising within ourselves, and even the women who had never practiced Wicca before felt it coursing through them. We moved this holy force around the group, feeling it encircle and entwine us in a magical ring of light, energy, and love. The charge was palpable and observable—faces grew flushed, bodies warm, palms began to tingle, and we felt ourselves connecting to energy that was profoundly powerful and present. Slowly, we opened our eyes and beheld the Goddess shining forth from each woman. "Thou art Goddess," I said to the woman to my left, and the blessing and acknowledgment passed swiftly around the circle.

❈   *The Functions of a Circle*   ❈

Casting a magical circle is an electrifying and empowering experience—you can feel the power running through you the minute you start. When you cast a circle, you know you're a Witch because you can *feel* yourself working with divinity. A sacred circle is your temple and you don't need stones, mortar, or money to create it.

Contrary to the dominant religious models of the West that require worship in a church, temple, or mosque at an appointed hour guided by God's designated representative—a priest, rabbi, minister, or mullah, who is generally or exclusively male—Wiccan practitioners need neither building nor ordained representative in order to experience the presence of divinity. *Casting circle demarcates sacred space where you encounter the Divine and work with divine energy.*

There are many more layers of meaning and purpose within the act of casting a circle. I would like to dive deeper into the question of why Witches cast and work in circles, for with this understanding you can tap into the full power and potential of this important spiritual practice.

THE CIRCLE AS A CAULDRON

So why do we cast a circle? The most common explanation is that you need a container to hold the energy you raise for magic, just as you need a pot in which to boil water. *The circle is a container, made of elemental, psychic, and sacred energies, that holds magical energy.* This is not an abstract principle but a physical fact that becomes very apparent as you cast circles. You may not be able to *see* the circle that you cast, but you will certainly *feel* it and its effects, and so will others.

I'll never forget how powerfully I learned this lesson—it was the very first circle that I led for others, the summer after my initiation. I and a covenmate had decided to conduct a Summer Solstice celebration for a group of friends at Mystery Hill in New Hampshire, where there is a very old stone circle that was probably constructed by early Scandinavian or Celtic visitors long before Columbus arrived.

It was a very chilly but beautiful night and I was exhilarated by the countless stars in the sky. We set up our altar and everyone sat around it in a circle. We explained the meaning of the Sabbat and what we were going to do. We also explained that the circle would act as a container to hold the energy that would build as we worked within it, and that it was very important not to "break" the circle by getting up and walking out. We showed everybody the simple technique for leaving the circle while it is still erected, called "cutting out." To cut out, you stand facing away from the center of the circle (looking outside the circle) and literally cut a "door" in the shape of an arc from left to right (following the pattern of an energy wave as it moves deosil [clockwise, the direction of increase] around the circle). You then step through the arc, and close it behind you by moving your hand behind you from left to right. When it is time to return to the circle, you cut another arc—this time from right to left (again, the direction in which the energy would be moving)—enter, and seal the "door" behind you.

We cast circle, and celebrated the Summer Solstice with a wonderful ritual. We'd been working for quite a while and everyone was really enjoying themselves, when suddenly we all realized we were absolutely freezing!

"What's going on?" one of my friends asked. "There's no wind."

And then I noticed that someone was missing from circle. I immediately suspected that he hadn't cut out and had broken the integrity of the circle that had been containing all of the energy we'd raised, thereby keeping us warm. We scrambled into our sweatshirts, and waited for his return. Sure enough, when he came back a few minutes later, he walked right back in to where we were still sitting in our circle, without cutting a door. I asked him if he'd "cut out," and he acknowledged that he hadn't. We were all stunned and impressed by the very tangible change in the energy—and the temperature!

Over the years I have always noticed that I feel warmer in circle as the activities progress, and I've also observed that the temperature will often drop after the magical work is completed and the energy has been released from its "container."

Some traditions of Wicca have inherited the view of the old ceremonial traditions that the circle is not just a container to keep energies in, but is a protective barrier to keep negative energies out. My tradition does not emphasize the need for protection against invading negativity, but it's certainly true that there are all sorts of annoyances—from bothersome roommates to the blare of a neighbor's television—that belong outside your circle, and casting has the remarkable power to keep them out. Sounds from the distant world diminish, and there is a definite feeling of enhanced privacy and security. Cats, some dogs, and babies can move in and out of circles without breaking them, and my dog, Webster, who is always with us in circle, often places himself between the circle and door as our guardian!

THE CIRCLE AS PERSONAL SACRED SPACE

A circle is also your temple where you make magic. It can be created anywhere—your home, your garden, your place of power in Nature, even your workplace. You can also cast a circle around yourself for immediate protection or energy anyplace or anytime you feel the need—just by visualizing and sending out a ring of light. *Working in circle teaches you that the temple exists within each of us, and is everywhere around us.*

It's wonderful to be able to dedicate a space in your home as your temple, the place where you cast circle. But most of us don't have this luxury, so we work in our living rooms, our bedrooms, or our backyards if they are private. When working in space used for other purposes, it's always a good idea to begin by purifying the space to clear away energies that aren't appropriate to your sacred work (we'll explore this shortly). It's amazing how just turning off the phone, setting up your altar, lighting candles in each of the four directions, and burning some terrific incense will transform a room used for watching television or sleeping into a mystical temple. (But I can't overemphasize the importance of properly closing, or "banishing" as it is traditionally called, your circle afterwards! I have countless stories of all the electronic equipment in my students' homes going on the fritz after a few weeks of intensive circle casting. The energies we work with are potent, and if they can change the world, they can certainly fry your electronics!)

Wherever your circle is cast, before entering this sacred temple where magic is made and a Witch is crafted, you must pass two tests: First, you must meet the challenge posed at the temple of Delphi: Know Thyself. If you have not read Chapter 2, Divination, and completed its exercises, please do so now. Second, before entering a sacred sanctuary, you must purify yourself. Purification prepares you to encounter divinity, unburdened by the cares of the day, chaotic thinking, distracting anxiety, offensive egotism, or inhibiting self-doubt.

BASIC PRACTICE
PURIFICATION

Make a purifying scrub of sea salt, rosemary, sage, lavender, and a few drops of eucalyptus oil. Take a bath (or shower if you are pressed for time), using your purification scrub to wash away the stresses of the day. Try not to rush. Let the water run over you and cleanse you, body and soul. If you don't have time for a bath or shower, use the scrub to wash your hands and face—be careful not to get the eucalyptus oil in your eyes! If you don't have all the ingredients, you can also use plain old salt.

You can also purify with the herb sage. Used by Witches and Native Americans to cleanse themselves before sacred ritual, sage is burned and the smoke used to purify the user and the space—a process called "smudging." Wave the sage smoke all around yourself, then carry the burning sage all around the perimeter of the room, or outside area, where you will cast circle, beginning in the east. Since you are banishing negativity, move widdershins (counterclockwise, the direction of decrease).

These purification techniques can be used anytime you need them, not just before casting circle.

PURIFYING AND CONSECRATING THE ELEMENTS

When you are ready to cast a circle, set up your altar with representations of each of the four elements, as well as your images of the Goddess and God, your working tools, flowers, fruits, and whatever you will need for making your magic (see diagram on page 235). If you have your athame, you will use it to purify and consecrate the elements. If you don't have an athame, use your active hand (right hand if you are right-handed, left if you are left-handed).

Meditate, ground, and center. When you are ready, start to purify and consecrate the elements on your altar, beginning with the element of air. Place a lit incense charcoal in a brazier and place some homemade incense on the burning charcoal (see, for example, the Mental Concentration Incense box in Chapter 3, page 86). As the incense burns, sending up a fragrant billow, draw an invoking pentagram in the smoke using your athame or hand. Start at the top of the star, and move down to the lower left point, then up to the upper right point, across to the upper left point, then down to the lower right point, and finally back up to the top of the star.

Invoking Pentagram

As you draw this invoking pentagram in the element of air (the incense smoke), say: *"I purify and consecrate this creature of air. May all good enter herein in the names of the Goddess and God."* (We often use the terms "Lady of the Moon" and "Lord of the Dance" to refer to the Goddess and God, and you may use the specific names of Goddesses and Gods with whom you will be working as you make magic.)

Next, draw an invoking pentagram over the candle flame (be careful not to burn yourself by getting too close!) and say: *"I purify and consecrate this creature of fire. May all good enter herein in the names of the Goddess and God."*

Then draw an invoking pentagram in the bowl of water, and say: *"I purify and consecrate this creature of water. May all good enter herein in the names of the Goddess and God."*

Finally, draw an invoking pentagram in the bowl of salt, and say: *"I purify and consecrate this creature of Earth. May all good enter herein in the names of the Goddess and God."*

Return your athame to the altar.

PURIFYING AND CONSECRATING THE CIRCLE

The next step in casting your circle is to purify and consecrate it. If you are working with others, this is a wonderful task to share. Each person takes a representation of an element from the altar and carries it around the circle. At the beginning, it's natural and easy for astrological signs to work with their elements (see the Table of Correspondences on page 78) —in other words, the air signs Aquarius, Gemini, and Libra work with air; fire signs with fire, etc. Group members might also choose to work with the element that they need to create greater inner and outer balance: For example, someone who is working on becoming more assertive would work with fire, while someone who is trying to manifest their ideas and passions and bring them to fruition would work with earth.

Note that though you are cleansing the circle with the elements and banishing negativity, you won't be walking widdershins (counterclockwise) but deosil (clockwise) because you are consecrating and charging the circle with the elements.

Begin and end in the east, starting with air (incense), and be sure that you have something like a potholder to hold your brazier, or whatever you are using to burn the charcoal and incense in, as the charcoal gets *very* hot. Put some more incense on the charcoal so there's a nice cloud of smoke. Now pick it up from your altar, and walk to the east. (If you don't know which direction is which, get a little compass—it always gives me such a kick to see how disoriented folks are, especially we urban Witches!) Lift up the brazier in salute to the east. Then, holding the brazier comfortably before you, walk slowly deosil, defining the outer shape of the circle (traditionally, a circle is nine feet in diameter, but you may be limited by the size of your space, or you may have to make it larger to accommodate other people). Also, some people are allergic to incense, in which case using feathers or a fan is a wonderful substitute.

As you walk, if you are working outdoors, pay careful attention to how Nature responds to you—feel the breeze come up, the birds start to sing. Or, if you are working indoors, remember what it felt like to be outside on a breezy day. Bring those sensations vividly to mind, and as much as you can, to your body and heart. As you move from south to the west to the north, and finally back to the east, watch the billowing incense flowing around the circle and feel the air gently blowing the smoke as you move. Breathe deeply and allow your mind to grow clear. As you walk, say, *"I purify and consecrate this sacred circle with the element of air. I surround myself (or us) with the powers of insight and inspiration, laughter and wonder. Let the creatures of the air encircle me (or us) with clarity and imagination."*

When you return to the east, salute the east with the brazier, and then, walking deosil, return to your altar and place the brazier on it.

Next, pick up the burning candle, which represents fire, and walk deosil to the east and salute it. As you walk deosil around the circle with the candle, visualize a circle of flame springing up from your footsteps and see the circle ringed with dancing fire. Recall the heat of the Sun on a hot summer day and really *feel* it. Say: *"With the flaming powers of fire I purify and consecrate this sacred circle. I surround myself (or us) with its powers of passion and determination, courage, and energy. Let the creatures of fire encircle me (or us) with will and enthusiasm."*

Repeat this process with the element of water, sprinkling it as you walk and visualizing streams and rivers flowing from your footsteps. Remember the sensation of rain on your face, of waves against your body, of swimming in cool water. Say: *"I purify and consecrate this sacred circle with the element of wa-*

ter. I surround myself (or us) with its powers of love and compassion, dreaming and delighting. Let the creatures of water encircle me (or us) with joy and feeling."

Then do the same with the bowl of salt, representing the element of earth. Scatter the salt as you walk and visualize mountains and fields full of grain springing up from your footsteps. Feel the strength of your body, feel yourself move. Say: "With the powers of earth I purify and consecrate this circle. I surround myself (or us) with the powers of fertility and creativity, strength, and nurturing. Let the creature of earth encircle me (or us) with power and patience."

Once you have purified and consecrated your sacred space, sit before the altar and take a moment to visualize and *feel* the elemental energies circling you. Use your memories from your work in Nature to feel the breeze, the heat, the moisture, the solidity. Feel the inspiration, the passion, the love, and the strength that surrounds you.

THE CIRCLE AS A TOOL FOR ALTERING CONSCIOUSNESS

In addition to acting as a cauldron or container for magical energy or as a sacred space, casting a circle has another even more remarkable function in making magic: It alters your consciousness. It allows you to see what is usually hidden. My tradition of Witchcraft is devoted to living your life as your magic, and so we are constantly seeking the Sacred in life, in ourselves, others, and the world. Our primary magic is paying attention as deity expresses itself in our lives. But given the distractions and pressures with which we must also live, we all need techniques to help us pay attention. One of the most powerful ones is casting circle.

Casting circle helps you to craft yourself as a Witch because it shifts your consciousness from being distracted by ordinary, everyday matters to perceiving nonordinary reality, that is, the presence of divinity. When you first begin casting circles, you may feel absolutely no difference in your state of awareness. But the more you cast, the more you will overcome your self-consciousness and worries about "doing it right," and the more you will become attuned to the presence of deity. In this state of heightened consciousness, you will make and experience the most effective magic.

I first recognized the deep spiritual purpose of casting circle many years ago, when I was just starting to practice. Standing in the midst of my first coven—seeing their radiant, smiling faces, feeling their joyous energies merging with mine, beholding the generous bounty of the Earth on the altar before me, feeling divine power connecting us all—I realized that *when we cast circle we do not create sacred space—we discover the sacredness of the space we inhabit.*

And when you use Wiccan practices within circle, just as your consciousness and actions activate the latent energies of herbs, oils, colors, tools, your awakened consciousness and actions in sacred space activate the latent energies that reside within and all around you. With these energies, you make magic and craft a Witch. *The process of casting circle awakens the deity within, and creates a temple for the deity that surrounds us.*

A circle is also a portal that allows your energies to move about the Universe in entirely magical and utterly real ways. After my coven casts circle, we say, "Our circle is cast, and we are between the worlds"—a wonderful phrase that really captures this shift. Within circle, you are able to move outside the limits of time and space. You can return to the distant past, move ahead into the future, and literally "see" things and people that are physically out of sight of the circle. And you can influence future events.

One of the most personally moving experiences I have had involved a vision I received during a journey in circle. I was going to Italy, a place of profound spiritual meaning for me, for the first time and wanted to know what to look for that would guide my spiritual path. In my vision, it was nighttime and I was seated in a small piazza. There was a rounded, old wooden door in a stone wall behind me, and bushes filled with tiny white flowers on either side of the door. To my left was an ancient round temple. I heard bells ringing, and saw the Moon just above a tower in the piazza.

A few months after the vision, I arrived in Benevento, Italy, a city where practitioners of *la Vecchia Religione* (the Old Religion) were said to have settled to escape the Church's persecution. My husband and I wandered the city, and I was filled with a sense of déjà vu. Exhausted, we finally sat in the city's main piazza, drinking coffee as the sun set. I wondered about my future as a Wiccan Priestess—I was trying to decide if I should go public and was worried about the consequences. As I looked about, I suddenly realized I was sitting in front of a rounded door in a stone wall framed by two large potted shrubs with tiny white flowers.

My pulse began to race as bells began ringing, the unexpectedly huge sound filling the night air. I looked up to see the clouds part and the Moon appear just above the pointed roof of a bell tower. I was stunned as I suddenly recognized every element of my vision precisely as I had received it, including the beautiful round temple dedicated to Isis, now encased within a church! My decision was made.

BASIC PRACTICE
CASTING CIRCLE

Method One: Casting with a Wand, Athame, Sword, or Hand

In a traditional coven, a circle will often be cast by the Priestess or Priest who uses a wand, an athame, or a sword with which to cast the circle (please read the sections on wands and athames in Chapter 9, Potions, Notions, and Tools, if you are unfamiliar with these items). I have also used my hand, a tree branch, and a bouquet of flowers to cast. Holding and lifting one of any of these tools or natural objects before her/him, the Priest/ess walks deosil around the circle, outside of the seated members. In my tradition, we begin in the east, walk three times slowly around the circle, and end in the east.

If you are alone, or are chosen to cast the circle for your group, you too will begin in the east. Salute the east, and then walk slowly deosil around the circle. As you walk, visualize a circle of blue-and-white flame, or light, flowing from the tip of your wand or athame (or your hand if you are not using a tool). Feel the energy rising from the Earth and flowing through you to shape the circle in which you will work. Take your time.

You may read the following, though it is best to memorize it first so that your concentration will be free to work with the flow of energy. Don't worry about making mistakes because there aren't any. As you walk, say: *"I conjure this circle as a sacred space, a place between the worlds where the worlds meet. I conjure this circle as a boundary and a protection to preserve and to contain the energies that I (or we) shall raise herein. Thrice do I conjure this circle as a safe space, a sacred place where the Divine resides, where spirit and matter are one, in perfect love and perfect trust. As I do will, so mote it be."*

As you return to the east at the end of the third circle, see the energies connecting. Visualize the three lines of blue-and-white light that you have spun around the circle spreading into a sphere that surrounds the entire area with energy. When you have accomplished this, walk deosil and return to the altar, or, if you are going to invoke the four directions, remain in the east (in my circle, Calling the Four Directions is the next step of casting and is often shared by four different people who each call a direction).

As discussed in Chapter 11, Solitary Practice, as you become more skilled at casting, or conjuring the circle, you should write your own casting language, and ultimately, you should speak spontaneously from your heart as you cast.

Method Two: Casting Circle Hand to Hand

Everyone should sit or stand together in a circle. Begin with whoever is sitting in front of the altar—traditionally, the Priestess or Priest, or the person who is facilitating the circle.

The person who begins turns to the person on her left, makes eye contact, takes her neighbor's right hand, and says, *"Hand to hand I cast this circle."*

This second person now turns to the person on his left, takes his hand, makes eye contact, and says, *"Hand to hand I cast this circle."* This continues all around the circle until everyone is holding hands. The last two people to take hands often give each other a small kiss. The person who began the casting then says, *"Hand to hand and heart to heart, we cast our sacred circle. Let us remember where we are, and why we are here."*

As you take hands, keep your thumbs to the left. This will create the best structure for the flow of energy—each person will have their left hand (their heart hand) palm up and their right hand palm down. Be sure that each person speaks so they can be heard, and that they make eye contact with each other. And it's not just okay—it's wonderful to smile.

A SACRED PLACE FOR COMMUNION

As a sacred space that unites the worlds of spirit and matter, the circle is a temple where divinity dwells. The Sacred arrives in many ways and many forms. Once circle is cast, we invoke the Goddess and God, in any of many forms, which we'll explore in Chapters 5 and 6. But before these invocations, there is an important part of conjuring the circle called Invoking the Quarters, or Calling the Four Directions. This is one of the magical practices we have inherited from various ceremonial traditions, including the Masons, which is shared by other indigenous faiths, including traditional Native American religions.

In my own tradition—the Ara tradition—the circle represents our intuitive faculties, and the square created by Calling of the Four Directions represents the intellectual and analytical faculties because in Nature, there are no visible right angles. It requires deduction and analysis to discover or to make a right angle. And so the square and the circle are joined in the process of casting the circle, as are intuition and intellect, spirit and matter, divinity and humanity.

Calling the Directions is also a practice where my tradition of shamanic Wicca and the ceremonial traditions tend to part company. I'd like to explore this last step in casting circle, and propose some challenges to the language and style many practitioners use.

In the Ara tradition, the Calling of the Four Directions is a process by which you *invite* the Divine—in the form of elemental energies that correspond to each of the four directions—to join you. Having sealed the circle by casting, you now open four portals between the worlds, through which the powers of each direction may enter the circle. You are responsible for the presence and participation of the energies you invite. *How you address the powers of the elements is very important;* and how we as a community address them is critical.

I was taught invocation language that has roots in ceremonial traditions, which in turn have roots in patriarchal, biblical models of magic. This language was to be spoken in a strong and forceful manner: "Hail Guardians of the Watchtowers of the East" —or whatever direction you're calling— "I summon, stir, and call ye up, mighty powers of Air" —or whatever element you are summoning—"to witness our rites and guard this circle, in the names of (Goddess) and (God)." Though the language rang with mystical power, from the very beginning I felt uncomfortable with its style of commanding and controlling because the language reflects the old idea of the magician as literally commanding spirits to appear and do his bidding.

I prefer the "shamanic" style of addressing the four directions, a style that has much in common with many Native American traditions. The powers of the four directions are not commanded to appear, nor are they summoned or stirred. Instead, they are invited, or called. And the language, physical posture, and tone of voice I use are all in accord with an invocation as invitation rather than royal summoning. In my tradition, when we call the directions to join us in circle, we are respectful, grateful, and poetic. Instead of acting superior or inferior, we greet our creative colleagues with joy, reverence, and appreciation.

Calling the elemental powers is like inviting a beloved and esteemed guest to your spiritual home. A quantum reminder: What you bring to the experience determines its outcome. It has been my experience that the energy with which you approach this process makes a tremendous difference in the kind of energy that responds to and works with you. Below you will find the language for the Calling of the Four Directions with which I, and the Tradition of Ara, work most comfortably. I encourage you to try a wide range of styles, to discover what works best for you.

As with all aspects of Wiccan ritual, you should begin by choosing the language that feels most comfortable for you and then memorizing it. Then, write your own invocations, and finally, speak spontaneously from the heart. I have always found that speaking from the heart, and not the head, is the most powerful, magical experience—and when I watch someone else work in this shamanic manner, I am always awed by the beauty, eloquence, and divine wisdom with which they speak. I know I am in the presence of deity.

INVOKING THE QUARTERS/CALLING OF
THE FOUR DIRECTIONS

Stand in the direction you are going to call, facing outward. If you have your athame, use it to draw an invoking pentagram in one continuous and fluid motion (start at the top and move to the left lower corner of the star, etc.). Use your active hand if you don't have an athame. As you draw, visualize a flaming star of the color that corresponds to each direction: yellow or lavender for east, red or orange for south, blue or aqua for west, green or brown for north. See and feel the power of each element coming to you through the star portal as you speak. If you are practicing in the Northern Hemisphere, begin in the east, then move to the south, west, and north. In the Southern Hemisphere, begin in the east, move to the north, then west, and south. (Note that the Northern and Southern Hemispheres also reverse the powers of north and south so that north is fire and south is earth in the Southern Hemisphere.) As you move to each direction, call upon its spirits:

> *I call the ancient spirits of the east*
> *Powers of air*
> *Where the Sun rises*
> *Powers of wonder and imagination*
> *Clarity and communication*
> *Powers of a child's laughter*
> *Powers of music and dawn breaking*
> *Powers of breezes blowing and birds singing*
> *Power of the eagle and the butterfly flying*
> *I invite you to this sacred circle*
> *Hail and welcome!*
>
> *I call the ancient spirits of the south*
> *Powers of fire*
> *Where the Sun is high in the midday sky*
> *Powers of passion and determination*

Courage and devotion
Powers of bonfires burning
Powers of trial and transformation
Powers of high Sun and lizards leaping
Power of the desert lion and the phoenix rising
I invite you to this sacred circle
Hail and welcome!

I call the ancient spirits of the west
Powers of water
Where the Sun sets
Powers of love and compassion
Of feeling and dreaming
Powers of waters flowing
Powers of the Mother's womb
Powers of deep oceans and gentle rains
Power of the whale and the dolphin swimming
I invite you to this sacred circle
Hail and welcome!

I call the ancient spirits of the north
Powers of earth
Where the Mystery dwells
Powers of fertility and creativity
Of strength and groundedness
Powers of fertile field
Powers of mighty mountains
Powers of the verdant plains and rich forests
Power of the bear and the wolf
I invite you to this sacred circle
Hail and welcome!

When you have called each of the four directions, return to the east, acknowledge the east, turn back to circle, and say: *"Our circle is cast, we are between the worlds."*

LIBATIONS AND BLESSING THE CAKES OR BREAD

A libation is a sacred toast that is offered after the magic has been performed. Facing each other in front of the altar, the Priestess holds the Goddess's chalice and the Priest/partner holds the athame (this can be performed by anyone in the circle, including members of the same sex). The athame is plunged into the cup as the Priestess says: *"As the cup is to the Goddess,"* and the Priest says: *"So the athame is to the God,"* and together they say: *"And conjoined, they bring blessedness."* They kiss over the cup and blade, the Priestess offers the first libation. Holding her cup, she speaks from her heart, inspired by the ritual. She pours from her own cup into the libation chalice (or bowl), drinks from her cup and passes the libation chalice to the person to her left. Each person offers their libation, as the cup moves all around the circle. If you are outdoors, you can pour your offering directly on the Earth. (This is my favorite part of circle, because as each person speaks the wisdom s/he finds in her/his heart, I know I am in the presence of divinity.)

After libations, the Priestess holds a plate of cakes or bread in one hand and the Goddess's chalice in the other. Her partner dips his/her athame in the wine and sprinkles it on the bread as s/he draws an invoking pentagram. The Priestess then speaks a blessing—the traditional one is: *"Bless this bread unto our bodies, bestowing upon us the gifts of health, wealth, joy, and the eternal blessing, which is love."* She breaks off the first piece of bread and puts it in the chalice as an offering back to the Goddess, then feeds a piece to her partner, who then feeds her. The bread is then passed around the circle for everyone to share. When you're outdoors, always leave some for the birds and animals.

Elemental Magic
✳   within the Circle   ✳

If you're having trouble really *feeling* the elements, and your connection to the Divine, I suggest you put this book down immediately and go out into Nature. Stop imagining and start experiencing! Once you're connected to the elements in Nature, you will find it much easier to feel them within the confines of a circle conducted indoors. Instead of imagining a breeze, or rain, or sunlight, or the feel of the Earth, you'll be working from powerful sense memories of your physical, emotional, and spiritual encounters with these energies in their natural state. You can't invoke a direction effectively if you are working from abstract, imaginary thoughts.

The first time I realized how real the elemental energies are occurred during a stifling hot circle one summer afternoon during my first year of studies. We were working in the apartment of one of our Priestesses, and though the windows were open, there was not a breeze stirring. As east was called, a sudden gust of wind lifted the heavy Venetian blind, startling all of us. It was the only puff of air for the entire day. But perhaps the most emphatic lesson was during my second year, when I had the responsibility for calling fire at the handfasting—the Wiccan marriage—of my Priestesses.

I had been working with fire for many months, in an effort to balance my personality with more willfulness and confidence. I wore lots of red, did lots of candle magic, and greeted the Sun every day. The proof of how thoroughly I'd conjured fire occurred in a terrifying, fiery moment as I reached for the fire candle on the altar to purify the circle. My hair fell forward from my shoulder into one of the altar candles and in seconds I was in flames! Luckily, I wasn't hurt—that was never the fire's intention, nor my own. But from that moment on, I began to be more aware and respectful of my own fiery-ness and the power of elemental magic.

You will experience all of the unique energies of the elements—the awakening power of air, the passionate power of fire, the emotions of water, the strength of earth—in your body and in your heart. Though the circle is the first repository into which the energies pour, *you* are their ultimate receptacle. Just casting a circle and Calling the Directions can be a powerful form of making magic. Whether you are a new or seasoned practitioner, I urge you to devote a circle to working only with the elemental powers of the four directions.

Each of us has a wide range of elemental characteristics (have your astrological natal chart done to discover yours). I'm an Aquarius, heavily weighted toward air and water signs, with enough fire to get things done. That means I enjoy communicating ideas (naturally I'm a lawyer, an author, a teacher, and a philosopher), whose feelings, intuitions, and spirituality run very deep (I'm a Priestess), and I've got a strong will, but need help getting organized and materialized (reflected in the relative absence of earth in my chart). When I first began practicing Wicca, I spent lots of time working with fire and earth invocations and did lots of fire and earth magic to bring these elements into my character and my life—and I still do when I need a boost! By working with each element as you cast circle, and by doing elemental magic, you can become more balanced, cultivating and strengthening the aspects that you are lacking. (See Chapter 3, Nature, and the Table of Correspondences for more guidance.)

ADVANCED PRACTICE
AT THE CENTER OF THE CIRCLE

Go to your place of power. Explain to the four directions that you wish to cast a circle and to learn from their powers. Do not set up an altar, because *you* will be the altar. Instead, stand, and remain, at the center of your circle, facing east. Ground and center. Stretch out your arm, and begin casting your circle from the center, three times around.

Call the east and invite the powers of air to join you, to teach you, to illuminate your mind, and inspire your thinking. Pay careful attention to the breeze, as it will respond to your invitation. Pay careful attention to the birds and insects that inhabit the air. Meditate on the gifts of air, and the role the qualities of the element—for example, working with your intellect and your intuition, writing, making music, seeking inspiration, communicating with others, exploring new directions—plays in your life. Do you need more, or less inspiration, mental acuity, communication skills, etc.? Do you think too much, or too little? Ask for balance. Feel that balance within you.

Remaining in the center, turn to the south and invite the powers of fire to join and teach you, to fill you with courage and determination. Pay careful attention to the feeling of the Sun's warmth on your skin, your closed eyes. Meditate on the gifts of your willpower, the role it plays in your life. Do you need more or less of it? Are you courageous enough, or not enough? Are you passionate enough? Do you suppress your anger, or express it too often and harshly? Ask for balance. Feel that balance within you.

Turn to the west and invite the powers of water to join and teach you, to fill you with love and compassion. Pay careful attention to your lips, feel the moisture on your tongue, the sweat on your brow. If you are near water, listen carefully to its sounds. Meditate on the gifts of your emotions, the role they play in your life. Do you need to be more emotional, or less? Are you compassionate, or not? Do you love, and receive love? Ask for balance. Feel that balance within you.

Turn to the north and invite the powers of earth to join and teach you, to fill you with strength and fertility. Pay attention to your body—feel your solidity, your muscles. Feel the Earth beneath you. Listen to the sounds of the Earth—the creatures of the Earth are always singing and talking. Meditate on the gifts of your body, the role it plays in your life. Do you need to be more physical, or less? Are you working to make your dreams a reality? Ask for balance, and feel that balance within you.

Take your time. Turn back to the east when you are done. Open your circle by devoking, or "releasing" and thanking each of the four directions (see Practice: Closing Circle, Devoking and Thanking the Directions, page 114) and giving thanks.

Write down what you learned.

✳   *Why a Circle?*   ✳

All energy moves in a circular manner, that is, in a spiral. We represent energy as moving in waves, but a wave is actually a two-dimensional image of a three-dimensional configuration. (If you can't picture this, take a spring and uncoil it slightly, or wind some wire or a twist tie around a pencil, then pull it off. Squint at the coil or spring, or look at its shadow, and you'll see that, in two dimensions, it looks like a wave.) So, *by working within a circle, you are working within the greater model of how energy moves in the Universe.* From the invisible quantum level of subatomic particles whirling in their orbits, to the glory of galaxies spinning in theirs, the Universe moves in circles.

When you work with energy within a circle you are working in harmony with the organic flow of all energies. That's how magic works— you learn from Nature and harness the natural flow of energies in the Universe. A circle symbolizes infinity, for it has neither a beginning nor an ending. When we say that *"Our circle is cast—we are between the worlds,"* this means that our circle is actually a nexus joining the worlds of spirit and matter, divine and human—it is the point of connection between the two. A circle joins the infinite with the immediate—and literally shows us the meaning of the old occult maxim, "As above, so below."

We work in a circle because we live within the eternal circle of life— the cycles of the seasons, the Moon, the Sun, the tides, and the heavens moving above us. Working within a circle helps our psyches attune to the natural rhythms of divine energy that animate and regulate the order of the natural world. As we work within the circle, and as we study Nature, we see how its cycles relate to the cycles of our own lives, and we begin to recognize divine patterns of change and transformation at play (we'll talk more about this in Chapter 13, Sabbats).

When you take your place in a circle, the physical shape—the roundness—literally and immediately changes the energy dynamics with which we have been conditioned to approach spirituality. When we work together in a circle we create a new model of social relationships. In the old biblical traditions, the passive parishioner sits in the pew, and is subordinate to the spiritual professional at the podium, who is subordinate to the transcendental God in his heaven above. The structure of the church reflects the power relationships, and the energy dynamics, of patriarchy. But everyone is equal in a circle—there is no elevated podium separating the Priestess and Priest from the rest of the community, and no hierarchy between you and the Divine.

The shape of the circle also places each individual within view of everyone else, so just by participating in this simple organic form we create an immediate intimacy, connection, and sense of community. And even in some of the enormous circles that I have participated in, with hundreds of people, the circle connects everyone present—it creates community.

And indeed, the physical shape of a circle facilitates the movement of energy, for just as cooking pots are round to provide for equal distribution of heat throughout whatever is being prepared, a circle distributes divine energy equally throughout the practitioners, though each of us responds in uniquely personal ways.

BASIC PRACTICE
CLOSING CIRCLE, THANKING THE DIRECTIONS/CLOSING THE PORTALS

Before closing circle we often like to end by sending a kiss deosil around the circle with the blessing, "Thou art God/dess," depending on whether you are addressing a woman or man. Then starting in the east, you move widdershins around the circle (remember, that's counterclockwise in the Northern Hemisphere, clockwise in the Southern) to thank the powers of the four directions and close the portals (traditionally referred to as banishing the quarters). This process allows the energies to depart the circle and closes the star portals.

Facing east, draw a "banishing" pentagram in the air before you with your athame or hand (start at the lower left point, then move to the top of the star, etc.). As you draw your devoking ("banishing") pentagram, say farewell and give thanks to each direction:

Devoking Pentagram

> *"Mighty powers of the east (or north/west/south)*
> *Thank you for your presence, and your blessings*
> *And 'ere you depart for your fair and lovely realms*
> *I bid you hail and farewell*
> *Blessed be!"*

An alternative devoking:

> *"Ancient Spirits of the east (or north/west/south)*
> *Thank you for your presence, and your blessings*
> *By the air that we share (by the fire that we are/by the water*
>   *that flows through us/by the earth that unites us)*
> *I bid you hail and farewell*
> *Blessed be!"*

Return to the altar, pick up the candle, and return to the east. Carry the fire candle around the circle, three times widdershins, blowing out all the candles as you walk, and reciting three times:

> *"Fire seal the circle round*
> *Let it fade beneath the ground*
> *Let all things be as they were*
> *Since the beginning of time."*

When you have circumnavigated three times, and all the flames are extinguished, say:

> *"Our circle is open, but never broken*
> *Merry meet and merry part and merry meet again!"*

TEMPLATE FOR CASTING CIRCLE

- Purify and cleanse yourself.
- Set up your altar.
- Purify and consecrate the elements.
- Purify and consecrate the circle.
- Cast circle.
- Invoke the quarters/Call the Four Directions.
- Invoke the Goddess and the God.
- State the purpose of the circle.
- Raise energy.
- Spellcast, if you choose.
- Offer libations.
- Bless the cakes or bread.
- Give thanks as you close the portals and the circle.

THE CIRCLE AS THE EMBODIMENT OF DEITY

Finally, perhaps one of the most important reasons we cast a circle, and its greatest power, is that *a circle is an embodiment of deity* —it is a symbol of the Goddess, but it is also an actual manifestation of the Divine Feminine. When you work within a circle, you are working within the womb of the Goddess. Circles are indeed cauldrons to contain energy—they are the Goddess's cauldron of rebirth, where you make magic to change yourself and your life. The energies of new life flow through you as you are immersed in the infinite potential from which all life springs.

Casting a circle is an important spiritual practice in which you learn to take responsibility for your growth, transformation, and magic. It is a place to encounter your own holiness, to welcome divinity into the world, and to discover the magic that dwells between the worlds. What shape will deity take when you invite it to your circle?

The Goddess

Every woman you meet is the Goddess. If you are a woman, look in the mirror, and you will see Her. And if you are a man, look in your heart and you will find Her, for She is in each of us. Go out tonight and stand beneath the arc of star-filled space, and you will see the Goddess, for you are looking into the womb of all creation. She is the infinite potential from which all existence emerges. She is the life force that gave birth to the galaxies, the stars, and we humans who are made from the stuff of stars. She is the ground of all being, the "quantum energy field" and all within it.

Unlike the biblical model of transcendent, masculine divinity, the Goddess resides in the world. She *is* the world, in all of its myriad forms and expressions. *You do not "believe" in the Goddess, you experience Her.*

The Goddess is visible in the rhythm of women's bodies, and in their capacity to give birth, and in a man's capacity to create, love, and nurture. The Moon is the Goddess's shining face, the ocean is Her womb, the Earth Her body, the Universe Her infinite spirit. She has countless names, faces, powers and gifts, and She has been present with us from the birth of human culture, throughout the ages, and all over the world.

Surrounding you with unconditional love, or rising within you as the inspiration for your life, the Goddess awaits you with open arms. Leave your home, walk out into Nature, and you will experience Her. Look into your soul, and you are Her temple. *The Goddess dwells within your heart. When you speak from your heart, you speak to Her and for Her—you also cultivate Her presence and your relationship with Her.*

BASIC TO ADVANCED PRACTICE
A GODDESS SPELL

Each day for the next week, stand before a mirror, cross your arms over your chest, look into your own eyes, and recite the following spell:

> *"Great Goddess who dwells within and all around me,*
> *Goddess of the Shining Moon and the Fertile Earth,*
> *Goddess of the Starry Heavens and the Infinite Womb,*
> *Goddess from whom all blessings flow,*
> *Bless your child."*

As you finish, close your eyes, uncross your arms, keeping them loosely to your sides with elbows bent, hands up—about even with your shoulders—and palms facing out or upwards. This is called the Goddess position and is used when you Draw Down the Moon to signal the Goddess's presence within you. Let the feeling of Her presence come to you, from within, and without. Open your eyes, and see the light of the Goddess shining forth from you. When you are done, close your arms, and give thanks.

Wicca is the only religion in the Western world that conceives of the Divine as female as well as male, and the Goddess is a primary reason that Wicca is now one of the fastest growing religions in the United States. The fact that Wicca recognizes the female aspect of the Divine was certainly important to me when I started practicing, and it has been important to many women and men I have worked with over the years. Women have created a spiritual home in modern Witchcraft, where they have an image and experience of divinity that honors, liberates, and empowers women, and where they are also spiritual leaders. For men, the Goddess is an equally powerful symbol and transformative spiritual force—which we'll explore more fully below.

THE MANY NAMES OF THE GODDESS

In my tradition, the Great Goddess is revealed to us in an infinity of forms and aspects, which we experience through many Goddesses, such as Diana, Brigid, Kali, Yemaya, Tara, Spiderwoman, Kuan Yin, and even Mary, to name just a few. Just as each of us is a drop of water from the infinite ocean of divine life, so too are the countless Goddesses integral parts of the infinite Goddess. The Great Goddess contains all aspects of being, and so there are Goddesses of mothering and of war, of hunting and of animals, of sexuality and virginity, ecstasy and civilization, creation and destruction, and much more.

This range of possibilities and capacities is one of the Goddess's greatest blessings, especially for women. It's also an important contribution to breaking down the tired old ideas about what's feminine and what's masculine. Ancient Goddesses played all sorts of roles our culture has confined to the masculine realm: They were warriors, hunters, philosophers, magicians, and makers of civilizations. And it's so empowering to discover how often the same Goddess will preside over entirely opposite realms—like the Greek Artemis, who protects women in childbirth but is a virgin, or the Celtic Maeve, who is one of the fiercest Celtic warrior Goddesses and also a Goddess of sexuality. These Goddesses teach us that we women can be complicated: We can be aggressive without ceasing to be sexual, we can be maternal without losing our carefree "Maiden" self or our warrior nature. And so the Goddess in Her many forms also shows us how to think beyond dualities—beyond the limitations of either/or.

For some Witches, rather than a single Goddess with numerous aspects, there are simply numerous Goddesses. The Goddess is both one and many at the same time, and Witches respect both experiences and perceptions.

GODDESSES: A SELECT LIST

Goddesses are multifaceted, so while this list is a good starting point, I suggest you learn more about their many qualities.

Goddesses of Love: Aphrodite *(Greek)*, Oshun *(Yoruban, Voudoo)*, Venus *(Roman)*, Freya *(Scandinavian)*, Bronwyn *(Welsh)*, Shakti *(Indian)*

Goddesses of Culture and Wisdom: Athena *(Greek)*, Minerva *(Roman)*, Hokmah *(Hebrew)*, Isis *(Egyptian)*, Minerva *(Roman)*, Brigid *(Celtic)*

Goddesses of Magic and Transformation: Hecate *(Greek)*, Cerridwen *(Celtic)*, Isis *(Egyptian)*, Tana *(Etruscan/Roman)*, Thorgerd *(Iceland)*, Freya *(Scandinavian)*, Luna Diana *(Roman)*

Goddesses of Healing: Brigid *(Celtic)*, Isis *(Egyptian)*, Hera *(Greek)*, Kuan Yin *(Chinese)*, Tara *(Buddhist)*

Goddesses of Creation: Hathor *(Egypt)*, Shakti *(Indian)*, Spiderwoman *(Native American)*, Ishtar *(Babylonian)*, Amaterasu *(Japanese)*, Al-Lat *(Arabic)*, Nu Kua *(Chinese)*, Tara *(Buddhist)*

Warrior Goddesses: Durga *(India)*, Athena *(Greece)*, Artemis *(Greece)*, Kali *(India)*, Sekmet *(Egyptian)*, Bellona *(Roman)*, Freya *(Scandinavian)*, Morrigan *(Celtic)*

Goddesses of Earth, Prosperity, and Fertility: Demeter *(Greek)*, Ceres *(Roman)*, Freya *(Scandinavian)*, Fortuna *(Etruscan/Roman)*, Lakshmi *(Indian)*, Mokosh *(Slavic)*, Yemaya *(Yoruban)*, Sovereignty *(Celtic)*

Goddesses of Justice: Themis *(Greek)*, Maat *(Egyptian)*, Sekmet *(Egyptian)*, Shait *(Egyptian)*, Hecate *(Greek)*, Kali *(Indian)*, Oya *(Yoruban, Voudoo)*

THE GODDESS IS EVERYWHERE

Witches, whether we are women or men, *experience* the Goddess within us and in the world all around us. I love what Starhawk said about this: "People often ask me if I believe in the Goddess. I reply, 'Do you believe in rocks?'" The Goddess is as real as the air I breathe because She *is* the air I breathe, the water I drink, the Earth that feeds me. She *is* all of that, and more. Because we've been raised in a culture that taught us that God is not present in the world, this reality of a living and present Goddess may seem unfamiliar and unlikely when you are first embracing Witchcraft. But as you work with Wiccan practices I promise you will encounter Her. I saw Her first in my dreams, then in the women in my first coven, and finally, in myself.

THE GODDESS AS ACTIVE CREATOR

The influence of patriarchal thinking in our culture is so strong that even Witches may think of the Goddess as the maternal counterpart to a Father God, or as being passive and inert rather than active and creative. I find it's helpful to remember the Hindu conception of the Goddess as the active, energetic principle of divinity that surrounds, provokes, and ignites the energy of the God. In contrast to the Western view, in Hinduism, it's the masculine force that is unmoving and passive. The Goddess is the (often erotic) initiator of creativity without whom the God cannot function. In Hinduism, the Goddess Maya is the source of all that exists and the active, creating principle in the Universe—the constant movement of the subatomic energy field. Maya is often called the "veil of illusion" because what we see is Her creation, rather than Her force—a force that is constantly creating. We focus upon the infinite variety in Her creation and fail to see the unifying identity and divinity behind all those forms (just as we are unable to see the quantum energy field). As a Witch, your practices enable you to both understand and appreciate the "veil," and to see beyond it.

When you make magic and craft yourself as a Witch, the Goddess is your creative partner. She may be invoked in any of Her many aspects to guide, inspire, and assist you. And one of the most powerful aspects is specifically as a Goddess of magic and transformation. Among these Goddesses are Hecate, Cerridwen, Fata Morgana, Maya, Devi, Tara, Tana, Diana, and her daughter Aradia.

BASIC TO ADVANCED PRACTICE
CERRIDWEN'S CAULDRON, A CHARGING SPELL

At the next full Moon, cast your circle. If you can work outside, do so. You don't need a full altar for this, just your cauldron, the symbol of the Celtic Goddess Cerridwen, or your Goddess/libation bowl. Put your cauldron or bowl in the center of your circle and fill it with objects of personal meaning and power, such as jewelry, a statue of a Goddess, your diary, your Book of Shadows, a talisman, or magical tool, etc.

Ground and center, and connect with the sacred Earth. Then invoke Cerridwen: *"Great Cerridwen, Goddess of magic and transformation, keeper of the cauldron of change and rebirth, come to me, bless me, energize and transform me. Hail and welcome."*

Raise energy (See Chapter 10, Energy) by chanting and "stirring" the object within the cauldron as you chant: *"One thing becomes another, in the Mother, in the Mother."* Feel Cerridwen's power flowing through you, into the cauldron and your objects. Visualize the changes you wish to make in yourself and your life, and see and feel them manifesting. Ground any excess energies. Make an offering, give thanks, and close.

THE GREAT MOTHER EARTH

How old were you the first time you heard the phrase "Mother Nature"? No matter what their religious persuasion, everyone knows and uses that phrase because it touches us at the deepest levels of our souls. Nature, and specifically the Earth, is in every respect our mother. We were born from Her ocean womb, and each day are nourished at Her breast. Without Her, we would perish. Most of us live such modern and comfortable lives, so completely cut off from Nature—buying everything we need at the grocery or department store—that we've lost touch with how totally dependent upon Her we really are. And living within our artificial environments and gated communities, we have cut ourselves off from Her endless gifts—the inspiration of Her beauty, the wisdom of Her ways, the empowerment of Her elements. We have forgotten that Nature is indeed the gown the Goddess puts on in order to be seen.

The Earth has long been revered by indigenous peoples, and by Witches, as an embodiment of the Great Goddess. Spend time in Nature and you will recognize that She is the power of fertility, the source of all life, giving birth to and nourishing all of Her children: plants, animals, humans. Realizing this profound spiritual truth can come in such personal and simple ways. When I began living in farm country I suddenly wanted to learn to cook, and I did, because I was so captivated by the beauty and power of what was growing all around me. Even when we experience Mother Earth at Her most challenging—the heat-scorched desert, the frozen tundras of the poles, the barren landscapes of winter—the magic of life exists and persists.

We personify the Earth in the character of Goddesses, such as Gaia, Demeter, Rhea, Ceres, Sovereignty, and Freya, just as our ancestors did when they created the earliest examples of religious art: round bellied, large-breasted statues that were often found where grain was stored and in burial sites, symbolizing the Goddess's powers of birth and rebirth. Call upon these Goddesses to bless you with fertility, creativity, prosperity, strength, and the capacity to make your dreams come true.

But Witches need to be careful not to fall into the literal mindedness of the biblical religions and just change the gender of deity so that instead of calling upon a white-haired Father God you worship a beautiful Mother Goddess who sits on her earthly throne. When you think of deity *only* in human terms, literally visualizing a woman (or man), you make the vast mystery of the Divine more accessible and understandable to yourself, but you also narrow your ability to experience divinity in all of its expressions.

The priest and rabbi I discussed in Chapter 1 mistakenly believed that Witches "worship" rocks, but in fact we understand that rocks, like all of Nature, are an embodiment of divinity. Wicca recognizes a difference between plants and animals, which, according to science, have a mysterious "life force," and rocks and water, which have energy that, like the bones and blood of your body, are *part* of a greater life force—that of the Divine, and particularly the Divine Mother Earth. (This distinction helps us to live in the world, and to make ethical choices. For example, you'd push a rock off a cliff to save your dog, but you would not pollute a river to make money, nor would you bulldoze a hillside to erect a home without first consulting and receiving permission from the spirits of the land.)

When you work in Nature, you realize that the Great Mother Earth is present in every stone and every cliff, every morsel of food that you eat, in the wood from which your house was built, and the oil that heats your home. She is present in the love of a mother wolf for her cubs, the crone elephants who assist and midwife a mother elephant giving birth, in the mother swan that each year builds her nest in the creek in front of my house where she gives birth to and nurtures her cygnets. She is present in my garden, and the farms and vineyards that surround my home, now barren beneath a mantle of snow, and She is present in the snow itself. And when the snows melt, it is She who will stir to green and flowering life in the spring. The Great Mother Earth, Mother Nature, teaches us the rhythm of life.

Paying attention to Her embodied wisdom, and using your practices to help you, you'll see that life is freely given and generously supported by the Earth. *The Great Mother Earth teaches one of the most important of all spiritual lessons: The natural flow of energy is one of abundance and generosity. This energy is ever-present for making magic, and life.*

BASIC TO ADVANCED EXERCISE:
THE POWER OF THE GREAT MOTHER EARTH

This exercise will help to get you in touch with the Earth's nurturing powers, which are always bestowed bountifully and gracefully.

Go into Nature and look for a place where the Earth opens and reminds you of the shape of a vaginal opening. This could be within a tree, or the roots of a tree, or where a tree has fallen over, between large boulders, in a cave, or within a grassy hollow. Ask for permission to work here, and to learn. If you feel accepted, you may cast your circle, though you don't need to. Use your breath work to quiet and open yourself. Smell the richness of the soil, feel its endless strength supporting you. Observe how everything around you is growing. Watch the birds, animals, and insects feed. Lie back upon the earth, curving into the opening. Feel the gentleness of the grass, the softness of moss, the texture of rocks or bark, the fineness of sand. Ask the Great Mother Earth to nourish and transform you with the powers of Earth.

Now ground and center. Feel the power of the Earth running through you, healing and empowering you, providing you with all the energy you need to live, grow, change, and create the life you long for. Leave an offering for your sisters and brothers. Give thanks. Close your circle.

❈   *Men and the Goddess*   ❈

After working with men for many years, I know that the Goddess is as powerful a spiritual force for them as She is for women. Just as She offers treasured qualities long denied women, She restores aspects of men's humanity, and divinity, which have been sacrificed to an unbalanced and unhealthy conception of masculinity. The Goddess represents many aspects of men that have been denied, suppressed, and neglected.

For men, the Goddess is a force for healing, creative inspiration, and love, and She offers many other blessings as well. Men, it's up to you to discover which gifts you most need, and how you will retrieve them. Finding the Goddess will help you do both, for in finding Her you find what you need.

Perhaps one of the Goddess's greatest blessings is the "waters of life": the fountain of feelings, the Holy Grail so long withheld from

THE STORY OF THE HIDEOUS HAG

Once upon a time when the trees grew tall and thick in the forests, the seas were filled with leaping salmon, and the sky with songbirds, hawks, and swans, the land needed a king, for he was the power needed to keep the fields fertile and the people safe. Three knights— all brothers—set out upon a quest, determined to prove that one of them was worthiest to be crowned king. Two of the knights were well-tested in battle, strong, and confident. The youngest had only just begun his journey to manhood, and often bore the brunt of his older brothers' scorn.

One night on their journey to the castle where the king would be crowned, they made camp within a dark wood. As the three brothers sat around their campfire eating the fine venison they had hunted, an ugly, sallow-skinned, and toothless hag appeared.

"Have you fine knights some morsel of food for an old woman?" she asked.

men. In the wasteland of emotional suppression, the Goddess offers the healing, freedom, refreshment, and empowerment that connecting to your feelings will give you. She also offers sexuality and eroticism that is whole and integrated into the realm of feelings, instead of isolated and objectified in body parts, magazines, porn flicks, one-night stands, and strip clubs.

She is the muse to man's creativity, and inspires culture, honoring your capacity to feel deeply instead of requiring you to repress it. Men have long denied Her, for they have been taught to fear emotions as crippling, irrational, overwhelming forces. Men have also been taught to fear women—their sexuality, power to give birth, menstrual mysteries, intuitive gifts, and strong emotions. Long ago I found an old pre-Christian, Celtic tale, part of the ancient Grail myths I suspect, which brilliantly captures this challenge, and that of the Goddess for men.

The Goddess tests a man, and She rewards him with gifts far beyond

"Away with you, hideous creature," the oldest brother exclaimed. And the second brother tried to drive her off with a shove.

But the youngest brother offered her his food, and when she had eaten, he opened his warm woolen cloak and wrapped it about her frail shoulders. She nestled beside him, smiled up at him with a weird and toothless grin, and asked, "Have you a kiss for a hideous hag?"

Without hesitation he tenderly kissed her upon her hirsute cheek, and then, together, they both fell asleep beside the fire.

In the morning the young man awoke and was stunned to find lying beside him not the hideous hag, but the beautiful Goddess Sovereignty, the sacred power of the land incarnate. She smiled, took his hand, and rose to stand before the three astonished brothers.

"It is you who shall be king," She said to the youngest, "for only a man who is compassionate is fit to serve and to protect the land and its people."

his expectation or imagining. The Goddess provides men with their greatest opportunity to face their encultured fears and to transform them, and themselves. As you discover the Goddess, you discover that Her presence does not weaken you, it strengthens you. She actually brings forth what is best in a man—as the Charge of the Goddess wisely says, power must be accompanied by compassion, honor by humility, and mirth by reverence. The Goddess restores balance to a man's soul.

Your journey to discover the Goddess, and Her contribution to your life and your spirituality, will be facilitated if you spend as much time as you can in Nature, for the Goddess you are seeking surrounds you. She also dwells within you. Finding Her inside may be the most difficult quest of all for men. As you know only too well, men have been taught from their earliest years to separate themselves from their feelings. But your feelings are like a hunting dog: Follow them and they will lead you into the sacred grove within your heart where the Goddess dwells.

GRAIL MAGIC—A GUIDED VISUALIZATION TO FIND THE GODDESS WITHIN

This practice can be used by anyone seeking to meet the Goddess within, but it is particularly helpful for men. In this visualization you are going to awaken and honor your inner Goddess, releasing Her healing and inspiring gifts. You may wish to tape this guided visualization to listen to.

Find a comfortable and quiet place, preferably outdoors in a feminine Earth spot (see the Power of the Great Mother Earth exercise). You may cast a circle around yourself, but it is not necessary. Sit or lie against the Earth and close your eyes. Breathe, meditate, ground, and center. See yourself rising and walking down a path toward a forest. You carry a leather pouch in which you have an offering for the Goddess. Surrounded by magnificent trees, you are walking through a great and ancient forest. As you walk, a hawk flies overhead, swooping downward to land upon your shoulder with a powerful beating of wings and stirring of air. You feel its sharp talons graze your skin as it says, "You have begun the quest for the Holy Grail. It is a journey filled with challenges—are you prepared?"

You feel the warm sunlight on your face, a sense of confidence floods you, and you reply: "I am ready."

As you walk through the silent wood, the bird asks, "What do you seek?" and you answer from your heart.

"When you are ready," the hawk replies, "enter the sacred grove at the end of the path." And with those final words it thrusts away from your shoulder and explodes into flight. The path narrows, the woods grow closer and darker. From a distance you hear a woman singing. You follow her voice to a clearing that is surrounded by a ring of oaks. In the center of the clearing is a stone altar.

You enter the grove and slowly approach the altar. On it stands a shining silver goblet. And beneath it, carved in stone, is a spiral. You reach forward, lift the goblet, and drink. The taste is extraordinary, rich, smooth, and warm as it rolls over your tongue and through your body.

Your heart begins to open and feelings long forgotten flow through you.

You look down into the cup, and as you do so you see yourself, as a younger person, looking back. You hear a woman ask: "What is it you seek?"

You look up, and standing before you is a woman, radiant and stunning. It is the Goddess. She may appear to you as Maiden, Mother, or Crone—or all three. Tell Her what's in your heart. Speak honestly and do not fear Her judgment. Listen carefully to what She says. When She is finished, kneel before Her and feel Her hand touch the top of your head. Let the energy of Her blessing flow into you. Open your heart. Let your wounds be healed.

When you look up, She's gone. Place the chalice upon the altar. Reach into the pouch and place your offering on the altar. Express your thanks.

Leave the sacred grove, head back through the woods and to the place of beginning. Feel yourself within your body. Stretch your fingers, toes, arms, and legs. And when you are ready, open your eyes.

Be sure to write about your encounters in your magical journal.

For men, the Grail is the Goddess within themselves and the world who inspires, challenges, and transforms them. You may see Her first in a vision during a meditation in Nature, or in a dream. She may come to you in human form—you may recognize Her aspects in your mother, grandmother, or significant other. But as you find Her within yourself, you find your muse, your heart, your healing.

Today, perhaps more than ever, the world, the Goddess, and women need valiant knights to go forth once again in Her service and in service to the land and its people. Are you willing?

BASIC TO ADVANCED PRACTICE
AN OFFERING TO THE GODDESS

Create an offering to the Goddess who lives within you. An appropriate offering would be anything that expresses your creativity and what you feel to be your finest qualities, talents, or gifts. You can write, paint, sing, dance, play an instrument, cook, plant, sew, or whatever best expresses the best about you.

Cast a circle, and invoke the Goddess with your own written invocation.

Place your offering upon your altar or—if it is something to be performed like a chant, dance, or piece of music—perform it. Feel the Goddess's presence. You may wish to write in your magical journal what comes to you during this Goddess rite. Give thanks and close your circle.

The Moon, the Triple
✳   Goddess, and Women's Mysteries   ✳

Look up at night into the shining, silver Moon and you will be dazzled. The sharp arc of a new Moon can pierce even the thickest armor of cynicism with a sense of promise. The radiant full Moon is an ancient power for making magic, and a night without a Moon will remind you of the infinite abyss where dreams, death, mystery, magic, and rebirth all dwell. For a man, the Moon is a portal to the realm of his inner Divine Feminine, his subconscious, instincts, intuitions, and his deepest feelings. For a woman, the Moon is a mirror, reflecting the most holy truth that resides within all women.

The Moon's monthly cycle mysteriously reflects women's menstrual cycles, and its phases predict the stages of our lives. From earliest time, women have understood the fascinating connection between the Moon and themselves, for both share a twenty-eight day cycle. Just as the Moon regulates the tides of the Earth, so it regulates the blood tides of women. Make magic regularly with a group of women, and you will soon be sharing this mystery in the joined rhythm of your menstrual cycle. Pay attention to how the cycles of the women in your circle move in and out of rhythm together. It's a sacred, joyful, and occasionally grumpy bond! When I began practicing Wicca, I was astonished at how susceptible my menstrual cycle also became to the magic I was making: Often my period would be delayed until the night of some great ritual.

Working with the lunar mysteries reminds us that our bodies aren't sinful but sacred. And though menstruating women were isolated in patriarchal cultures, and treated as taboo, women are rediscovering what indigenous Goddess-worshipping cultures recognized: Women are particularly receptive to profound visionary states during their menstrual cycle. In some Native American cultures, women retire to a "Moon lodge," where they can experience these natural, altered states of consciousness without interruption or the responsibilities of daily life.

I was recently reminded of how divorced we've become from the connection between the Moon's cycles and our own when I went to a new doctor. He asked me when my last period had been, and I replied that it had begun two days before the dark of the Moon and ended three days after the dark Moon. He looked up, startled, and asked me if I was interested in astronomy, and then proceeded to tell me that he wanted to buy a telescope! Of course, he didn't realize that it's an integral part of my spiritual work to note where the Moon is when my "Moon" begins (when I begin menstruating) and ends.

BASIC TO ADVANCED PRACTICE
WOMEN'S MYSTERIES— OR YOUR MOON LODGE

Get a lunar calendar, one that is devoted entirely to the phases of the Moon every day throughout the year. The next time your "Moon" begins and ends, go outside and look at the Moon. Then mark these days on your calendar. Also, begin learning about lunar goddesses such as Luna and Diana.

Start watching the Moon every night. Notice how your mood and mental focus shifts with the phases of the Moon. Observe yourself over the course of several periods and pay attention to your body also—are your cramps greater when the Moon is full, and less when the Moon is waning to dark?

Set aside the first day of your cycle for psychic, visionary, and spiritual work. Try not to take any painkillers or other menstrual medications. Begin with a cleansing bath, then spend the day outdoors, preferably in your place of power, meditating, resting upon the Earth, and seeking visions beneath the Moon. Allow your mind to wander freely. You may also wish to use various divination tools to converse with the Goddess. Write down your visions and impressions in your magical journal.

The Moon is one of the most ancient symbols of the Goddess, and there are many Goddesses of the Moon, such as Diana, Selene, Heng O, Ishtar, and Luna. When the Catholic Church became the dominant religious power in Europe, Mary was often depicted with the lunar crown that had once belonged to the Goddess Diana.

The Moon is also a long-standing symbol of the unconscious, the sacred spiritual powers that reside deep within your mind, where many feel the Divine dwells without inhibition or repression. But as much as it is a symbol of your inner life, the Moon is also a powerful force that governs the tides of women's bodies and the oceans, as well as the tides of the Earth's growing cycles. Farmers have long planted and harvested by the Moon and its phases, and there is an elaborate folklore associated with the Moon's magical influences on the Earth. Every Moon during the year has a name that harkens back to our Pagan forebears and their deep relationship with the cycles of Nature. I love the evocative poetry of names like the Milk Moon of May, Strawberry Moon of June, Hunter's Moon of October, Cold Moon of December, and the Wolf Moon of January.

Women in particular have a profound spiritual relationship with the three phases of the Moon, for they represent the three aspects of the Goddess—who is referred to as the Threefold Goddess (the Maiden, Mother, and Crone)—and three stages of a woman's life.

NEW (AND WAXING) MOON: THE MAIDEN

She is the active principle awakening to Her power, defined only by Herself and Her hunger to explore and experience. She is free, independent, often a Goddess of wild animals and the hunt, and She is a warrior. She is Artemis, Diana, Kore, Athena, Nimue, Sekmet, Luna, and many others. She is a virgin, which means a woman unto herself. In the Celtic tradition, Her color is white. She is associated with the magic of liberation, courage, and becoming.

NEW MOON MAGIC

New Moon magic is generally dedicated to beginning new projects, recapturing your independence, preparing yourself for battle, feeling your strength, gaining inspiration, or honoring your instincts. The following may be practiced by women and men. Choose any one of these or any other goal associated with the Maiden Goddess (examples of specific Maiden Goddesses are listed above).

Write, create, or select something that symbolizes your goal. When the new Moon appears in the sky (a crescent arcing from right to left in the Northern Hemisphere and from left to right in the Southern), take a purifying bath. Then, dress in white, decorate your personal altar with any items sacred to the Maiden Goddess, and prepare this **Inspiration/Instigation Potion:** Starting with one tablespoon of each, grind together verbena, vervain, mugwort, rue, hyacinth, clove, moonwort, and bay leaves. Add a few drops of Dittany of Crete oil and a few of jasmine oil until the scent pleases you. This formula can also be used as an incense, or a bath.

Place your symbol/creation on your altar. Cast a circle. Invoke the Maiden Goddess, saying: *"I call upon the powers of the mighty Goddess Diana, power of the new Moon, Lady of the Wild Things. Strengthen and free me to live the life I want. Charge and bless me."*

Raise energy by dancing and chanting, "Lady of the Wild Things, free me, strengthen me." Direct the energy into the herbs and your object. Place some of the herbs into a square of white cloth, bundle it together with white ribbon, hold it to your heart, and feel the young, confident energy of the Maiden Goddess filling you and charging your amulet. When you feel ready, give thanks and close your circle. Then start your new project, new life, new attitude—and act in accord.

FULL MOON: THE MOTHER

This aspect of the Goddess is active power purposefully channeled into creativity, whether it is birthing a world, a child, a business, or a work of art. She is powerful, creative, fruitful, sexual, pregnant with life. She is Semele, Isis, Hathor, Shakti, Yemaya, Cybele, Demeter, and many others. She is the power of a woman in the middle years of her life, capable of creating life and culture. She is also the power of women's sexuality. Her Celtic color is red. She is associated with the magic of creativity, fertility, manifestation, and sexuality.

ADVANCED PRACTICE
FULL MOON MAGIC, OR DRAWING DOWN THE MOON AND CHARGING MOON WATER

Traditionally this is done by women, but can be done by men as a very advanced practice.

Solo Practice

This practice is meant to be done solo, although the invocation and process can be done with a partner (see below). Your first experience of the Goddess should be outside, beneath a full Moon, if possible. If you must work indoors, try to do so where you can see the Moon from a window. On a full Moon night, go outdoors to a place of safety and privacy where you can see the Moon. If you can, go to a body of water. Bring a small, empty bottle, which you will fill with water when you are done. If you can't work by a body of water, bring a large bowl with you and enough water to fill it. If you are a woman, pay attention to where you are in your monthly cycle so that you can attune your psyche to the Goddess—Are your energies waning, waxing, full? Are they in sync with the Moon's?

You do not need to set up an altar. Cast your circle in a spot where you can see the Moon and its reflection on the water. If you are using a bowl, place the bowl where you can see the reflection and cast your circle around it. You may wish to sit the first time you do this. Look out upon the water along the silver path of light made by the Moon reflecting on its surface. Open your arms and call upon the Goddess to be with you. You might say: *"Gracious Goddess of the Glorious Mother Moon, by all that is holy I invoke you. By the blood of life that will flow/flows/flowed* (depending on your gender and what stage of life you're in) *through me, let your shining light flow into me, let your power and beauty flow into me, let your wisdom and grace flow through me."*

What is most important is not that you speak the words that I have written, but that you speak from your heart. As you speak, look slowly along the path of moonlight until you are looking up into the shining orb of the Moon itself. As you are visually "walking" along the Path of the Moon, or as you look into the Moon's reflection in the bowl of water and then up into the Moon itself, say: *"Great Goddess of the silver Moon, I look into your mirror bright. I seek a blessing and a boon. I seek the gift of inner sight. Bless me with your power."*

Or write your own request. Repeat the verse softly until you feel yourself opening to the presence of the Goddess. As you feel Her coming to you, allow yourself to receive the feelings, images, and words that flow into you. You may lose all track of time, or find yourself a little unsteady. If you feel any lightheadedness, breathe deeply. Allow yourself to be filled by the Goddess. It may feel as if a presence, and voice, is coming to you from very far away or is wrapped all about you. You may experience an overwhelming rush of deep emotions or a powerful surge of energy. When you feel the presence of the Goddess wane, or actually depart, cross your arms over your heart. Ground yourself: Place your hands upon the Earth and let any excess energies drain away. Advanced practitioners should release the energies into the water.

You may feel somewhat dazed, light-headed, and cold after the experience. It's important to ground by eating something and by drinking water (never alcohol) and to wrap up in something warm. Your memory may be foggy and you may not be able or want to talk, your senses may also be particularly acute and you may experience deep feelings of love and awe. You may remember every word in detail, or nothing at all, which is very common. Write down whatever you do recall.

Fill your bottle with the moonlit water, then hold it up and look at the

Moon through the glass and the water. You now have Moon-charged holy water to work with in making magic (for example, you can use it for scrying).
When you are ready, thank the Goddess for Her visit, and close your circle.

Your experience may range from the very intense to the barely discern-
able, though the power of the full Moon in a natural setting generally produces
at least some strong feelings. You can repeat the experience, preferably working skyclad on a balmy night in a place of safety and privacy. Bring a white or
pale sheet that you can wrap around yourself—as you invoke the Goddess
(Draw Down the Moon), open it to catch the moonlight and the Goddess's
energy. Later at home, make your bed with the sheet and record any dreams
that you have.

Drawing Down the Moon with a Partner

Drawing Down the Moon is also frequently done by working partners, or
members of a circle who will work as partners for the Drawing Down. After
circle has been cast, the partners should take a few minutes to ground and
center and connect their energies by holding hands and circulating energy.

Let's suppose you're the one being drawn into: Stand in the center of the
circle, arms folded across your chest, eyes closed. Your partner (this can be
done by a man or woman) stands in front of you, grounds, and gets in touch
with his/her own longing and desire to be in the presence of the Goddess.
With a wand, s/he draws an invoking pentagram on your body, starting with
the tip of the wand placed lightly upon your third eye (in the middle of your
forehead), then moving to your right foot, then up to your left shoulder, across
to your right shoulder, down to your left foot, and back up to your third eye.

As the invoking pentagram is drawn upon your body, the partner invokes
the Goddess using the invocation above, one s/he has written, or the traditional invocation used in the Tradition of Ara: "*By seed and by root I invoke thee.
By stem and by leaf I invoke thee. By bud and by flower I invoke thee. By fruit and
by seed I invoke thee. Great Goddess* (state the name of the particular Goddess
you are invoking, or general title, such as Lady of the Moon), *descend into this,
the body of thy Priest/ess. See with her eyes, speak with her voice, kiss with her lips,
that your children may know your blessings.*"

As the wand comes to rest upon your third eye, you may feel a shock of energy entering you. As the sense of the Goddess's presence becomes clear, open out your arms into the Goddess position.

It takes time to develop the skills to invoke, and to be Drawn Down into, so don't worry about or expect instant results. It also takes time to be able to speak the words of the Goddess while in the trance state created by Drawing Down, so don't worry if you don't speak. It's an incredible, profound experience—don't judge it, just feel it. And don't be surprised if members of your circle report real changes in your physical appearance and your voice when you are Drawn Down into. Most recently, while communing with the Goddess, one of the women in my coven appeared several inches taller to everyone present.

Again, when the energy begins to wane or the Goddess clearly departs, close your arms. Your partner should ground you with a warm, long hug, and then help you to sit. Ground, eat something, and keep yourself warm.

You will never forget the ecstasy of this encounter with the Goddess, and it will change your life, and your perception of yourself, forever.

WANING MOON: THE CRONE

She is power in contemplative repose, creativity turned inward at will, but able to be turned outward as well. She is wise, introspective, and contains within herself all the powers of the Maiden and Mother. Thus She is also independent, sexual, and creative—the opposite of the image of older women imposed upon them by a patriarchal culture. I saw this so clearly when, after my father died, my mother fell in love again at the age of seventy: She embodied the confident and playful Maiden and the sexual Mother as well as the Wise Crone.

The Crone is the agent of change and transformation who understands the mystery of death, of endings and letting go into the darkness. She is Hecate, Baba Yaga, Morrigan, Grandmother Spiderwoman, and others. She is the power of a woman who is postmenopausal, who owns the power of a full life and its wisdom. Her Celtic color is black. She is associated with the magic of transformation, wisdom, banishings, choices, and death.

WANING MOON MAGIC—HECATE'S POWER TO BANISH

Hecate is often depicted as a Crone, but the ancient Greeks actually knew her as a Maiden Goddess. This capacity to be more than one aspect simultaneously is part of Her power, and is a gift of the Crone, who is also Maiden and Mother. Hecate is an ancient and very shamanic Goddess who predates the Olympian gods. She shared with Zeus the unique power to grant the wishes of human beings but Her association with magic was unique. And She was the only deity with the power to move between all three realms of being: the world of spirits and the dead (the "underworld" or Lower World), of mortals (the Earth or Middle World), and that of the gods (Olympus or the Upper World). Often depicted with the three faces of Her totemic animals—the dog, pig, and horse—Hecate is the Goddess of transformation, for it is She who is invoked at the crossroads of life when a choice must be made. She is not only a Goddess of magic, protection, and justice, She is also a Goddess of liberation. Summon Her to guide you as you become a Witch and to guide your meditations on the wisdom that comes with age.

When the Moon is dark, cast your circle. Use your favorite method of divination to help you see clearly what you have outgrown, and call Hecate to help you see clearly and to choose wisely. You will need a piece of black yarn and a cauldron in which to burn it. Use purple candles.

Prepare a **Dark Moon/Banishing Incense:** Make the New Moon incense described on page 133 and add two tablespoons of Low John, one tablespoon of sandalwood, a pinch of hellebore root, and a pinch of dirt taken from a crossroads where three roads converge. Burn the incense.

Hold your black yarn and recite the Invocation of Hecate:

"Hecate, Goddess of magic at the crossroads, you I invoke:
You walk in all the realms: heaven, earth, and world of the spirits.
By your secret names I call to you:
Chthonia of the Earth, Phosphoros—the light bringer,

Propolos—the attendant who leads,
Persephone's guide, Protector of women,
Patroness of ancient Rome,
I entreat your presence
At the crossroads of my life."

Now take the black yarn and tie a knot in it for each thing you wish to banish. As you tie each knot, ask Hecate to help you banish your self-doubt, or your fear, or that which you've outgrown, etc. Then say, *"Help me to relinquish that which holds me back. Help me to transform decay into rebirth. Banish (state whatever it is). Hecate, force of magic, you I invoke."*

Now, place the yarn in your cauldron and use your candle to set it aflame. As it burns, chant: *"Burn it away, Hecate, burn it away, Hecate!"*

And when it is gone, say loudly and with conviction: *"Be gone! By Hecate's power, so mote it be!"*

Thank the Goddess. You may also wish to speak with Her, asking Her counsel as to which road to take into your future by again using divination. Be sure to write down Her advice, and to follow it. Close your circle.

✳   *The Goddess Who Guides You*   ✳

It is impossible to explore the Goddess in all of Her many forms, but over the years I have seen that there is usually one Goddess in particular who calls to each of us, women and men. Each Goddess has Her own unique powers, gifts, symbols, stories, animals, plants, colors, invocations, energies, and mysteries. She will reveal Herself to you through all of these and more, and as you learn and use them in creating magical rituals, Her powers will grow within you, and will fill the world around you.

There are many magical paths for finding the Goddess, many of which you've now explored, and which are not just the information-based, logical path of the mind (though there's nothing wrong with good research to help you discover which Goddess has come to you). They are the paths of Nature and the Moon, intuition and dreaming,

SOME GREAT GODDESS SPELLS

Womb Goddess of the Sea (Water)

Go floating—preferably in the ocean. Bring seven white carnations as an offering to Yemaya, fertile Goddess of the ocean. Scatter them around you as you enter the water and call Her to be with and bless you. Stay close to shore, and especially if you're not a skilled swimmer, use something designed to keep you afloat. Feel the water beneath you supporting and cushioning you. Let your emotions rise to the surface and flow through you, let the Goddess rock you, restore you, and renew you. Float in the womb of the Goddess, from whom all life on Earth was born, just as you floated in your mother's womb. Feel Her love.

The Mother's Heartbeat (Earth)

Take a drum, head out to Nature, sit upon the Earth, listen to the music around you, ask the Mother to be with you, and then beat softly upon the drum in the tempo of a heartbeat: *bum bump* pause *bum bump* pause *bum bump* pause.... Let the drumming open your heart to the Earth's heart.

symbols and the stirrings of something sacred within. She is welcomed by poetry or meditation, chanting or invocation, Drawing Down, or other powerful techniques. And most of all by your desire to encounter Her and your ability to open yourself, like a sacred chalice, to receive Her. *Just as casting circle reveals the sacredness of the space in which you stand, invoking the Goddess reveals Her presence, which has been with you all along.*

Cultivating your relationship with the Goddess takes time, but once you open your heart to Her, She will fill your life with magic.

Igniting the Fires of Love (Fire)

For women: *Aphrodite Oil.* Wear this for love and passion, to draw love irresistibly toward you. Mix four tablespoons of almond oil with one tablespoon each of rose oil, musk oil, and ambergris oil. Add a pinch of ground cinnamon.

Keep your oil in a lovely bottle placed on a beautiful shell. Pamper yourself: Have a massage, buy a sexy outfit, get a new hairstyle, go dancing!

For men: *The Lady of the Lake.* This spell will inspire you to chivalrous acts of courage, passion, and romance.

Read the Grail stories, particularly the tales of Gawain and the Green Knight. Create a ritual in which you pledge yourself to honoring your creative spirit and the Goddess who is your muse.

Music Magic (Air)

Listen to Billie Holiday, Ella Fitzgerald, and Lena Horne. Sing along shamelessly and play their music as you write an invocation of the Goddess.

BASIC TO ADVANCED PRACTICE
CREATING AN OFFERING AND AN ALTAR FOR THE GODDESS

Create an altar to your Goddess using Her colors, fruits, vegetables, flowers, herbs, symbols, and objects that represent Her gifts and powers. Create or find an image of Her for the altar. Create a potion using herbs that are special to Her. Create an offering for Her. Meditate at Her altar, and ask Her for guidance. Ask to be shown how to integrate Her powers into your life, and how to receive and create Her blessings. Cast circle, raise energy, and direct it to the visions of your growth. Write in your magical journal and act in accord with the guidance you receive. Integrate the wisdom, power, and blessings of the Goddess into your life as you craft yourself as a Witch.

THE CHARGE OF THE GODDESS—ARA TRADITION (ADAPTATION OF LELAND/ GARDNER/VALIENTE VERSION)

Read by Priest: "Listen to the words of the Great Mother, who was of old called Artemis, Astarte, Dione, Melusine, Aphrodite, Rhea, Cerridwen, Arrianrhod, and by countless other names. The youth of Sparta made due sacrifice at her altar."

Priestess: "Whenever you have need of anything, once in the month, and better it be when the Moon is full, then shall you assemble in some secret place to call upon me, for I am the Great Goddess. Beneath the Moon shall you assemble, you who wish to learn all the mysteries yet have not won the deepest secrets. To you shall I teach things that are as yet unknown. And you shall be free from slavery, and as a sign that you are truly free, you shall be naked in your rites, and you shall dance, sing, make music and love all in my presence. For mine is the ecstasy of the spirit and mine also is joy upon the Earth. My law is love unto all beings.

"Keep pure your highest ideals, strive ever toward them. Let naught stop you nor turn you aside. For mine is the secret that opens

At the most critical moment where we face annihilation, the Goddess restores balance to a toxically unbalanced world. She heals by returning to both women and men the lost qualities of divine connection, nurturance, compassion, and abundance. The Goddess changes the rhythms of life and culture from endless and destructive linear expansion to cycles of creation and repose that embrace growth, but temper it with harvest, rest, and renewal. She restores intuition to intellect, and retrieves and redefines ideas about what it means to be active and passive, masculine and the door of youth, and mine is the Cup of the wine of life, and the Cauldron of Rebirth, which is the Holy Grail of Immortality.

"I am the gracious Goddess who gives the gift of joy unto the hearts of humanity. Upon Earth I give knowledge of the eternal Spirit, and beyond death I give peace, freedom, and reunion with those who have gone before. Nor do I demand aught in sacrifice, for behold! I am the Mother of all things, and my love is poured out upon the Earth."

"I am the beauty of the green Earth, and the white Moon amongst the stars, the mystery of the waters, and the desire of heaven and of men. I call unto you to come to me who is the soul of Nature and who gives life to the Universe. From me all things proceed and unto me all things must return. Beloved of Gods and men, let thine inmost self be enfolded in the rapture of the infinite. Let my worship be in the heart that rejoices, for behold, all acts of love and pleasure are my rituals, and therefore let there be beauty and compassion, honor and humility, mirth and reverence within you. And know, you who think to seek for me, that your seeking and yearning is of no avail unless you have learned this mystery: That if that which you seek you find not within yourself, you will never find it without. For behold, I have been with you since the beginning, and I am that which is attained at the end of desire."

feminine. The Goddess returns bearing the promise of new life, and so She brings us hope, inspiration, and joy.

The reborn Goddess, and we, require a very different God from the one who has scorned and oppressed Her. One of the most precious gifts that the Great Mother Goddess brings us as She emerges from the Underworld is a new God. Who is this new God, born of the Great Mother?

The God

There is a wonderful Scottish expression that a student of mine taught me: "Never give a sword to a man who can't dance." In defiance of all the biblical images and edicts we've been raised with, when you make magic crafting yourself as a Witch, you're going to encounter a God who dances. In Wicca, the God is not just warrior, king, and father. He is playful, joyous, erotic, and ecstatic.

Where can you find this God? If you are a man, look in the mirror, and you will see Him. And if you are a woman, look at your life and you will find Him. Go out today and stand beneath the warm and shining Sun and you will see and feel Him. The God is the fire that fuels creation, the force that inseminates the ground of being, and the seed from which all life grows. The planets, the comets, and the star stuff from which all humans are made are the God, for every atom in our bodies was once a part of a star.

Like the Goddess, the God is the life force flowing through creation, and He is present in the ground of all being. He resides within all of us, and like the Goddess, He too has countless names, faces, powers, and gifts. Like the Goddess, the God is one and many simultaneously.

The Old and New Testaments of the Bible have provided our dominant stories of the Divine Masculine as an absent, single parent/angry father, or a sacrificed son of God. But there are countless stories and myths about Gods which have survived, showing us the tremendous range of qualities the God actually encompasses. There are Gods who are sons and lovers of Goddesses (Tammuz, Adonis), who are so present in the world they are actually part animal (Herne, Cernunnos, Pan), or are the green plants growing from the Earth (Tammuz, Baal, the Green Man, Mescalito). There are Gods who are as famous for their lovemaking as their warmaking (Mars and Ares).

But standing between us and these other experiences of the Divine Masculine is the presiding presence of the God with whom we have all been raised, even if we were not raised in religious homes—Yahweh, the God of the Abrahamic religions (Judaism, Christianity, and Islam). Until modern Witchcraft reappeared on the Western religious scene, the word "God" conjured the image so beautifully captured in Michelangelo's paintings on the Sistine Chapel's ceiling: a barrel-chested, bearded patriarch looking down at us from his heavenly realm. Read the Bible and the image of a stern deity becomes more vivid, and far more frightening. For all of his wisdom and divine power, Yahweh was a self-proclaimed jealous God, who demanded that animals be sacrificed to him and who angrily smote anyone who disobeyed him. And he ordered his followers to do the same and worse, all from his distant throne, far away from the world in which we live and struggle.

In the context of this punitive and distant Father God, and the surviving, patriarchal Pagan deities who were also supplanting the Goddess, it is easy to see how Christianity could arise. The figure of Christ presents a very different conception of masculine divinity—he is tolerant, forgiving, compassionate, the soul of gentleness. He is actually quite feminine (having taken onto himself many of the qualities once ascribed to the now suppressed Divine Feminine) and, according to many New Testament stories, atypically sympathetic to women. But like his mother, Mary, he is also without sexuality, or a sense of humor. Jesus is not playful, Jesus doesn't dance, and like his father, he too is capable of self-righteous anger.

Ultimately Christ is the embodiment of self-sacrifice, which elevates him to the holiness and power of his Father God. Christ is not only the son of God, but is himself divine. While the symbol of the crucifixion is a profound and complex religious metaphor (rooted, in part, in the pre-Christian agricultural mysteries such as those of Attis, Tammuz, Diony-sus, and Adonis), I can't help remembering my reaction as a little girl to the sight of Christ upon the cross. I recoiled when I saw the spikes ham-mered into his hands and feet, the blood running from the wounds and from an open gash beneath his heart and down his face, where a crown of huge thorns cut into his skin. The image alone terrified me, and as I grew older I was increasingly disturbed that Jesus was in this state because of his father's decision to sacrifice him. To allow your child to be violently sacrificed, even for a "good" cause (saving mankind from "sin"), is still vi-olent and cruel—and you can't escape the harsh fact that this morally amounts to murdering one's own child.

The crisis of the absent father and the sacrificed son is everywhere present in our modern culture, and could not have been more violently and painfully evoked for those of us who lived through the Vietnam War. Reflecting the actions of their God, men sent their sons off to slaughter rather than work at solving the problems in Southeast Asia in a peaceable way. We have been raised with such wounded, brutal, and brutalizing conceptions of the Divine Masculine. How do we move beyond suffering and the infliction of suffering? And most importantly, how do we find a living, present God who dances in joy and embraces life and the Goddess? Where does the journey begin?

TEARS OF POSEIDON

Since the 1960s, many men have struggled to find a new definition of masculinity, one that does not involve shutting down emotionally only to burst out in anger or violence once those feelings surface. In the 1980s,

Robert Bly, a leader of the men's movement, wisely and sadly noted that men don't talk about their feelings because when they look inside, they cannot find them. And the common experience of the absent father is also a reflection of that distant God whom we can't access—He came, He procreated, He went to the office, so obey the rules while He's gone and He'll be back on Judgment Day to punish you if you were naughty.

Expressing most feelings other than anger is taboo for men, and many of us women also have this problem of repressed emotion, especially when we enter the once-forbidden work realms of men, where strong emotion is considered a weakness. Bly's other great and wise suggestion was that the appropriate response to such an absence of feelings is grief.

Having spent many years "stuffing" my feelings, especially as a lawyer, and having had cause to grieve, I know Bly's counsel is wise. As you allow yourself to grieve—awkward, frightening, and difficult though it may be at first—what you discover is that *the grief is a barrier, blocking the rest of your emotions.* Like the water that melted the Wicked Witch of the West in *The Wizard of Oz,* tears and expressions of mourning—like speaking, writing, ritual, or using therapy (*not* abusing alcohol or drugs)—dissolve the obstruction of grief and allow *all* your feelings to begin flowing freely. And so as you begin your journey to find the God who dances, summon the aid of a God who resides in the saltwatery realm of emotions, and who can help you to grieve.

BASIC PRACTICE
THE RITUAL OF GRIEF

Combine one cup of salt and three cups of water in a bottle or other container and bring it with you to the water's edge (even a small stream will do), preferably at sunset. Let yourself grieve. Think about your losses and reasons to mourn: relationships that failed, friends and family you have lost, opportunities that passed you by or dreams that died, time that was wasted caretaking for unappreciative people instead of spent nurturing yourself, the loss of permission to cry, the absence of your father, or whatever haunts you.

Allow your feelings to surface. Cry if you can. Invoke Poseidon, the ancient Greek God of the Sea, whose myths are filled with emotions as deep as the ocean, and who is a God of male emotions. You might simply say: *"Mighty God Poseidon, whose feelings are as deep and powerful as the vast sea you rule, hear my lament, accept my tears, help me to cleanse my heart and free my soul to feel."*

Speak your grieving out loud, stating your regrets and sufferings, your fears and losses, your pain and sorrow, and each time you acknowledge aloud something that you are grieving, pour some of the salt water into the water before you. When you're done, wash your face in His waters, and thank Him.

Repeat this practice as often as you need to, until you feel your grief breaking up and dissolving and your feelings beginning to flow.

✳ *Rebirth of the Dancing God* ✳

Working with the God in any of His various forms, you will find that whatever you have lost or longed for—your feelings, your sexuality, your spontaneity, your passion, your courage, your determination to live your life on your own terms, your authenticity—will all be reborn with Him. He leads you to a different expression of masculinity—not stoical and humorless but playful, in touch with your emotions, intuitions, and instincts, free enough with your body to dance and to experience your sexuality as sensuality, attributes we were taught weren't masculine. *The dancing God is always present in the magic of daily life.*

Saying God is a potent force present in the world is just an abstraction if you don't bring Him into your life. Personal ritual is one of the most powerful ways of accomplishing this. And just as casting a circle is itself an invocation of the Goddess, in a very real sense, creating a ritual within that circle can invoke the God. As you invoke Him, you will discover one of His greatest gifts—His powers of rebirth.

But how do you discover which Gods to invoke? Once your feelings are more fully available to you, you'll find they're a powerful guide to recognizing, encountering, and experiencing the God in His many guises. The God who first comes to you may take any one of many shapes—don't superimpose your intellectual expectations or you may miss His appearance entirely. The God is not abstract, He's visceral and the place to encounter Him is not in books or ideas, but within yourself and in the world. Invite Him to join you and He will appear.

Passion, erotic or otherwise, is the force that opens your life to the God of Wicca. Let your longings and fascinations guide you to Him. A student of mine always loved music but never learned to play. After years of prowling the club scene, he finally picked up a guitar, and it was then that the God really came to him. Making music got him out of his head and in touch with his strong feelings, and his feelings were the fuel for his music. He had found his bliss, his divine gift, and in the process he found the God within himself. He was soon working with Gods of music, dance, and ecstasy—such as Dionysus and Apollo. He learned to play drums, and brought all of these, and the God energy that they expressed, into his magic and his life.

BASIC TO ADVANCED PRACTICE
A GOD SPELL

Each day for the next week, standing before a mirror, arms crossed over your chest (this is called the God position), look into your own eyes and recite the following spell:

> *"Great God who dwells within and all around me,*
> *God of the shining Sun and the fertile forest,*
> *God of the stars above and the seed of new life within,*
> *God from whom inspiration comes,*
> *Empower me."*

As you finish, close your eyes and let the feeling of His presence come to you, from within, and without. Open your eyes, and see the light of the God shining forth from you. When you are done, lower your arms, and give thanks.

GODS—A SELECT LIST

As with the many Goddesses, these Gods embody more than one quality, but here is a short list of Gods you can work with in making magic. I encourage you to learn more about the various Gods.

Love: Eros, Dionysus (*Greek*), Amor (*Roman*), Osiris (*Egyptian*)

Culture/Wisdom: Baldur (*Scandinavian*), Chokmah (*Hebrew*), Ganesha (*Indian*), Hermes (*Greek*), Thoth (*Egyptian*), Elleggua, Ogun (*Yoruban, Voudoo*)

Magic and Transformation: Amathaon (*Welsh*), Osiris (*Egyptian*), Shango (*Yoruban, Voudoo*)

Healing: Apollo, Asclepius, and Chiron (*Greek*), Chango (*Yoruban, Voudoo*)

Creation: Bumba (*Congo*), Zeus (*Greek*), Jupiter (*Roman*), Shango (*Yoruban, Voudoo*)

BASIC EXERCISE:
HEROES

Another way to find the God is through your heroes—who are they? What have they accomplished? Why do you admire them? What is their power, their gift, their talent? How does it inspire you? You can see and identify and begin to experience the God energy by answering these questions.

A DANCING GOD

Because Wicca is the only religion in Western culture that honors the Divine as female as well as male, the feminist community has made a substantial contribution to its rapid growth. Witches have emphasized the

Warrior: Ares (*Greek*), Mars (*Roman*), Chango (*Yoruban, Voudoo*)

Prosperity: Dionysus (*Greek*), Adonis/Tammus/D'Umuzi (*Middle East*), Enki (*Middle East*), Frey (*Scandinavia*), Ganesha (*India*), Herne (*British*), Ogun (*Yoruban, Voudoo*)

The Green Man/Fertility/Nature: Jack-in-the-Green, Jack-in-the-Pulpit (*British, Celtic*), Dionysus, Tammuz, Adonis (*Middle Eastern*), Mescalito (*Native American*), Ochossi (*Yoruban, Voudoo*)

Music and Dance: Apollo, Dionysus (*Greek*), Shiva (*India*)

Justice: Odin (*Scandinavia*), Zeus (*Greek*), Jupiter (*Roman*), Shango (*Yoruban, Voudoo*)

Trickster: Loki (*Scandinavian*), Coyote (*Native American*)

Fertility/Instincts/Sexuality/Horned Gods: Dionysus, Pan (*Greek*), Cernunnos (*Celtic*), Herne (*British*), Apis, Osiris (*Egypt*)

Power/Wisdom/Sun Gods: Helios (*Greek*), Sol (*Roman*), Ra, Horus (*Egyptian*), Shango, (*Yoruban, Voudoo*) Baldur (*Scandinavian*)

Goddess, and some Witches, particularly those who practice in the Dianic tradition, do so exclusively. As the Taoists say, if a tree has grown all of its life bent in one direction, and you wish it to grow straight, for a time you must bend it in the opposite direction.

But working with a God who has as much range as the Goddess can also be religiously revolutionary. He is a force of profound empowerment for men, and for women—which we'll explore more fully below. As with the Goddess, there is great diversity within the Wiccan/Pagan community as to how the God is viewed and experienced. In my tradition, we experience Him as the Goddess's complementary partner, the other half of the dynamic process out of which the Universe was born, and which continues to drive its movement and creativity. And we experience the many Gods as integral aspects of the Great God.

DIONYSUS

Because the many manifestations of God energy are so richly varied, they have the power to impregnate our culture with utterly new definitions and experiences of the masculine, and the feminine. One of the most radical examples is the Greek God Dionysus. He's a terrific God to work with for many reasons, most importantly Dionysus introduces us to a very different Divine Masculine. Qualities once confined to the feminine belong to Him, and He points the way for men and women to find the lost parts of themselves, and to integrate the masculine and feminine. He's also a God of ecstasy who will help you to get in touch with your ecstatic self, and guide you as you experience spirit and flesh meeting as one. He's the God that teaches you to dance, and He's as close as a great rock 'n' roll concert or the passion that makes you feel truly alive.

Dionysus's "feminine" qualities stem from the fact that He was disguised as a woman to hide Him from the wrath of the Goddess Hera. She was enraged that Her husband, Zeus, had fathered Him with Semele (sometimes depicted as a mortal, other times as an Earth Goddess). An earthy God, Dionysus was found in the grapes from which holy wine was made, and the bull who has long been a symbol of the God's fertility. He is a God who dies and is reborn, and He is a profoundly shamanic deity because, like Hecate, He moves between realms of existence—the earthly realm where He lived amongst humans, the spiritual because He is a God, and the netherworld of death because each year He died, and was reborn from death.

Dionysus is also a shamanic deity because, above all else, He is a God of ecstasy, which is the state beyond duality, the state in which you are united with divinity. He is a God you *feel* within yourself, and as Joseph Campbell said: "The power of Dionysus is to ride on the full fury of the life force." He is also a God of madness—which strikes only when you deny Him. Contrary to stereotype, He is not a God of alcoholic excess; in fact, His followers did not indulge in drunkenness, for it dulled the senses (in fact, alcoholism is a form of madness for it obscures the God), though He is a God of intoxication by divine bliss.

If you're a man, you certainly don't have to dress in drag to encounter Dionysus! You just need to let go of the need to always be in control, and integrate the traditionally feminine qualities of intuition, emotion, and the capacity to be open, to receive, and to rejoice, which are part of experiencing ecstasy. Working with Dionysus you will realize that these are also masculine qualities. For women, He also represents the freedom expressed by His Priestesses, the Bacchantes, to independently revel in wild abandon.

BASIC TO ADVANCED PRACTICE
THE GOD WHO TEACHES US TO DANCE

You can work alone, or for even more energy, with a group. You will need seven purple candles: four for the quarters and three for the altar, a drum, some music that makes you want to dance, a bunch of grapes, a bottle of grape juice or Greek wine, a pitcher of water, and a glass or glasses. If you have an image of Dionysus, you should put it on your altar.

Cast your circle, and invoke Dionysus, saying:

> "I invoke you Dionysus
> By the grape and the drumbeat,
> By the dance and the heartbeat,
> By the bull and the dancer,
> Hear me, dancer in the darkness,
> Shining Dionysus, by vine and by horn I invoke you,
> Bless me and teach me to dance."

Pour yourself a small glass of wine or juice. Rub some on your lips, your feet, the palms of your hands, and over your heart. Drink some.

Put on your music, pick up your drum, and beat it in time with the music. When you are ready, get up and dance. Don't stop when you feel exhausted—push through it and keep dancing. (If you have any physical problems that would make dancing dangerous, you should not dance, or if you can dance somewhat, do so slowly and within your physical limitations.) Call out to Dionysus to dance with you, and in you. *Feel* His presence.

When you are beyond exhaustion, and you know that He has been with you, drop to the floor and feel your heart pounding, your blood rushing, your energy dancing. Ground the excess energy. Drink some water to rehydrate. Then, give thanks and close your circle.

You'll also find Dionysus wherever you find rock 'n' roll and raves. But remember, experiencing ecstasy doesn't mean taking the pharmaceutical. It's illegal, it depletes your serotonin levels thereby creating a posthigh depression, and the long-term effects are unknown. You don't want to be under the influence of anything but the God when you invoke Dionysus.

Dionysus was often depicted as a bull, and the Minotaur—the bull headed man/God—is another of his forms. As Greek culture became increasingly devoted to the rational mind, Dionysus fell from favor and the Minotaur was depicted as a monster hidden in a labyrinth on the island of Crete, who was ultimately slain by Theseus. The myth expresses the tragic change in Western culture as the ecstatic became demonic. Western culture has a very old fear of "losing control" and looking foolish. Some have theorized that men are addicted to orgasms because it is the one ecstatic experience they have that allows them to feel intensely; afterward they shut down again. Similarly, abusing alcohol seems to allow some men to release repressed feelings, but ultimately leads to depression. Dionysus defies the social edicts that men ought to keep their emotions in check and women should rein in their sexuality and anger if we are to "fit in" to society.

The Dionysian ecstatic experience ruptures this repression. A Wiccan Priest in the Tradition of Ara encountered Dionysus at a critical time in his life and was deeply transformed. Several years into his recovery from alcohol abuse, he had a profound visionary dream. He found himself awakening on a dune, high above a beach where a crowd of frightened people were pointing out to sea. There he saw a huge, black sea creature moving toward the shore. Terrified, he knew that everyone would be taken by it, and he rose to run.

He saw he was on an island, and knew there was nowhere to go, but still he thought he could get away. He ran toward a copse of trees at the far end of the island where he might be able to hide.

He was almost at the trees when suddenly he felt something staring at the back of his neck. He turned and there, standing on top of the dune where he had been sleeping, was a gargantuan black bull with red eyes. It was staring right at him. He realized it was the creature from the sea and it was after him. He turned to run again. In two quick leaps the bull vaulted across the island, standing between him and the trees. The bull stared at him, and he realized he couldn't escape. There was nowhere to hide.

Suddenly, feeling his rage at being prey, he began screaming: "All right, you son of a bitch! What's the worst you can do to me? Kill me? Well, all right, then fuck you, you bastard!" And he charged the enormous creature. He thrashed against the beast, flailing and kicking wildly, but the creature, which now had the body of a man and the head of a bull, did not harm him. Instead the Minotaur wrapped his immense arms around the Priest, holding him to his chest, cradling him like a father holds a child. The Priest stopped fighting, and was suddenly swept by overpowering emotion. He began crying as he felt tremendous love coming from the beast. The bull God carried him to the water, and held him gently in the salty waves. And as he cried, his sadness, fear, and anger disappeared. There was nothing but release and love. And then he woke up.

He woke up within his life as well, and rapidly began making the changes he had always longed for. Years later, when he became a Wiccan Priest, he discovered that the Bull/Minotaur of his dream was Dionysus. He recognized his period of alcoholism as an initiatory spiritual journey, a death and rebirth. And his dream was a signal that he had moved from the madness of excess and denial, to the ecstasy of divine connection.

As you walk the labyrinth of your life, you will learn to dance with the Bull God, and you will discover that at the center of the labyrinth you will find, not a deadly monster, but a God of love and ecstasy who awaits you with open arms.

A Different and
✳   *More Complete God*   ✳

There are countless sources for reconceiving of and reconnecting with the Divine Masculine in new and very liberating ways. One source of inspiration is the Hindu tradition. The God is the passive principle, acted upon and animated by the Divine Feminine. For example, Shiva, the Lord of the Dance, is often provoked to destructiveness, but when He is in the presence of the Goddesses Shakti or Parvati He can also be a divine creator.

This dynamic is most graphically depicted in sexual imagery in which the Goddess straddles the God by sitting on top of Him. Guys get a vacation and girls get on top! (This essential interdependent relationship exists in all partners, regardless of gender, sexual orientation, or preference—how the polarity is expressed is unique to each individual, and couple.)

The God becomes a very different being when approached in this matter—far more contemplative, receptive, and reactive than we have considered Him in the West, even in most traditions of Witchcraft. Rather than disempowering men, this new model can liberate them from society's singular emphasis on competitiveness, aggression, and domination. It also frees them from always having to be in charge, to initiate sex, and otherwise "run the show." By working with these very powerful Gods, men can embrace these other parts of themselves that will in turn help them to fully experience both masculine and feminine divinity.

These broader conceptions and experiences of God don't negate or deny the hunter, the warrior, the king, and other more traditional positive qualities of masculinity. But they provide a balance to those qualities, and a widening of all the possibilities open to you. They will also help you to reconceive what is "masculine" and what is "feminine." Ancient Gods were lovers, partners, dancers, musicians, and poets, as well as warriors, hunters, fathers, and kings.

Many Witches see the God as existing *within* the Goddess, in keeping with the early agricultural motifs of the Old Religion. The God was the son and the lover of the Goddess. He was the seed which grew from the Mother Earth, was harvested, and then replanted in the Earth, fertilizing Her to grow once again (the Gods Tammuz and Adonis are two of the most vivid examples of this dynamic). And He was the Sun, reborn from the womb of the Goddess. Others work with the God as the Goddess's co-equal, cocreative partner (Chapter 13, Sabbats, explores their relationship). The Ara tradition appreciates the wisdom in both perspectives.

As with the Goddess, you will discover that *you don't believe in the God, you experience Him.*

THE GREEN MAN

Going outside and into Nature is a sure way to experience the God. But in our culture, we've almost completely forgotten about the God who dwells in Nature. Even in the midst of the "Bible Belt," Mother Nature remains a cultural icon, but the Green Man is a mystery to modern folk. He's one of the most ancient and magical Gods. Call upon him—the Green Man, Jack-in-the-Green, Jack-in-the-Pulpit, Dionysus, Tammuz, Adonis, Mescalito, Ochossi—and He will teach you to dance, get your feelings flowing, and help your magic manifest.

The Green Man is the God of Vegetation, the life force embodied in the plant creatures of the natural world. He is corn and grain, vine and fruit, and the magical spirit of peyote and the other psychotropic plants. He wears a leafy crown, and his image is found all over the churches and cathedrals of England and Europe, a surviving reminder of the Old Ways. His energy is gentle, patient, and joyful, and like the Mother Earth, He nourishes.

Just as the Moon teaches women about the inherent divine wisdom of their bodies, the Green Man teaches men about the holy rhythm of theirs. He embodies and teaches the cyclical certainty of the life force. All plants start as seeds within the Earth, grow, and finally bear fruit, which dies by being harvested. We eat the fruit, and once again the seed is returned to fertilize the Earth and the cycle begins again. The Green God is in every seed—He is the Sun's energy, the blueprint of the future, the spiraling DNA. He dies and is reborn and His spirit is eternal. He is the teacher of the mystery of time, and He is infinite. Like Dionysus, who is also God of the Vine, He teaches you about the natural cycle of life, death, and rebirth—in the short cycle of growing plants.

In the life cycle of the Green Man, a profound spiritual mystery is revealed. Though the form changes, the spirit (or life force) remains constant. So if you want to make his acquaintance, I suggest you step out into Nature.

BASIC TO ADVANCED PRACTICE
DANCING WITH THE GREEN MAN

On the first nice day when you can take some time to go hunting for the Green Man, head for the woods and hike into your place of power. Begin with a sensitivity exercise or two: Pay attention to what you see and what you smell. Ground and center. Feel the power of life that makes all the plants grow flowing through and empowering you. Feel yourself grow healthier, stronger, more joyful. Realize all the good things you are creating in your life. Ask the Green Man to be with you, and to show Himself to you. If you have a pentacle, you might place it upon the Earth and stand or sit upon it. Cross your arms over your chest, clear your mind, and when you are ready, invoke the God of the Earth (in my tradition, this is called Drawing Up the God). You might say: *"Green Man, power of the forest, power of the grain, power of all things that grow, Green Man who feeds us, feed my spirit, teach me how to grow."*

Open your eyes very slowly, so that your eyes are like slits. Pay careful attention to the first thing you see. If you perceive a shimmering, sudden movement, you've just seen the Green Man dancing. Open your eyes quickly—see if you can catch another glimpse as He slips back into the green around you.

Move off of the pentacle and dance, even if it makes you feel silly or self-conscious at first. Give over, let go, free yourself, and let the Green Man show you the steps. There is a wonderful chant that will help you to dance: *"Corn and grain, corn and grain, all that falls shall rise again. Hoof and horn, hoof and horn, all that dies shall be reborn."*

Dance until you're exhausted and you fall upon the Earth. Lie there and recharge your batteries. Then, when you're rested, thank the Green Man and leave your offering (birdseed, nuts, grain, etc.).

As you did with the Great Mother Earth, let the Green Man move you beyond confining deity to human forms. Let Him show you the fertility, prosperity, strength, and wisdom that are abundant in Nature. Let Him teach you how to move through the cycles of your life, creating, harvesting, resting, and beginning again. And remember, every time you eat a vegetable, a fruit, or a slice of bread, you're receiving the gift of life from the Green Man—give Him thanks.

✳ Women and the God ✳

The relationship between women and the God is just beginning to take shape. It has been natural for women to cleave to the mysteries of the Goddess, for She is such an important part of our liberation and our empowerment. Part of women's resistance to working with God energy has been, of course, the dominant, and dominating, patriarchal model with which we have all been raised. And though Jesus had some fairly feminist things to say, they are rarely invoked in most Christian denominations. Not only do these old models of masculine divinity belittle women and their spirituality, they exclude women.

But there's so much more to the Divine Masculine than these outdated and incomplete ideas. In fact, the God is a tremendously important force of transformation and empowerment for women's souls and lives. Just as the Goddess represents aspects of men that have been denied, so the God represents aspects of women that have been denied, suppressed, and neglected.

He can be a force of creative genius, of personal strength, courage, and determination. There are numerous traditions, both spiritual and psychological such as the Taoists and the Jungians, that recognize that there is a feminine aspect within men, and a masculine one within women. One of the greatest journeys of my life has been to stop seeking the God in others, particularly men, and to instead cultivate His gifts in myself.

Writing my first book was one of the most important steps that I have taken on my spiritual journey. Instead of pouring my energy into the current man in my life to help him fulfill himself, I focused on meeting my own challenges and fulfilling my talents. I had to find warrior skills to fight demons of self-doubt. I had to courageously enter the male-dominated realms of culture, religion, and media. I drew on Goddesses to guide and empower me, but I also realized I was often calling upon God energy. And it was there for me!

The God that dwells within women is the white knight that we have all been waiting for. As we discover Him within ourselves, we tap into a powerful source of creative energy and self-confidence. We can draw not only upon the Goddess's active power, but also the God's, and that is particularly empowering in a male-dominated culture. The God offers many other gifts as well, and as you realize what you most need and want, you will be able to create meaningful rituals that connect you to the God and to the gifts you have within you.

Perhaps one of His greatest blessings is the "fire in the belly," for the Goddess may be the belly, but the God is the fire within it. The "fire in the belly" is the power to create, engage, analyze, and assert. It is the power that breaks down barriers and brings forth a new vision of life. It is also the power of unbridled lust and sexuality (interestingly, it's the "male" hormone testosterone that gives women their sex drive). The God is the fuel to your fire, and the fire that burns within you. Find Him within you and you can burn down the house, and then build a new one constructed according your own design, and with no need for locks.

The God restores to women the power to do all the things we were told good girls don't do, and all the things the culture wouldn't let us do: the power to be smart, funny, loud, outrageous, badly dressed, devastatingly dressed, fat, skinny, strong, athletic, independent, passionate, pissed off, visionary, difficult, easy, and yourself. And doesn't it feel good?

WAND MAGIC—A GUIDED VISUALIZATION TO FIND THE GOD WITHIN

As with the Grail Magic visualization in Chapter 5, The Goddess, this practice can be used by anyone seeking to meet the God within. However, this practice is particularly helpful for women. In this visualization you are going to activate your inner God, unleashing His active and creative capacities to aid you in crafting yourself as a Witch. Please use the text of the Goddess visualization to guide you into and through the sacred forest. Answer the hawk's questions, but visualize a stag asking them instead of the bird. And hear a man's deep voice singing.

Enter the glade but this time, as you approach the altar, see a shining golden wand. And beneath it, carved in stone, is a lightning bolt. You reach forward, lifting the wand. You hold it before you, dazzled by how it reflects the shining Sun. As you hold it, a rush of energy begins to flow from the wand into you, running down your arm and through your body. You feel yourself fill with fire.

Your heart begins to beat and power long forgotten courses through you. You look up into the Sun, and as you do so you see yourself, as a younger person, looking back, and you hear the deep voice of a man speaking to you: "What is it you seek?"

Standing before you is a man, tall and powerful, with antlers growing from His head. He is fierce but His eyes soften with kindness as He looks at you. It is Herne, the God of the Forest, the power of the animals, the power of the Earth. As He looks at you, you can feel the fire growing within you. Tell Him what's in your heart. Speak honestly and do not fear His scorn. Ask the questions you long to.

Listen carefully as He responds to what you have said. When He is finished, step into His powerful arms and feel them wrap around you with strength and power. Let the energy of His blessing flow into you. Let your heart open, let your wounds be healed, let your belly know its fire.

And then, He's gone. Place the wand upon the altar. Reach into the pouch and place your offering on the altar. Express your thanks. It's time to leave the sacred grove. Head back down the path, through the woods and back to the place of beginning. Feel yourself within your body. Stretch your fingers, your toes, your arms, and legs. And when you are ready, open your eyes.

Be sure to write about your encounters in your magical journal.

The wand is the power of the God within you—woman or man. And the God of the Forest is always present in the world, and the natural world, to strengthen and empower you.

✳ *The Sun and Men's Mysteries* ✳

The prebiblical cultures of the Middle East honored the Sun as the fertilizing partner of the Great Mother Earth. The Egyptians called Him Ra, the Greeks Helios, the Romans called Him Sol, the African Yoruban tribe called Him Shango, and the Scandinavians called Him Baldur. He is also an ancient embodiment of spiritual fire and wisdom. The early Pagan appreciation of the Sun's energy as the force that draws forth the Earth's capacity to bear life is a powerful model for men seeking to retrieve their own power, and to create positive, dynamic relationships with women. If the Green Man is the God of Growth, the Sun is the power that makes the Green Man grow. His energy is powerful, invigorating, wise, and illuminating.

You'll find that just as the Moon phases are reflected in the lives of women, the phases of the Sun are reflected in the lives of men. The Sun is said to wax during the period from the Winter Solstice to the Summer Solstice, the period "ruled" by the young and virile Oak King. The Sun wanes during the period from the Summer Solstice to the Winter, ruled by the Holly King, the wise, old philosopher. The rhythm of a man's life also waxes (as he grows in strength and maturity) and wanes (as he ages, declines, and dies). But just as the Moon returns each month, so the Sun returns each year. And as you work with this profound cycle, you learn to make magic that brings in new life, new opportunities, new people, and to let go of old relationships, jobs, and projects that you've outgrown. There is a great cyclical lesson for men, and women, in the Sun's waxing and waning, for the Sun becomes the Lord of Death and Rebirth.

The Sun teaches us that power and growth is followed by decline and rest, which will inevitably be followed by a return to action and growth. The Sun's cycle is the fastest, providing us a daily lesson as it rises and sets to rise again, but it is also the slowest, for its journey is the measure of our year. By working with these rhythms you can learn to let go when you ought to let go, and embrace the new when it is time to do that.

The Sun God teaches you the natural movement of energy—expansion followed by contraction followed by expansion. This is quite a contrast to our culture's preoccupation with a constant movement upward—for example, we take for granted that every year business has to generate bigger profits, which completely denies the cyclical nature of life. Imagine what it would be like if the Sun shone twenty-four hours a day, every day of the year. The world would be a desert!

Learning to attune your psyche to the Sun's great energies enables you to make magic that can fertilize and empower your spells, and your life. As the light of the Sun God shines on both your creative surges and periods of decline, you recognize that there is a seed of wisdom in your experiences, even in the hard lessons of failures, dreams that did not come true, and disappointments. Shining the light of truth and courage on your life, you can learn from your experiences, and so begin again with greater power, confidence, and maturity.

Like the Sun, you become a being of light, transforming loss into courage and mistakes into wisdom. This process is the means by which you, as a spiritual person, and maker of magic begin to transform the nature of God—He is no longer just a warrior, a punishing father, an abstract principle, a sacrificed son. He truly becomes a force of fertility and joy.

ADVANCED PRACTICE
DRAWING DOWN THE SUN GOD

As with the Drawing Down of the Moon for women, this is designed primarily for men, but can be performed by women as an advanced practice.

Please read and carefully review the Drawing Down the Moon practice, page 134, as a guide for this practice. The best time to Draw Down the Sun is anytime after it begins to wax. While most Drawing Downs are conducted in circles, which are generally cast at night, the first time you Draw Down the Sun you should be outdoors in bright, warm sunlight at noon, when the Sun is highest in the sky. Since you won't want to be disturbed, I suggest you work in your place of power. Choose a goal to work on.

Prepare a **Solar Incense** to be charged and used in later rituals:

Grind together two ounces of frankincense, two ounces of myrrh, five pinches of cinnamon, three pinches of red pepper. Bring the incense with you in a small jar you can open to the Sun's heat and light.

Carve a red, orange, or yellow candle with your name, the names of Sun Gods, a symbol of the Sun, and your goal for the next solar cycle.

Cast your circle, ground, and center. Stand in the center of the circle with your arms outstretched toward the Sun. If you are working with a partner and are being drawn into, your partner will draw an invoking pentagram on your body (see Drawing Down the Moon practice in Chapter 5) as s/he speaks the invocation.

Say:

> "By fire and by light I invoke you,
> By heat and by energy I invoke you,
> By wisdom and by passion I invoke you,
> O mighty God of the Sun,
> Descend into this the body of your child (name)
> Speak with his tongue, kiss with his lips,
> see with his eyes,
> So that your children may be made wise."

When you feel the God entering you, close your arms across your chest in the God position, bringing the fire of the Sun into you.

Feel the energy of the Sun God empowering you. Remain open to His presence. When you feel the energies wane, bow your head and drop your arms. If you feel drained, rest and rehydrate.

Light the candle, transferring some of the fire energy you received into the flame of the candle. Speak your goal and ask the Sun to bless and empower your efforts. Visualize your goal manifesting. If you feel up to it, you may raise energy by chanting, drumming, dancing, or by surrounding yourself in a circle of lit candles (be sure that nothing can catch fire!). Send your energy into the candle, the incense, and yourself. When you are done, ground any excess energies in the Earth. Blow out the candle—you can use it in future rituals as a fire/God candle. Give thanks, and close your circle.

As you proceed to empower your life with the energy of the Sun, note your milestones and accomplishments in your magical journal.

✳ *The Horned God* ✳

The Horned God is almost as ancient as the Great Earth Mother. He is the God of Nature, the Lord of the Forests and the Animals. He dances upon the walls of the prehistoric caves of Lascaux, France, part man, part stag. Surrounded by the animals upon whom life depended as much as the plants of the Earth, He is the God of their life force. His figure, as God or shaman, is painted upon the walls of this deep cavern, for He is also a force of fertility, inseminating the Great Mother Earth from whom the animals are born. Horned Gods are Gods of animal power, of sexuality and strength, freedom and instincts, wildness and the body (embodying these qualities in ways that you won't find in the Green Man and the Sun God).

When you make the acquaintance of this powerful force, anything can happen, for He is a power you invoke to make the most pleasurable magic of all. The Horned God expresses the holiness of the Earth, the presence of the Divine Masculine in the world. He is the stag or antlered God called Herne or Cernunnos amongst the Celts and the British; and He is depicted as a bull by the Greeks, Romans, and Egyptians: as Dionysus (and the Minotaur); Poseidon, Neptune, Apis, and Osiris. And He's the randy Goat-Foot God, and Pan, known all over the pre-Christian world and bearing no resemblance whatsoever to the Biblical demon Satan (but His goat image was misappropriated by the Church to depict Satan, as a way of demonizing the Pagan God).

Like the Goddess, He too draws together opposites—for He is both the hunter and the hunted. He is the reminder that we too are part of the circle of life, and that though we hunt and kill animals, we too are their prey, as we are also the prey of time. The Horned God is the force that unites us with our animal brothers and sisters, reminding us of our obligation to them, for they honor their obligation to us by sacrificing their lives so that we can live. His form, part man, part horned animal—whether bull, or stag, or goat—reminds us that we too are part animal.

And in that animal aspect, as all shamans know, there is a divine wisdom, power, and magic that you as a Witch can't live without, and that we, as a species, can't survive without. Every shaman works with spirit guides and power animals, who guide them in their journeys between the worlds. Animals have profound spiritual wisdom and will share their knowledge of how to make magic with us, if only we learn to ask, and to pay attention.

The Horned God is the power of our instincts, our ability to "smell" danger, and to immediately know all we need to about a situation or person. The Horned God is present on a weekly basis with my husband as he drives out from New York City to Long Island late at night. His instincts have become uncanny, and he can sense the presence of a Smokey sitting in his squad car with his radar gun miles ahead of us!

And the Horned God is the power of passionate sexuality who inspires and drives us as we become more animalistic when in the throes of passion. *The world is full of magic, but we need our animal selves to sense and enjoy it.* The Horned God is your guide. Call upon Him, and let your journey be filled with His magic.

DRAWING IN THE HORNED GOD

The best place to meet the Horned God is, of course, the forest. But you will find Him within you as well, and so you may draw Him in wherever you are. Again, follow the basic guidelines set forth in the Drawing Down the Moon practice.

You may wish to use a pair of antlers which have been purified and consecrated, holding them in your hands as you Draw in the God. You may also wish to do this at night, when stags are freer to roam. Again, you may draw into yourself, or have a partner do it. The invocation I have provided is the traditional one used in my tradition. And as with Drawing Down the Sun, this exercise is primarily for men, but may be done by women. I recommend using green or brown candles, and either of these **Horned God incenses**, depending upon which God you wish to call:

Stag/Cernunnos, Herne:	Bull/Dionysus, Apis, Osiris:
Pine	Pine
Deer's tongue	Sandalwood
Valerian	Valerian
Musk	Musk
Cinnamon	Cinnamon
Frankincense	Dittany of Crete oil
Oak leaves	A few drops of red wine
Cedar	

Cast your circle, ground and center, and assume the God position in the center of the circle. Your partner should draw the Invoking Pentagram on your body. Invoke the God:

> "By hoof and by horn I invoke you,
> By hide and by bone I invoke you,
> By sinew and by muscle I invoke you,
> To descend into this the body of your child (name),
> Speak with his tongue, kiss with his lips,
> Dance with his body,
> that your children may be empowered with freedom
>   and joy"

Let the God come to you and fill you. Allow yourself all the time you need. You may or may not wish to speak. You may feel a noticeable change in your physical sensations—as if you had suddenly gotten much taller, or stronger.

You may wish to dance, to snort, to laugh. Do whatever you are moved by the God to do (once when he was drawing in the Horned God, one of the Priests in my coven asked for a drum and began drumming in the tempo of galloping hooves—the sound was thrilling, and we could all feel the God's presence in him, and in the circle).

When you feel His energy departing, bow your head and drop your arms. Ground yourself, and eat and drink something (not alcohol). Thank the God for the blessing of His presence and close the circle.

✳ *The Warrior King God* ✳

The only God who can be trusted with a sword is a God who dances, for only a God who loves life can be entrusted with the power of death. There is a very powerful moment in the rituals that I learned, where the God places His sword at the feet of the Goddess. What does it mean? It means that death—as a warrior, as a hunter, as time, as part of the cycle of energy in the Universe—serves life. The warrior's power does not serve drug lords, polluting multinational corporations, imperialistic excursions, nor corrupt politicians. It doesn't serve greed, terror, oppression, misogyny, tyranny, a lust for violence, nor jingoistic patriotism. It serves life. The God as Warrior protects, defends, nourishes as a hunter, and above all reveres life. And so the Goddess embraces Him, and the God becomes a God of love whose gift is the power of rebirth.

BASIC TO ADVANCED PRACTICE
HONORING THE WARRIOR WITHIN

Meditate on your experiences where you have defended yourself or others, or a noble cause. Create a ritual that honors the Warrior God within yourself. Work with your athame, or sword. Pledge yourself to life and to the best of who and what a warrior is.

SOME GREAT GOD SPELLS

The Horned God's Hoofbeats (Earth Magic)

Take your drum, head out to Nature, sit upon the Earth, listen to the music around you, ask the Horned God to be with you, and then beat upon the drum in the tempo of hooves galloping upon the ground. Let the drumming stir your passions and your courage, your strength and creativity. And go make love.

Sun God Spell (Fire Magic)

Build a bonfire at the end of the day. As the Sun sets, light a torch, holding it to the setting disc. Set the logs afire, drum, dance, raise energy, and direct it to become a power of light that guides you.

Singing the Song of the Dancing God (Air Magic)

Sing shamelessly, in the shower, or elsewhere, preferably in public. If you don't know what to sing, try this wonderful song, "Simple Gifts," written by Elder Joseph Bracket in 1848. Many Wiccans have adapted the refrain from a later set of very Christian lyrics called "The Lord of the Dance" written in 1963 by Sydney Carter. Some of his verses, however, have been criticized as anti-Semitic and, also due to copyright issues, they are not published here. The lyrics may, however, be obtained from the Internet. Here are the original, magical lyrics of "Simple Gifts":

> 'Tis the gift to be simple,
> 'Tis the gift to be free,
> 'Tis the gift to come down where you ought to be,
> And when we find ourselves in the place just right,
> 'Twill be in the valley of love and delight.

When true simplicity is gained
To bow and to bend we shan't be ashamed,
To turn, turn will be our delight,
'Till by turning, turning we come round right.

Making Love in the Water (Water Magic)

Make love in the shower, the pool, the lake, the ocean. Or love your body by exercising until you've worked up a good sweat.

With these new experiences of divinity—as Goddess and God, and as immanent—you have an invaluable compass to guide you as you Witch craft.

❊   *An Altar to the God*   ❊

You may wish to create an altar honoring the God with whom you are working (see the Goddess chapter, page 117). But remember, *you* are the God's altar. A man, or woman, who has drawn in the God as Horned God, Sun God, Green Man, or any other form will be forever changed. You must be prepared to have Him shatter the confining constraints that society has placed upon you, whether you are a man or a woman. A living, present God grounds you in the magic of your life, your emotions, your desires, your impulses (both creative and destructive), your instincts, your body, and your sexuality. Invite Him into your life, and He will come playing pipes and dancing in wild and ecstatic welcome. Leave your home, walk out into Nature, and He is everywhere. Look into your life, and you are His magic. *The God dwells dancing within your life. When you live it fully, joyfully, and courageously, you are expressing His power and His presence in yourself and in the world.*

Witchcraft without Rules

I t's exhilarating to realize that magic is real and that you have the power to bring your dreams to life. But most of us are a little afraid of our own power—afraid that, like the sorcerer's apprentice, we won't be able to control it. With all the other kids in the audience of Disney's classic *Fantasia,* I watched with envy as Mickey Mouse commanded the broom to do his chore of carrying water from the well to the sorcerer's magical cave. And then I watched with real fear as the broom refused to respond to Mickey's commands to stop, drowning him in a whirlpool of water. The message was clear—Don't mess with magic!

Every book on Wicca will tell you there's no need to fear Witches abusing their power because we have a rule that keeps us, and others, safe from the power that we wield. It's called the Threefold Law: Witches never use magic to harm or manipulate others because whatever you send out magically will return to you three times over. But I have some very serious problems with the Threefold Law, and the ethics of making magic is one of the most important subjects our growing religion must tackle. In fact, the troubles with the Threefold Law pervade a lot of contemporary Wiccan practices and ideas. There is another Wiccan precept called the Wiccan Rede: "Harm none, do what you will," which is, unfortunately, popularly explained in terms of the Threefold Law. I want to propose an entirely new basis for Wiccan ethics, which will also provide a better explanation of the Rede in the process. But first, we need to look at where some of the problems began.

✳   *Why Do We Fear Power?*   ✳

Fear of the power of magic, Witchcraft, and the "occult" (which simply means "hidden") has kept too many people from entering an Aladdin's cave of spiritual riches. It has cut off our culture from a heritage of wisdom and empowerment, and it continues to plague us. We are surrounded by the prejudices and fears of others—as an activist and attorney I see far too many tragic consequences of these forces of oppression. And on a more subtle yet important level, we Witches have absorbed some of this fear into our own psyches and our ideas about magical power. We cannot practice our religion in fear, so let's figure out how we can get rid of it. Let's look at the real morality of making magic.

Most people don't realize that the source of real magic is sacred, and so they are frightened by the prospect of human beings accessing such amazing power. They fear that we aren't worthy of such a gift, that we couldn't possibly do anything but abuse it. They wonder whether we humans are innately good or evil, and fear that we are the latter. Given what we've done to one another and to the planet, people have good reason to worry, and to doubt that we can be trusted with such godlike power.

The irony, of course, is that we unleashed a power that is beyond our control that is not associated with magic, but with science and technology. The splitting of the atom led to the nuclear arms race that hangs like the sword of Damocles over our heads, threatening us with imminent destruction and making us understandably terrified. And our technology has generated so much pollution that we face extinction. So much for the skeptics' fear that "irrational" beliefs in the numinous and magical pose the greatest danger to humankind!

The other irony is that Witches themselves, far from having used their power to control or oppress others, have been the victims of some of the most inhumane and evil acts in human history.

FEAR OF WITCHES

For centuries, millions upon millions of people have chosen not to look at where their fears come from, which would allow them to transform those fears into freedom. Instead of confronting their own shadows, they have projected their terrors onto others. As a result, throughout the Middle Ages, Witches—and women who were not Witches—were accused of using their "demonic" powers to harm, to seduce, and to impose their will on others, to control the weather, to kill cows and crops and other people. They were even accused of making a priest's penis disappear, according to the *Maleus Malifacarum*, the Church's official edict on Witchcraft, in which Pope Innocent VIII authorized the use of torture to elicit confessions. Village herbalists, healers, and midwives were accused of killing instead of curing. The village shamans, wise women and men, were now accused of diabolic instead of divine communion.

These distorted stereotypes arose six hundred years ago during the Church's Inquisition against the Jews and its crusade for religious domination. Jews were accused of worshiping Satan, and of murdering Christian babies as part of their supposedly satanic religious rituals. They were brutally persecuted and falsely accused, and their tormenters turned their violent attention to women and the remnants of surviving Paganism and shamanism in Europe, which we call the Old Religion. Even the demeaning image of the big-nosed, ugly Jew was recycled as an image of the evil Witch.*

Hundreds of thousands were tortured and killed, falsely accused of being Satan-worshiping Witches, and hysteria was fanned as the Church used fear and blame to make sense of sources of unrest like the black

*The brilliant and devastating book *Witchcraze: A New History of the European Witch Hunts* by Professor Anne Llewellyn Barstow is required reading on this subject.

plague. Most of these victims were women. It was, in fact, the women's holocaust, and the legal status of women underwent a radical subversion. Women were no longer people but property controlled by their fathers, husbands, or nearest male relatives. Women could no longer inherit or own property. They were forbidden from receiving an education. They could no longer practice medicine as herbalists and midwives. And the struggle that women have today—for equal rights, employment, and education, for healthcare, and control over their own bodies—stems in significant part from the persecutions of the Witch burnings, and the charges that women, and Witches, were agents of the devil.

But of course, there is no devil in the Old Religion and Witches certainly do not worship him. He belongs strictly to the religions of the Bible. He's their demon, their personification of evil, their shadow, and it is time for members of the biblical faiths to stop projecting him onto others and simply deal with their own darkness. As long as people continue to avoid confronting their fears, they will be controlled by them. And that, as the history of the Inquisition, the Witch burnings, and the Holocaust tragically demonstrates, only leads to disaster. It has taken a tragic and deadly toll even in this modern era.

Aside from misogyny, one important reason the Church persecutions during the Witch burnings were so ferocious is that Pagan shamanic practices enabled people to communicate with the Divine and have access to sacred power. *If everyone is capable of communing with deity, and of living divinely empowered lives, the entire hierarchical, and much of the theological, basis of the Church is rendered irrelevant.* For a hierarchically based institution, that's very threatening.

The success of those medieval persecutions are the primary reason that, to this day, people view Witches with tremendous fear and hostility and have very distorted ideas about magic as satanic, supernatural, manipulative, and destructive. Those in power get to rewrite history, and the Old Religion, the shamanism of Europe which preceded Judaism, Christianity, and Islam by thousands of years, was demonized, and the old Gods and Goddesses were either coopted as "saints" or demonized as well.

FEAR OF MAGICAL POWER

For hundreds of years we have suffered under the misunderstanding that magic is demonic. And even those who don't believe in the devil fear that, just maybe, fooling around with magic can unleash supernatural powers beyond our control. Skeptics, of course, scoff at magic because they think that it is irrational, and given human history, they're understandably afraid of people who zealously embrace the irrational. Skeptics feel a sense of security in "knowing" that the unexplainable can be explained away as foolish, superstitious nonsense, but they fear what they feel they can't explain or control. As humans, we have an age-old fear of the unknown, and that's certainly what magical power seems to be: an unknown force from an unknown source. We're afraid we will lose control of ourselves, and of the world in which we live.

We are also taught to fear that if we don't have authorities—specifically, a religious hierarchy—to stand between ourselves and such extraordinary power, we will go mad, or blind, or both in the face of it. (Many of our most ancient myths are about this fear, such as the story of Semele, who is destroyed when her lover, Zeus, finally relents to her pleading and reveals himself to her, or Moses, who is blinded by the sight of Yahweh when he receives the Ten Commandments.) And for thousands of years, we in the West have been taught that we are indeed undeserving of power, and that we are unworthy, or incapable, of being in the presence of deity. It's time to leave that myth behind.

❋ Separation from the Divine ❋

There's a terrible wound at the center of our civilization and at the center of our souls that gives rise to all of these fears. It comes from the central myth of our religious culture that we have been cast out of paradise and must struggle each day with our "sinfulness" and "the temptations of the devil." Many of us were raised to believe that we can never achieve paradise on Earth again because we separated ourselves from the Divine. And even those who are not religious live in a culture influenced by these ideas.

These false beliefs have many dangerous implications for ourselves and for our planet, and have even crept into our own Wiccan thea/ology and practices. As I explained in Chapter 1, Real Magic, the biblical religions have taught that divinity is not present in the world. They claim that God is, as the rabbi and priest I met explained, like a potter who created a pot (the world), and that "worshiping" the pot is idolatry. And in the biblical creation story, God gave us the right to use and exploit this "pot" as we please, and to dispose of it as we see fit.

This attitude has been one of the principal causes of the tremendous environmental tragedy that we've created, particularly over the last hundred years. In less than two centuries, humans have increased the total amount of carbon dioxide in the atmosphere by over 25 percent—just by burning fossil fuels and destroying forests. We have contaminated the groundwater in every state in the United States. Less than 3 percent of our coral reefs remain. And these are just a few of the results of this old cosmology, and industrialization, that are contributing to the destruction of the planet and the human race.

This fundamental idea that the world is inanimate, without value, and devoid of divinity, has resulted in people having no compunction about killing off entire species, wiping out old-growth forests, polluting the water, and destroying the ozone layer. When we think this way, we do not recognize that the forests are in fact the lungs of the Earth and without them we will die. We don't see that the waters of the Earth course through our veins, because we do not perceive the precious connections between ourselves and the Earth. Worse, we have failed to recognize the innate and sacred value of the Earth and Her creatures. And so we are destroying divinity.

ORIGINAL SIN

"But that's not me," I can hear you protesting. "That's not what I believe! I'm a Witch! I recycle!"

Terrific, but you're going to be surprised at the extent to which the beliefs of this old cosmology have carried over into the ideas and practices of modern Witchcraft. I don't want to demonize the old ideas, but if we don't look at them very carefully, we will remain unconsciously under their influence, repeating the same old mistakes that keep us separated from the Sacred.

Most of us were taught that because Adam defied God by eating from the Tree of Knowledge, brought about by Eve's susceptibility to the devil and her seductiveness, man is alone, expelled from paradise and from the presence of God. He is born with the stain of original sin and condemned to a realm that, like man, has fallen from grace. Spirit and matter are eternally separated and the Divine is forever outside of us and our world. The best we can hope for is to come to God's favor through living a "pure" life in accordance with the teachings of the Bible, Torah, or Koran—or through vicarious redemption via Jesus. But the assumptions beneath all of these "paths to salvation" are that we are devoid of divinity and in need of saving. In this patriarchal and tragic worldview, at best we humans, separated from God's guidance, just sort of blunder about.

RULES AND AUTHORITIES

When God is not present in the world, you are living in a *Lord of the Flies* reality. And when you yourself are "sinful," you need something to tell you the difference between right and wrong. You need rules—a Bible, and the Ten Commandments, a Torah and a Koran—that come down from some transcendent, supernatural (masculine) source. You need saints to intercede on your behalf, and because God is not present to consult with you, you need a church, temple, or mosque with a hierarchy of authority figures who know better than you do. You can't be trusted to interpret those rules by yourself. And so religious institutions quickly become institutions of power over others.

The rules stipulate that if you do not behave, you will be punished. If you murder, covet your neighbor's wife, or steal, you'll be punished here or in hell. But people violate those rules all the time. When we see endless wars and hideous persecutions and unbelievable amounts of crime and violence, when we look at our materialism, greed, and moral hypocrisy, we see that a rulebook is obviously not enough. Nor are threats of damnation, hell, and punishment.

Is it that we are just so selfish and prone to evil that even the rules can't save us from ourselves? Given how bad things are already, where would we be without the rules? Certainly, that was the concern expressed by the rabbi and the priest as they concluded the show, acknowledging that they had learned a great deal about Wicca that they'd never understood, but also worrying that we did not have a Bible to tell us how to determine the difference between right and wrong, that Wiccans don't have religious rules for moral and social conduct.

❋ The "Rules" of Making Magic ❋

Of course we Witches are taught, primarily by books, coven training, or word of mouth, that we *do* have rules that govern our magic and keep us from practicing so-called black magic (an implicitly racist term that Witches condemn), or using it for evil, manipulative, or destructive purposes, referred to by Witches as "baneful" magic. The very first rule any aspiring Witch (or neo-Pagan) learns is the Threefold Law, which I have recently taken to calling the Boomerang Whammy Rule, because it says that whatever you send out magically will come back to you threefold. It's a sort of magnified karma—you'll not only get your due, you will get it in spades, and that threat will certainly keep your temper, and your magic, in check.

The next rule that is often cited is the Wiccan Rede (rede actually means "advice," but many think of it as a rule), which states, "And ye harm none, do what thou will." This is generally interpreted to mean that we all have tremendous freedom but are constrained by the consequences of our actions. And those consequences are generally explained in terms of the Threefold Law. Another interpretation, without the Threefold Law, is that you are free to say what you think, but it's not ethical to yell "Fire!" in a crowded movie theater when there is none. I can get angry at you, and even express my anger, but my freedom to do so stops an inch away from my fist connecting with your jaw.

Another moral rule of magical conduct (often applied to spellcasting) has evolved from the Rede and the Threefold Law: Witches do not make magic to have power over anyone but themselves. Therefore, Witches would never cast a spell to harm or have power over someone else—for example, Witches would never cast a spell to break up another couple, or to cause a competitor to fail. Witches wouldn't cast a love spell to make a specific someone fall in love with them lest they end up more emotionally entangled than the love interest. In fact, by this rule, Witches won't even do a healing spell for someone who is ill unless they have permission from this person, because it would be imposing one's will on another.

But are these rules of ethics really a part of Witchcraft? And if they're not, what's to prevent us from casting a baneful spell on anyone who crosses us and using our power to control others?

JOURNAL EXERCISE:
THE THREEFOLD LAW

In your magic journal, answer the following questions, and as you write, pay attention to how you're feeling about your answers.

When and where did you first learn about the Threefold Law? How did you react to it?

When was the first time you thought about making magic that might have manipulated someone else—such as a love spell, or a baneful spell? Did the Threefold Law stop you from making manipulative or baneful magic?

Were you afraid that something bad would happen to you if you went ahead with the magic you'd been thinking about? What were you afraid might happen?

Were you tempted to act anyway, because you doubted the

consequences, or figured you could deal with them, or were willing to "pay the price" in order to get what you wanted? Did you
ignore the Threefold Law? If you did, what happened?

WHAT'S WRONG WITH THE THREEFOLD LAW

There's no doubt that the Threefold Law isn't traditionally Wiccan. It reflects the influence of the Hindu concept of karma—what you do returns
to you—as it was popularized in this country during and after the 1960s.
It also reflects an old magical principle of cause and effect, derived in
some measure from Eastern philosophies, and incorporating various
Western models of philosophy and even scientific thought: There *are*
consequences to our actions. The fact that these philosophies bled into
modern Wicca isn't the real problem.

I believe the Threefold Law is an inadequate, inaccurate, and inap-
propriate basis for Wiccan ethics. It is not and should not be the reason
that Witches do not "hex,"* harm, or manipulate or do baneful magic. I
want to propose something that I believe is critical to our growth and maturity as a spiritual movement, and which I hope will be valuable to you
as you make magic. *Witches do not require rules in order to practice Witchcraft ethically.* We need something else entirely, something that we have
but which we overlook because of our enculturated fixation with rules.

The primary problem is that *the Threefold Law is basically a theory of
punishment*: I won't misbehave because if I do, something (three times)
worse will happen to me; therefore, I behave myself because I don't want
anything bad to happen to me.

I have always had a problem with punishment as a basis for ethics
because it is not an ethical precept—avoiding punishment is simply ex-
pediency and self-interest. It's the weak cousin of morality because it's
conduct based purely on deterrence. Punishment really doesn't make us,
or our magic, moral. It just teaches us to be motivated by fear, and fear—

---

*"Hex," frequently misused to refer to baneful magic, is derived from the Middle German *hexe*, which simply meant
"a Witch."

as we've seen-—is not a good thing. It also creates a peculiar mind-set: Hey, if I can get away with breaking a rule, why not?

This is thinking carried over from the religions and the culture in which we were raised. It's a remnant of patriarchal religious ideas about punishment, damnation, and sinfulness. It's a rule based on fear that stems from the idea that God isn't present in the world. It doesn't flow out of Wiccan cosmology and it's just not good enough. But if we don't have the Threefold Law, what is our ethical precept, and where does it come from?

The Real Morality
✳ of Making Magic ✳

The real reason that Witches do not and should not harm, do baneful magic, or use magic to have power over others, is because they experience immanent divinity. Through Wiccan practices, you will commune with the Divine, and once the Numinous has entered and touched you, filled and transformed you, it does not even dawn on you to do harm in any way. It is not within the realm of your experience or your consciousness to hurt anyone, because you know that the world in which you live is holy, and sacred, and divine. *All of our behavior, our magic, and our ethics flow from this epiphany that the Divine exists within ourselves, in others, and in the world.*

The way in which we make magic, how we cast spells, how we work with the power that is available to each of us, is very simple once you've experienced communion with the Sacred. *You would simply never harm, or manipulate someone else because you recognize that they are an embodiment of the Divine.* This is also part of the mystical experience of Oneness—for everything is a part of, and an expression of, deity. All is holy, and all that is holy is to be treated as sacred.

The experience of being in the presence of divinity changes everything—your perceptions of yourself and everything around you. And it changes your relationship to the world. Your conduct is motivated not by fear of punishment, but by respect, awe, appreciation, and, most of all, reverence for the innate divinity of the world. Your generosity and compassion flow as naturally as the Sun rises in the morning and sets in the evening. You live in a state of grace. And just as our magic flows from our connection to divinity, our ethics flow from this state of grace. We don't need a book of rules to know the difference between right and wrong because "living in right relationship," as Native Americans and Buddhists say, is *natural*.

Unlike in the old biblical model of reality, magic is not something we do to manipulate or control the Universe—it's about communing and cocreating, about bringing your own sacred power into fullest expression or manifestation. *The only person we ever seek to control with magic is ourselves.* Magic, when done properly, brings you into alignment with the powers of the numinous Universe, so that they may assist you in giving form to your true purpose, your reason for being. *The energy with which you make magic is sacred and so how, and why, you make magic is sacred.* As you continue to work with the practices in this book, this spiritual approach will become increasingly clear and empowering.

And this personal, universal experience of immanent divinity as the source of our ethics is the real explanation of "Harm none, do what you will" as a Wiccan precept. Witches harm none, not because they fear the consequences of the Threefold Law, but because all is sacred. With this profound experience and insight to guide you, you are free to make your own decisions about what is right and wrong for you as you craft yourself as a Witch.

DEALING WITH NEGATIVITY

Because you live in a sacred world and are a practicing Witch, when you are confronted with harm, or behavior that is destructive or cruel, your impulse should not be to respond with greater harm, destruction, or cruelty. You may get angry or be hurt—we're only human, after all. But don't *act* out of rage, hurt, or an impulse to harm or have revenge. Your actions should be tempered and guided by your awareness of the everpresent Divine, and you should seek to rectify that which is out of alignment with that numinous reality. *Witches learn to make magic to heal where there is a*

wound, to provide love where there is hate, compassion where there is cru-
elty, to respond to what is wrong with what is right. And so we make magic to
restore balance, to transform negative energy into positive energy.

Transforming challenges into strengths and negatives into positives can
be the greatest trials of your life, but they are also one of life's greatest spiritual gifts. Every negative reveals the positive: Anger shows you the need for
love, war shows you the need for peace, hurt shows you the need for healing. One of the greatest challenges I faced was the source of the most positive change in my entire life: For years I was idealistically caught up in "Pagan politics" and had become the target of a lot of negative, malevolent
energy. Finally, it was so overwhelming and toxic that I walked away.

At the time I thought I was giving up on my commitment to embody
my spirituality through community activism, which made me very disappointed in myself, but I soon realized that I had freed myself to accomplish what I was really here for. I began filtering out the negativity and
drawing on the purified energy, and I used it to push further away from
my entrapment and to transform my life. I looked at where I was and why
I was engaged with people who behaved in such cruel and destructive
ways. I realized that I wasn't going to change them—but I could change
myself. I could liberate myself from their endless games and free my energy for truly productive and sacred purposes. I ended up blessing and
thanking them because they were my teachers: They showed me that I
could change myself, and that I belonged somewhere else.

If I had not been able to connect to the Sacred that resides in the
world and in myself, and receive its healing and guidance, I would never
have been able to stand back and to view them, and myself, with compassion. I would have remained engaged in negativity, locked in conflict with
them. Instead I was able to separate myself, and their energy actually
helped me to move out of a bad situation and to draw on my own gifts
and talents—I write, lecture, teach, advocate, work at "Witch crafting,"
and participate in many worthwhile community building efforts. Now I
get to travel the world and meet and work with the most amazing and
wonderful people who inspire me and enrich my life. I get to make real,
divine magic and I am endlessly grateful.

There are many wonderful magical practices that can help you to deal with negativity in a variety of nonharmful ways: protection spells, sending negativity back to its source, banishing negative energies, and binding them and transforming them. It always helps to precede any of these choices with a good purification and cleansing—of you, your home, your office.

MAGIC FOR DEALING WITH NEGATIVITY

Protection Spell. Take a purification bath, ground, and center. Hold the energy in your heart and send it outward to surround your body with a shining, white sphere of light. With each breath, exhale more power into the shield. Visualize and *feel* it growing until it stretches out about three feet from your body. As the protective sphere strengthens and glows, visualize all the negative energy that might be directed toward you being absorbed by the shield and feel it being transformed into positive, empowering, loving energy that you can use for your own growth and success. Feel the positive energy flowing into you.

When you feel the protection shield securely in place around you, name your power "Radiant Shield." The next time you encounter attacks from your foes, just summon your power with the words "Radiant Shield" and visualize and feel the sphere forming around you. Any negativity coming at you will be deflected and transformed.

Return to Sender. Purify and consecrate a small, round mirror—about four inches in diameter is a good size (if you don't know how to do this, see the section on purifying and consecrating your tools in Chapter 9, Potions, Notions, and Tools). Place the mirror on your altar, cast a circle, and then pick up the mirror and hold it to your heart. Say, *"With this tool of light and truth I send back all negativity that is sent to me. Let it return to its sender, may s/he be held in the light. May s/he see, and may all see, the truth of her/his actions and her/his thoughts. May anger be turned to peace, injury to healing, confusion to clarity. I work this spell three times three, as I do will, so mote it be."*

Carry the mirror with you. If the negative energy is coming from an antagonistic coworker, place it on your desk, facing your foe. Or you may want to flash the mirror at your least favorite fascist politician the next time he appears on television!

Banishing Spell. When the Moon is waning, prepare an object that represents what you're going to banish. It could be a photograph, an object that belonged to someone you want out of your life, or something that represents your bad habit, your broken heart, or your failed business endeavors. Place it on your altar. Light white candles on the altar and in the four directions. Cleanse the circle with the elements of earth and water—scatter water (from a bowl of salt water) around the circle. Then cleanse the circle with fire and air by waving the smoke of burning sage around the circle ("smudging" it).

Cast a circle and call upon the aid of cosmic recyclers such as Hecate, Anubis, Cerridwen, or Hephaestos. State what you wish banished. Sprinkle the object with the salt water and pass it through the sage smoke.

Express the positive situation you want to turn the negative into, for example, "I want to transform my broken heart into one filled with love." Move widdershins around the circle (counterclockwise—the direction of decrease), chanting: *"Farewell farewell to the loss of the past/No pain or sadness ever lasts/Healing my spirit/I release the past!"*

At first you may feel sluggish and strangely slow, but gradually you'll feel the energy building. Raise the energy by moving and chanting faster. As you feel the spell coming to a climax, direct your energy into the object and say: *"I cast this spell now three times three/As I do will, so mote it be!"*

Quickly tear, break, burn, or otherwise dramatically dispose of the object. Ground yourself, thank the spirits, close the circle, and throw whatever's left in the trash or toilet, bury it, or toss it into moving water—and give thanks to Mother Nature for her recycling powers. Open the doors and windows of your home and let the negative energies exit. You can use a broom to sweep them out and use burning sage and salt water to recleanse your space. And finally, act in accord.

Binding Spell. Follow the directions for banishing, but instead of destroying the object, you're going to bind it. Wrap it in red cord, chanting as you do: *"No harm be done to anyone/No harm be done by this one."* And when you're ready to set the magic, say: *"I bind this (*say who or what*) so no harm may be done. By the power of three times, as I do will, so mote it be."* You may also wish to soak your object in water, wrap it in aluminum foil, reflective side facing inwards, and put it in your freezer. (At a later date, you can banish it, and clean out your refrigerator!)

Binding is one of the few magics performed without the consent of another person, and is used very conservatively under only the most dire of circumstances to prevent someone from doing great harm—for example, you would bind a rapist, murderer, or perpetrator of other forms of violence. The magic is done not to harm but to prevent them from harming. Usually, the object you make and bind will be a poppit (a cloth doll) representing the perpetrator.

EXERCISE:
SMILE!

A simple way to practice the magic of transforming negative energy into positive is to spend the day being positive. Choose a day, preferably a Saturday or a day on which you tend to do a lot of chores and interact with strangers, and make a point of smiling at everyone you meet: the bus driver, the grocery store clerk, the waitress. Pleasantly engage everyone you meet, smile, crack a joke, ask them questions, radiate positive and warm energy—and watch the effect you have on everyone you meet. See how they brighten, how they respond with surprise and with friendliness.

Write about your experience in your magical journal.

DEALING WITH EVIL

Turn on the TV and you'll hear about human beings committing acts of astonishing evil. It's an appalling litany that makes us ask why.

Some say that we are innately evil, others blame the devil. What does Wicca say about evil? To answer this question, I sought the wisdom of Nature because the natural world, as an embodiment of the Divine, is our greatest spiritual teacher. Looking to the Earth, we see that *there is no evil in Nature.* If you are walking in the jungle, and a tiger should decide to eat you, that doesn't make the tiger evil, it makes him a tiger. And it makes you lunch! Unquestionably, that's a tragedy for you and those who love you, but there's no cruelty or evil in the tiger's actions. In fact, relationships within Nature are actually based on affinity—on mutual support, attraction, and interactions that facilitate the sustainable balance of life. By serving as the tiger's lunch, you're part of a natural relationship (even if it is small consolation!). And in fact, animals who hunt perform an important service to the overall health and well-being of the species they prey upon: They take out the sick, the old, and the young, thereby controlling the size of the population in extraordinarily precise ways that ultimately serves the survival of their prey, and themselves. They help maintain Nature's balance, and like the God who places his sword at the feet of the Goddess, in doing so they serve life.

But what of the terrible cruelty in the actions of human beings—the way they exploit and torture, rape and murder each other? Again, the answer comes from Nature: I believe this horrific behavior is the result of their separation from the Divine, and from the natural world. This separation has created a condition of profound psychological and social woundedness, a sickness and even a loss of soul, that manifests in the aberrant behavior we recognize as evil. Such acts rarely occurred in indigenous cultures that lived intimately connected to the Earth. In other words, *human "evil" is a symptom of our separation from the Sacred, and not something inherent.*

It's not hard to see how we can find solutions to problems of evil that have, for thousands of years, seemed unsolvable. We have to find ways of reconnecting to deity, within ourselves and the world. When you engage in Wiccan spiritual practices you reconnect to the Divine and heal the wounds in your soul.

It doesn't matter whether you are Wiccan, neo-Pagan, Tibetan, Native American, Jewish, Hindu, Christian, Muslim, or of any other faith persuasion, as long as your practices reconnect you to the Sacred. Once you reestablish that connection, a healing can begin. It begins with each one of us individually and spreads out into the world from there.

And what about those religious zealots who claim they have found the one true God and the one true way—yet continue to kill, oppress, and terrorize? Witches are quite open to the metaphors, wisdom, and experiences of the Divine in other faith traditions—we not only tolerate other religions but appreciate their positive qualities (after all, Nature teaches us that a healthy environment is a diverse one). But we vehemently reject those views and practices that are justified as religious, but that are used to oppress others through violence or other means. Those who harm others, particularly if they do so in the name of religion, reveal that they have no connection to the Divine. If they did, they would treat all of life with reverence.

When you experience the immediacy of the Sacred, you begin to craft a rich and vital system of values that influences the way in which you practice your religion, make magic, and live life. These values are beautifully summarized in the conclusion of the Charge of the Goddess: *"Let My worship be in the heart that rejoices, for behold—all acts of love and pleasure are My rituals. Therefore, let there be beauty and strength, power and compassion, honor and humility, mirth and reverence within you."*

Secrets of Spellcasting

Planted in our fertile imaginations by *The Wizard of Oz, Bewitched, Charmed,* or Harry Potter, the idea of a spell granting our every wish fascinates us. Thousands of people jammed Times Square to marvel at a man who'd "frozen" himself in ice for three days, and illusionist David Copperfield is the highest-paid entertainer in the world. Even phony magic captivates us.

When people think of Witchcraft, and magic, they think of spells. In fact, you may have skipped ahead to this chapter hoping to get to the "good stuff." I can't tell you how many lectures I've given on the real magic of Witchcraft, only to have someone raise his or her hand at the end of the talk and ask, "But can I just have a love spell?"

And that's to be expected—we live in a culture based on instant gratification. Instant cereal, instant communication, instant millionaires. What could be more instantly gratifying than a magical spell? This craving has resulted in countless recipe books on spellcasting and because so many practitioners of Witchcraft are self-taught from books, this approach has started to dominate people's thinking and practicing of the

Craft. Some people even say that Witchcraft isn't a religion, it's just a system for manipulating the Universe with spells—something I hope I've made clear is totally untrue.

So what's wrong with spellcasting? After all, isn't that what magic, and this book, are all about? Yes, spellcasting is an important part of Witchcraft, and it should be, but the fact is that the usual "gimme the spell, gimme the goodies" approach to Witchcraft *will not work.*

Why Magic Works but Most Spells Don't

Magic *does work*, and so do spells, but not in the ways or for the reasons many people believe.

There are hundreds of spell books that tell you what to say, what to wear, where to stand, what props to use, and what potions to mix. Some even describe how to raise energy and, at least to some extent, how to "change" consciousness in order to change reality. Along with all those books, I'll bet you've got the candles, herbs, oils, the parchment paper, and maybe even the iron filings, saturated snakeskin, and graveyard dirt. And concerned that by doing it wrong you might manifest a rat instead of a Romeo, you follow the instructions of your chosen spell to the letter. Then, when a ratty-looking Romeo shows up a year later, you wonder why the spell didn't work.

So, what happened? In the process of looking at why some kinds of spellcasting won't work, we'll uncover the real secrets for success. The problem is not with the reality of magic, but with the usual approach.

MECHANICAL MAGIC

Most people think of magic as if it were a mechanical process—say the secret word and the duck comes down (thank you, Groucho Marx)! They don't even realize that they are thinking mechanistically because it's so ingrained in their psyches by our culture. We Westerners are very much products of the twentieth century and scientific rationalism, so we see the world through the prism of Newton's physics.

From Newton's very wise perspective, the Universe is indeed a machine operating like a clock, with laws of motion, gravity, time, etc. That understanding has generated astonishing technology that we all benefit from—the computer I'm writing on, the oil burner heating my cozy home, the stereo playing Bruce Springsteen's CD in the background, the electricity that enables it all to run—all sorts of things that would have been considered "magic" a hundred years ago.

But Newton's laws only explain how *part* of the Universe works: The material world that we perceive with our five senses, or to put it another way, the world of gravity, matter, and time. Reality is bigger, and deeper, than that. There are other dimensions to reality (in fact, these days, current scientific theory holds that there are ten) and other laws of physics that operate in those dimensions. We're only just beginning to understand what these are and how they operate. But the most important aspect we need to understand for the practice of spellcasting is that at the (currently perceived) smallest level of reality, the level of the subatomic particle, everything is energy and interconnected. And we have an astonishing capacity to affect the outcome of subatomic particle energy events.

The implications are profound, and science is only just beginning to explore them. But already we're seeing remarkable applications in medical science—one of the most talked-about breakthroughs concerns the recent experiments showing that people who are prayed for by people they don't even know, and who themselves don't know that they are being prayed for, have statistically higher recovery rates from fatal illnesses than people who are not prayed for. Yesterday's magic is today's science.

We Witches have always worked with this idea that everything is ultimately energy. This understanding is one reason that we visualize when we spellcast. Working on this "pure" energy plane of reality apparently affects events on the "material," familiar, "Newtonian" plane. There are more fascinating discoveries emerging from quantum physics that affect our view of reality, and how we cast spells and make magic.

Quantum Consciousness
✳   and Casting Spells   ✳

Quantum thinking these days is that consciousness and reality require each other in order for both to exist. In order to exist, matter requires consciousness, and it responds to conscious interaction in phenomenal ways!

Consciousness is not just your mind—your thinking processes, your intellect, and analytical capacities. *Consciousness is our entire, holistic energy system and a wide range of mental capacities.* Our brains are constantly producing electrical impulses that are measured as waves: The power of the waves is measured by amplitude and the speed is measured in frequency. The frequency of a brain wave determines its category: beta, alpha, theta, or delta. Different brain waves are associated with different states of awareness.

In Witchcraft, many of our practices are intended to cultivate various states of consciousness, or brain waves. Beta is the fastest brain wave frequency, and we are in this consciousness when we are dealing with the mundane world of paying bills, preparing meals, and crossing the street. The next brain wave state is the alpha wave state, which occurs when we are meditating or visualizing. Alpha, which is a slower wave than beta, is a state of reverie and relaxation. When you achieve an alpha state, your heart rate slows, you relieve stress, and your body heals more quickly. The alpha state is a bridge between the conscious mind and the subconscious mind, but for all of that magical potential, alpha can also occur when you're daydreaming or simply watching television.

Next is the even slower theta wave state, which occurs when we are experiencing visions and journeying; it can also occur when we are dreaming, in deep meditation, or having a "peak" experience, such as those described by athletes. Theta consciousness is generally thought of as the subconscious mind, where many feel the Sacred resides along with our creativity and strong emotions. Theta is also the state in which you are most likely to experience your most powerful spiritual feelings and encounters.

And finally, the slowest wave is delta, the brain wave of deep sleep and the unconscious mind. But scientists such as C. Maxwell Cade (a Zen master) and Geoffrey Blundell have discovered that, in fact, delta waves can be produced when you're awake. They seem to serve as a kind of information-sensing system that provides you with intuition, empathic feelings, psychic insights, and warnings of danger—information that your conscious, thinking (or beta) mind doesn't perceive. Delta waves seem to be activated by practices in which you "reach out" to others. Healers of all sorts, particularly those who work with energy techniques, such as healing hands, Wicca, and Reiki, produce delta waves when they're working.

Practices such as meditation, journeying, and going into a trance help us to cultivate all of these brain waves, and to combine them into heightened states of awareness and sensitivity. In the higher consciousness of these combined brain wave states achieved by Witches, shamans, yogis, swamis, healers, and others, you can employ your ability to think, to experience empathy, use your intuition, gather information from the unconscious, draw on your creativity, and connect to your innate spirituality all at once.

But there is a quality of consciousness beyond the mind that also includes our emotions, our souls, and the energy of our bodies. In fact, brain wave production is powerfully influenced, or even generated, by these three additional states. This new idea of consciousness is very important to skillful spellcasting. Without it, we fall back into spellcasting from our heads instead of our hearts. When you feel the presence of deity, you'll experience true ecstasy and unleash countless other emotions too: joy, enthusiasm, exhilaration, awe, peacefulness, love, and more. You need all of these feelings to bring a spell to fruition. With this new quantum understanding of what a spell is, you can see that willfulness is only one form of energy—there are many other forms that can fulfill your longings.

QUANTUM SPELLCASTING

Quantum physics has also provided us with other insights about the nature of reality—about consciousness, energy, and matter—that can help us to understand how spells work, so that we can perform them with greater skill. One of these is the Principle of Instantaneous Nonlocality—which is a law of physics that behavior is linked across time and space (remember those two photons from Chapter 1?). The natural world is actually an event of pulsating energy, in which the vibrations of distant sources interact. Thus, it's possible for you to interact with the object of your attention no matter where it is. Focus on someone in Idaho who needs healing, and the energy of your consciousness is present with that person in Idaho.

Just as consciousness moves across "space," it also moves across time. This has direct application to your expectations and energy when you spellcast. When you see yourself in the future, your consciousness is there—your body will then follow the trajectory set by the energy of your consciousness. (Another reason why acting in accord is so important!)

A fun example of how I've used this principle in spellcasting involved a concert I was going to attend last year by one of my favorite performers. Two nights before the show, I cast a circle, put on his music, danced and played and raised a whole lot of very joyful energy, which I shaped into my desire—to be as close to the performance as possible. As I was raising energy, I focused on the fact that everything is local and everything is connected. I knew with absolute intellectual, intuitive, emotional, magical certainty that I was connected to the performer by joy, the political message of the music, similar social goals, etc. And it was such a great spell to cast! Two days later I arrived at the arena with my husband, a dear friend, and her fiancé, taking our seats at the very back of the stadium. It wasn't at all what I had visualized, but I refused to be disappointed. I was delighted just to have gotten tickets. Less than ten minutes after settling into our seats, a member of the concert team approached us and gave us four front-row seats, escorting us right to the stage where most of the solos were performed. Even I was stunned at how quickly and powerfully that spell had worked!

Obviously some states of consciousness are going to be more appropriate for this kind of magic than others—beta consciousness (daily task-oriented thinking) won't do it. But combining beta with alpha, theta, and delta states will provide you with astonishing, downright magical capacities. Alter your consciousness—through Wiccan practices like casting a circle, visualizing, breathing, grounding and centering, chanting, dancing, drumming, etc.— and add to it the energy of your emotions, soul, and physical body, and you can begin to accomplish extraordinary things. Just remember that spells come from the heart, not the head. The head helps the heart, but without your feelings a spell can't work. Even *with* your feelings—and your heightened consciousness and your understanding of quantum reality—you require one more critical thing for real magic, and spells, to work.

THE REAL POWER THAT MAKES A SPELL WORK

The power that makes a spell work is not to be found in some new recipe book. It's not in the secret ingredient, the ancient inscription, the newest invocation. *The real power that makes a spell work dwells within you, and surrounds you: It's the power of your connection to the Sacred. The real secret of successful spellcasting, as with all magic, is your connection to divinity, within and without.* Your thoughts, willpower, feelings, and physical exertions are actually all expressions or forms of this divine energy—just as air, water, fire, and earth are all forms of divine energy. When you understand the true nature of the energy you work with, you can make real magic.

A NEW KIND OF SPELL

Until recently, Witches rarely used the word "prayer." It simply wasn't a part of our vocabulary or our practices. Praying was seen as beseeching a male God to intervene on your behalf because you were powerless to affect the change you were praying for. At best, prayer was considered a kind of dialogue with God while a spell was an expression of your power. Like a prayer, a spell is a conversation with divinity, but when you cast a spell you are also going to the divinity within yourself. You are drawing up that innate power and grace from within and giving it shape and form in the world.

A spell draws upon your own sacred gifts, and upon the power of immanent divinity, which is infinitely greater than ourselves.(That divinity may be evoked in a variety of forms—which we'll explore further.) A spell is not an expression of powerlessness, but of empowerment.

But if you try to use spellcasting to have power over the Universe, it fails as a religious rite. Remember, the Universe is *not* a machine — it's *alive*, it's organic, and it's sacred. You certainly can't make magic by imposing your will on it, or treating it like a computer that you can program. That approach is not just unproductive, it's disrespectful and contrary to our spiritual values as Witches.

As you stop depending on externalized power—the herbs, the incantation, the magical tool—and focus upon the true source of a spell's empowerment, you will transform your spellcasting from simplistic and mechanical manipulation to divine communion and creation. And out of that communion you can craft a rich and magical life. You will also have a means of dealing with any of the challenges that life presents, transforming tragedies into strengths and losses into opportunities. Free yourself to approach spellcasting as a creative, religious ritual and you'll be amazed at how powerful the experience can be—whether or not your spell manifests. With this perspective about what a spell is, why we cast them, and why they do and don't work, you can vastly improve your ability to cast successful spells.

CREATIVITY

A good spell draws not just on information, but on your heightened consciousness, creativity, spontaneity, and inspiration. *Spells are forms of personal, creative, religious ritual. They are divinely inspired expressions that help you cocreate reality with the Sacred.* Instead of commanding the Universe, open your heart and soul to it. A spell can be used for ecstatic communion, or for very specific practical purposes. It can be a means of deepest spiritual transformation, or it can be a means of enriching your personal life. Once you begin to approach spellcasting from the spiritual principle at the heart of Witchcraft, an exciting new realm of possibilities opens up.

SOME OF MY FAVORITE SPELLS

All sorts of wonderful things can be used in spells, and as spells. Here are a few of my favorites:

The Serenity Prayer: *God/dess, grant me the strength to accept the things I cannot change, the courage to change the things I can, and the wisdom to know the difference.*

Your very first spell—wishing on a star!: *I wish I may, I wish I might, have the wish I wish tonight.*

Dance! Go to a rave, an empty beach during the full Moon, or crank up the stereo, take off your clothes, and go wild in your living room!

Creativity is an expression of your innate divinity, so it's essential to good spellcasting. The Universe is infinitely creative, and a spell is a microcosm of what goes on in the Universe. Spells can take many forms: planting flowers in your garden as a way of bringing greater fertility, beauty, and prosperity into your life; swimming beneath a full Moon to cultivate your psychic and spiritual powers; singing a chant that has come to you to help reenchant the world; or cleaning out your closet as a way of banishing the pain and disappointments of the past so they no longer influence your present.

Wicca is the jazz of religion—its beauty and power is in the freedom it grants you to play and improvise. There is a structure, and just as a jazz musician knows the key and tempo, you know how to cast a circle, invoke deity, etc. However, the purpose of the structure is not to confine, but to liberate you. Allow yourself the pleasure of spontaneity—to say what you feel, to move as you're inspired, to do what comes to you. And when you are careful not to overchoreograph a spell, you allow space for the Sacred to express itself.

A spell can also be a carefully planned ritual, using invocations written by others, magical oils and herbs for the creation of a potion, and a wide variety of techniques for working with and directing energy toward the intended goal. There's a lot of wisdom in the older forms of spellcasting, and once we've released ourselves from the constraints of how those spells were used, we can discover and employ their real power.

BASIC TO ADVANCED PRACTICE
GREEN GODDESS PROSPERITY SPELL

You may first want to read Chapter 9, Potions, Notions, and Tools (starting on page 213), to understand how to work with the power of herbs and other aids.

Gather together in a large bowl approximately a quarter cup (three tablespoons) of each of these herbs: bay leaves, rosemary, patchouli, cardamom, basil, cinnamon, heliotrope, vetavert. Add a quarter cup of allspice and sandalwood powder, seven coffee beans, seven anise stars, several pieces of frankincense, and a pinch of red pepper.

Cast a circle. Invoke Goddesses of the Earth by saying: *"Gaia, Demeter, Freya, Oestara, and all Great Goddesses of the abundant and nourishing Mother Earth, bless me with your strength, creativity, and prosperity. I welcome You to this sacred circle."*

Grind the herbs together, gradually adding a few drops of orris oil. You may also grind a piece of paper money into your potion (how much is up to you). As you grind them, invoke the Great Mother Earth and charge the herbs with Her power by chanting: *"As green all things grow/Your blessings I'll sow."*

Enjoy the fragrance as you work. Rub your fingers in the herbs, and rub some of the potion on your forehead, your chest, your heart, your stomach, your groin, your feet. Sprinkle some deosil around the perimeter of your circle.

Burn some of the potion as an incense (air and fire magic). And later, use some of the potion in a prosperity bath (water and earth magic). Wrap some of the herbs in a four-inch-square piece of green cotton cloth tied with a green cord. Hold the bundle to your chest, chant, and dance! Raise energy! And when you feel your energy is peaking, hold the bundle to your heart and charge it with all of your divinely earthy power. See and feel and know the prosperity and abundance that you will create.

Thank the Mother Earth and close your circle. You may place the bundle on your altar, or carry it with you for at least one full cycle of the Moon, or until your prosperity manifests or your strength increases.

A spell can be carefully planned or utterly spontaneous. It can employ a wide and wild variety of props and objects, or it can be as simple as a silent meditation. It's tempting to fall back on the old formula approach—after all, it's all done for you. Just open a book, whip up some energy, and *presto!* Resist the temptation: *Spells without creativity and divinity aren't real spells!* Spells have to be infused with *sacred* energy.

Does this new, "freewheeling" approach to spellcasting seem overwhelming, vague, or unstructured? Remember, you've got an invaluable aid in deciding how, and when, to proceed with a spell: divination.

✳ *Making Magic with Divination* ✳

Before s/he undertakes a ritual or casts a spell, a wise Witch takes advantage of the guidance, insight, and inspiration that come directly from deity through divination. Without divination you can make rash decisions, and rush into casting spells when you aren't clear about what you want. Driven by powerful emotions and shortsightedness, you can make poor choices. Divination assures you that when you make magic, you will make divine magic.

It's important for you, as a Witch, to ask yourself not just what your head wants, or tells you to do, but what your soul wants. In fact, this is another reason you learn to meditate, and to use divination, and to spend time in Nature: They are all powerful techniques for quieting your conscious and controlling mind (where all the habits and social conditioning assert themselves) and for checking in with your deepest and authentic self.

There's an added benefit of using divination when you make magic: Once you've mastered the symbols and vocabulary, not only can you receive sacred messages, you can send them. You can use the symbols, images, and metaphors in your spells and rituals and other forms of making magic to communicate your goals to the Divine, thereby bringing greater meaning, depth, and energy to your spiritual practice.

BASIC TO ADVANCED PRACTICE

GUIDANCE IN SPELLCASTING

Decide upon a goal for your spell or ritual.

Choose the divination tools with which you feel most comfortable.

Engage your oracle as described earlier, acknowledging its wisdom and role in guiding you to make magic. Then describe your reason for consulting it. There are a series of very helpful questions that I usually ask, and as you begin to practice, you're going to discover ones that are uniquely your own. For example, *"I wish to be united with my soul mate and to give and receive love with him/her. I know there is someone who will be as happy and fulfilled to be with me as I with him/her."*

Next, state your question about casting a spell. This can be done in a simple yes/no fashion: *"I would like to cast a spell to make this happen as soon as possible. Should I cast a spell?"*

Remember, casting spells is not always the right approach to manifest changes! If the oracle says no, you should ask, *"Why not?"* Depending on the clarity of the answer you receive, you may want to ask another question: "What can and should I do to bring love into my life?"

An oracle is a mirror that sees into the center of your soul—it sees things that you do not, or cannot, and it helps you to see them. For example, you may not be ready for love—in order to find your soul mate, you must first find your soul, or heal wounds from a past relationship, or learn to be more giving, or keep the focus on yourself and your other goals.

If the oracle answers that you should cast a spell, then ask for guidance in how to cast it. The answer will probably come in symbolic form, so it's important for you to be familiar with the language and symbols of your divination tool, and the symbols Witches use. (Some of these are in the Table of Correspondences on page 78.) Use your intuition and creativity in interpreting the symbol and you will be taking your next step to effective spellcasting.

You can also ask a more specific question. Spells commonly use one or a combination of elements—air, fire, water, or earth—to make magic. So, next you might ask the oracle: "Which element should I use in casting my spell?" Elemental magic is certainly one of the easiest and most effective approaches to spellcasting, especially at the beginning. And most divination tools—runes, I Ching, Tarot cards—use natural imagery. These images will guide you in determining an approach to casting your spell.

If you're using Tarot cards, I suggest you pull a single card from the minor arcana. (As your skills grow, or if you are an advanced practitioner, you should also work with the major arcana.) Each suit corresponds to an element — swords are air, cups are water, wands are fire, pentacles are earth. And the specific card may also contain further guidance, for example, the eight of discs/pentacles shows a little boy hard at work, carving a pentacle. I would interpret the oracle's answer to recommend that I do earth magic, that I create something using an element of earth such as clay, or dough. You could ask for further guidance on what to create— or engage your imagination. If you are looking for a loving soul mate, perhaps you'd create a clay statue of yourself and your beloved, or a heart.

And particularly if you are asking for guidance with a love spell, ask the oracle for a symbol that could be a sign that the spell is working. Because *our lives are our magic*, study the image you received as a possible clue. Also consider the symbols in the earlier cards, runes, or hexagrams. (In this example, because I pulled an eight of pentacles, I would keep my eye out for someone who was an earth sign, who was very hard-working, maybe at an early stage of his career, or whom I might meet through my work.)

Finally, ask the oracle if there is anything else you should know in creating your spell. Write down the questions and the answers you received. And make sure you end by thanking your oracle for its divine guidance.

You can also use the images as visualization tools, meditating on them to see what impressions come to you. Then, when the time comes to create your spell, you may wish to include the oracle's symbols into your magic by placing them on your altar, creating a talisman with the symbols marked on it, or by using them to meditate on and to focus energy in the spellworking.

MAGIC AND DAYS OF THE WEEK

Sunday—The Sun, success, power, the God

Monday—The Moon, transformation, intuition and psychic powers, the Goddess

Tuesday—Mars, courage, power, victory, protection

Wednesday—Mercury, communication, intellect, creativity

Thursday—Jupiter, finances, prosperity, confidence, happiness

Friday—Venus, love, romance, beauty, art, women's mysteries

Saturday—Saturn, lessons, hard work, goals, insight

SYMPATHETIC MAGIC, TIMING, AND ELEMENTS

There are other guides to creative and effective spellcasting. One is a practice called sympathetic magic. You've probably heard the Wiccan expression, "As above, so below," which refers to the unity of sacred and mundane, intent and form. The idea behind how sympathetic magic works is that your circle, and the work you do in it, is a microcosm of the world, which is the macrocosm. What occurs in circle occurs in the world.

Sympathetic magic uses an image and an action that symbolizes what you are seeking to manifest. For example, if you wish to have a life that is filled with growth and creativity, your spell might involve planting a seed, and raising energy and directing it into the Earth and the planted seed. Your spell will continue to work as the seed opens and a plant grows. As you tend the plant, you tend your spell, and your goal.

The natural movement of energy will help determine the timing of your ritual. For example, traditionally, spells for increase of any sort are done during the waxing to full moon, while spells for banishing are done when the moon is waning or dark. You'll also want to experiment with various forms of elemental magic (see Chapter 3, Nature), so that you can appreciate the different kinds of energies inherent in each of the elements.

This knowledge and experience will help you determine which is the most appropriate element for your spell. For example, a spell for artistic inspiration, to do well on an exam or an interview, or to make a new beginning in life would probably use the element of air, and perhaps the creation of an incense, a poem, song, or invocation, and the use of breathing, chanting, and singing to raise energy. It would also invoke spirits of the air, referred to as sylphs, and deities associated with air and with communication, such as the Egyptian God Thoth, the Greek God Hermes, the Greek Goddess Aurora, and the Greek Muses.

SPELL TIPS

There are some specific pointers that I want to share with you to help you craft spells that are powerful, meaningful, and effective. You'll find the specific techniques you'll need throughout *Witch Crafting*.

- Spells can be performed almost anywhere—though I don't recommend attempting it while in the midst of rush-hour traffic! You do need to work without being disturbed when you cast a spell. So find a quiet and private place, preferably outdoors.

- Divination will help you create spells that work, and will help you to understand, and thereby benefit, from spells that don't.

- Spells require energy, and so you'll need to learn how to work with it (see Chapter 10, Energy).

- Raising energy is like boiling water, so you'll need a container (that's one reason Witches cast circles) to hold the energy that you raise for casting spells, or performing other forms of magic (see Chapter 4, Sacred Space).

- Your expectations will affect the outcome of the experiment, so you need to be able to clearly visualize your goal (see Chapter 1, Visualization practice). As you raise your energy concentrate on a goal, and when you release it visualize your goal manifesting. A trick: Don't think about *how* it's going to come about, just concentrate on the final result. Let the Universe take care of the details. I was taught not to talk about a spell for at least twenty-four hours after casting it. In fact, I was taught that I shouldn't even *think* about it! The idea is that once you've done it, you must leave it alone—don't keep tinkering with it or worrying about whether it will work or not, or you'll interfere with and inhibit the spell's trajectory.

- The Table of Correspondences is a valuable tool for creating effective spells (see page 78).

- Remember, you should not do spellwork on someone else's behalf without their permission.

- There's an old axiom that spells should rhyme. It probably stems from the idea of enchanting the world—the magical practice of chanting a spell. A rhymed spell has rhythm and joyfulness in it, it's easy to remember and to repeat, and the repetition itself creates an altered, magical consciousness.

- Passion fuels a successful spell.

- Doubt kills a spell.

- When a spell works, it's important to give back something to the Universe. This is not only a form of giving thanks, it's also a way of maintaining the ecosystem of the Universe. Nature teaches us that a healthy environment is constantly cycling energy from one source to another, from one beneficiary to another. The rhythm of life is sustained by this ecological movement of energy. So when you've received, you must in turn give. After my successful concert spell, I passed on my blessing by making several generous donations of time and money to various worthy causes.

- And finally, remember that as long as you have creativity, divinity, and a pure and open heart, you'll be casting spells of incredible beauty and power.

Spells without Visualized Goals

Most spellcasting books recommend that you visualize your goal as clearly and specifically as possible: See your name on the company stationery, see yourself walking into your office, see your paycheck. This is a fine approach—sometimes. Over the years I've come to learn that open-minded spellcasting is also one of the best strategies for success and one of the most glorious spiritual experiences you can have.

What's open-minded spellcasting? Two things: First, rather than visualize capturing the heart of the gorgeous guy down the hall (who may well respond to your love, leaving you with the dilemma of what to do about his wife, his drinking problem, and his football fetish), ask for the love that's best for you, that will make you happiest, or ask for the love of a soul mate. Then trust the Universe and your "higher" self to creatively take it from there.

The other open-mindedness is just that—it's "Zen" mind. Some of the most powerful spells I've ever cast did not have a specific, detailed visualized thought form into which I projected energy. In fact, it was just the opposite—my mind was clear, free, and open as I sent the energy forth. I simply made an offering to divinity, and the Universe has blessed me with fulfillment beyond anything I could have imagined. Try it some time.

Acting in Accord

One of the most important parts of successful spellcasting is a principle we call "Acting in Accord." It means that once you've completed your spell, you're going to take specific, concrete actions in the material world to manifest your spell's goal. If you did a prosperity/money spell, you will take actions that will help you make money—whether it's going back to school, writing up a new résumé and going on interviews, asking your boss for a raise, or starting your own business. Our magic occurs not just on akashic planes of energy, but right here, on the plane where energy takes shape. Failing to act in accord confines your magic to abstract realms and prevents it from taking form in the world. *For a spell to work, you must ground it in material reality by taking action.*

To complete the process of casting the spell and to set it into motion so that it can manifest, you can use the techniques of binding, setting, and releasing the spell, which can be done in a variety of ways. This final step of the spell is like releasing a balloon with a message tied to it, or putting the cake in the oven, or tying the knot at the end of the thread you've been sewing with. It locks your energy and intent into place and sends it off to take form. But the most important step in setting your spell into motion is to act in accord.

Acting in accord reminds you that *your life is your magic.* Because this world, as an embodiment of deity, is sacred, at any moment you can experience the ecstasy and the magic of life—in the music of the wind in the trees, a flash of red as a cardinal flies past, the silver Moon rising in the night sky, the kiss of your beloved, the smile of a child. The sources of inspiration are endless if you are paying attention.

BINDING, SETTING, AND RELEASING A SPELL

To bind, set, and release a spell, speak these final traditional words—"As I do will, so mote it be!"—after you conclude the last action. What's the last action? Some examples are: If you are doing knot magic, tie the last knot; if you are burning something, wait until the last spark extinguishes and the smoke rises. If you are charging something, speak your concluding words as you hold the object to your heart. And as you speak, visualize your goal manifesting as you send out a cone of power into the image.

Here are other "final actions" that set the spell:

- Tying off the last ribbon on the Maypole
- Placing your hands over the spot where you've buried something in the Earth, and giving thanks
- Sealing a potion bundle, talisman, or sigil with wax or a cord
- Pulling the stopper to let the tub drain after a purification bath

And remember, act in accord!

When you cast a spell for love or money, health or inspiration, peace or empowerment, you are expressing your faith in yourself, and in the Universe, to create the life that you deserve—a life in which you are able to fulfill your destiny. A spell is an expression of your own sacred power to make that life. And so you must act in accord—fill out that school application, get rid of the clothes that no longer fit your new self, deal with your doubts so that you really can love someone else in a way that's good for both of you. Walk your talk. Ground your spirituality in action, joining spirit and matter, and the Sacred will work with you and honor your spells by fulfilling them.

CREATING SPELLS

Here's a simple step-by-step guide to help you create your own spells.

1. Decide on your goal.

2. Consult a divination tool or oracle for guidance.

3. Integrate the guidance you've been given into your spellcasting.

4. Consult the Table of Correspondence for guidance in choosing what deities, elements, herbs, etc., to work with.

5. Use your creativity, intuition, and information.

6. Gather your materials—this can include music, meditation tapes, and other aids—and set up your altar.

7. Prepare yourself with a purification bath.

8. Prepare your space—if you are working indoors, use a cleansing herb such as sage, or salt water, to clear the energy of where you will work. Turn off phones and other distractions. If need be, put up a sign so you won't be disturbed. Close the door.

9. Cast your circle.

10. Breathe, ground, and center.

11. Feel the divinity within.

12. Invoke/call upon deity from without.

13. State your goal—the intention of your spell.

14. Visualize your goal.

15. Raise energy.

16. Direct the energy into your visualized goal, or the object, potion, talisman, etc., that you are working with.

17. Set and release the energy of the spell.

18. Ground your excess energy.

19. Offer a libation and thanks.

20. Close the circle.

21. Break down your altar and carefully store your tools.

22. Act in accord.

23. If the spell comes to fruition, give thanks, and "free" your talisman, amulet, sigil, or potion. You can release it into Nature by scattering the contents into the air or the water, by burying it in the Earth, or even by burning it. If you have created a work of art, you may want to keep it in a place of honor, such as on your altar, or with your magical tools. If the spell doesn't work, determine why.

WHEN A SPELL DOESN'T WORK

Most Witches will tell you that spells work intermittently and they treasure and share the tales of those spells that were successful. A spell that works is proof that magic is real, that we can affect the outcome of events, not just at the mysterious level of subatomic particles, but at the level of daily life.

So what do you do when a spell doesn't work? With the old model, you just went out and bought another book, tried a different spell, used a different ingredient. And lots of people get discouraged and stop casting spells, convinced that magic isn't real and spells are just superstitious nonsense. Well, mechanical magic *isn't* real, and mechanistic spellcasting borders on superstition. It certainly keeps the power outside yourself, which is what superstitions are based on—powerlessness.

All your ingredients, including your timing, your energy, and your connection to deity, could be as right as they could be and your spell *still* may not manifest. Why not?

It's the magic of destiny working.

We often refer to Witchcraft as the Craft of the Wise. Wisdom is not just earned at school—it comes from living life, particularly living through life's trials and challenges. These tests are where the greatest wisdom comes from. And the failure of a dream to come true is one of life's greatest tests. Wisdom, however, has a unique way of transforming the bitter into the bittersweet, and ultimately, into the sweetness of life. And so, when a spell does not manifest, you should not ask, "What went wrong?" but, "Why not?" In understanding "why not," you become wise.

So when a spell doesn't work, use divination or meditation, and ask why not. I've never once had an oracle say to me: "Didn't I tell you not to use vervain? Next time use rue!" Oracles show us the *real* reasons: the deep, unseen, and spiritual currents moving through a magical life. Remember, *magic often works in unexpected ways*, and its timing is also not on the same schedule as yours, so be patient. I've been working on and waiting for and acting in accord with a very special spell for over twenty years.

Most of all, when events don't play out as our spell intended, remember that the Universe is a complex and *living* process. Just as humans behave unexpectedly, so too does the Universe. Chaos plays a far greater role in reality than we had thought when we viewed the world through the simple mechanics of Newton's laws. But chaos theory has also shown us something else quite amazing: At the furthest fringes of randomness, a pattern emerges. It is the pattern of spirals—the shape of DNA, the building block of life.

You live within an organic reality, your life is one of the spirals of beauty emerging from the infinite chaos of the quantum reality. That pattern is your destiny. Some spells advance the pattern, some do not. Those that do often manifest quickly and powerfully. Those that don't simply fizzle, or manifest in unexpected ways that are more appropriate to the pattern of your destiny.

Your destiny is not a fixed or unchangeable reality. Instead, it is a probability that requires your participation to come to fruition. A spell, some have suggested, helps change possibilities into probabilities. Wisdom, self-knowledge, love, and action advance your destiny. So does being connected to your inner divinity, and to the Sacred in the world. The failure of a spell may be filled with as much magic as its fulfillment. When you find the meaning behind a non-manifestation, you will find its gift, its magic, and its empowerment, for *you are the spell the Universe has cast.*

BASIC TO ADVANCED PRACTICE
THE SPELL FOR LIVING WELL

Go for a walk. Visit your place of power. Then ground, center, and meditate.

Look into your heart and ask yourself: "What do I want to be happy and fulfilled?" Pay attention to any images that appear to you that symbolize your desire and your goal. Thank the *genius loci.*

Collect objects that symbolize your goal—you may find them in Nature, you may already have them (such as photographs, books, works of art, etc.), you may acquire something that will help you accomplish your goal such as a briefcase, or a computer.

Write down a simple four-line spell that rhymes and that includes your goal and also the line: *"This is the spell for living well."*

Set up your altar and place your objects and your spell on or near the altar. (Be careful about electronic equipment in circles—the energy has a tendency to affect them in weird ways!)

Cast your circle (see Chapter 4).

Then chant your spell as you raise your energy, dancing deosil (clockwise) around your cast circle.

Direct the energy into your object(s) as you continue to chant the spell. Visualize clearly—see yourself living well. Feel the joy of the Divine flowing through you, into your life, and the world.

Set and release the spell by saying aloud and as loudly as your circumstances permit, preferably with a good shout: *"This is my spell for living well. As I do will, so mote it be!"*

Ground your energy, offer a libation, give thanks, and close your circle.

Act in accord—live well!

Potions, Notions, and Tools

Casting a spell is so much fun! And creating a ritual is an utterly magical experience. Part of the joy of Wicca is how deeply personal it all is. And creating emotionally and spiritually meaningful rituals and spells is very empowering and liberating. You discover that you are capable of producing transformative and numinous experiences that are very moving—and not just for yourself, but for others. You also get to draw on all sorts of artistic talents and interests, many of which you may never have realized you had.

Understanding the spiritual roots and purposes of magic should greatly enrich your confidence and skills. But as we turn to the subject of magical aids and objects, we run the risk of falling back into the old way of thinking about magic: that the power is outside of us, in tools and words and potions. Even experienced practitioners are susceptible to this mechanistic approach, so if you've been working for years, please don't skip over this chapter, thinking it's just "Wiccan bootcamp." I'd like to pose some ideas and approaches that might reinvigorate your thinking, and therefore your practices. And if you're just starting out, I hope this chapter will deepen your appreciation for why Witches do what they do and so enhance your skills as you practice.

When I began practicing Wicca, having been raised in an intellectual home that viewed religion with skepticism, I found myself very uncomfortable with rituals and spells, and especially with all the props and tools that Witches used, which seemed odd to me. Despite all of the mysterious experiences I'd had before I'd even met my coven, I still had a keen distrust of magic, ritual, and certainly spellcasting as a lot of superstitious mumbo jumbo.

Yet there I was, with a room full of women, standing around an altar with all sorts of unfamiliar stuff on it, listening as they called the names of strange deities, made all sorts of weird gestures in the air with knives, and polished it all off by drinking from silver goblets. I'm still surprised that I didn't go running out the door! But gradually I began to understand the meaning of the symbols, tools, and gestures they were using. I began to appreciate that the magical rituals they were creating weren't superstitious theatrics, but very moving, living works of religious art. My heart opened to the power of beauty and truth evoked by their rituals, and I felt a flood of emotions I'd never known.

I've been creating and participating in spells and rituals for almost my entire adult life and I'm never bored (unless I'm in a ritual conducted by an egotist!) because these very important ways of making magic and experiencing the Sacred are endlessly creative. Wiccan ritual is, as religious rites are intended to be, a profoundly aesthetic experience. My own perspective is that *spells and rituals are a gorgeous form of spiritual expression and, when done from the right heart space, they are charged with divinity and creativity. A spell or ritual is a process of discovering and expressing the deepest truths about the world, and yourself, through the highest human faculties—our aesthetic and divine sensibilities. It is the art of transforming ourselves and the world into something sacred.*

Like any artist, you learn to craft beautiful and effective spells and rituals by *doing* them—lots of them. The more you do, the better you'll get, and the more you'll enjoy yourself. Wicca is a celebratory and participatory tradition, and I know I've said it before, but I can't say it too much: If you're not having fun, you're not doing it right!

❋   *Understanding Your Craft*   ❋

My own approach to Witchcraft tends toward Zen simplicity and shamanic spontaneity—and natural inspiration. Then again, I also greatly enjoy crafting an elaborate ritual or spell, replete with specially prepared incenses, oils, talismans, candles, and wardrobe. And my coven has, for many years, sponsored large, carefully planned public rituals in New York City—one of our Beltaine rituals was the first public Wiccan ceremony to be performed in Central Park. So why, if the power is within, do I and millions of other Witches use all this stuff?

On a purely practical level, these aids help me focus and concentrate. And most importantly they help me to begin to shift my consciousness to the Sacred. But there's a deeper reason I use potions, notions, talismans, and tools.

As an Earth religion, Wicca is a sensuous spirituality that honors the wisdom that comes to us through our senses. Rituals engage all of your senses to enhance your experience of divinity. (If you haven't read Chapter 3, go to it right now, and do the Sensitivity Training exercise on page 72—you really need to expand your sensitivity in order to create fully effective rituals and spellcasting.) Rituals ground us and our spirituality in our bodies. When you participate in a ritual, you experience a powerful form of enacted meditation in which you are active, not passive, and deeply engaged emotionally, physically, and spiritually.

Magic *begins* with your preparation of the props, incenses, oils, and candles. When you use them, you awaken your senses, get out of your head, and begin to shift your consciousness and engage with divinity. That deity is embodied in plants (herbs), rocks (crystals), elements (water, air, fire, earth), and everything that you work with in creating a ritual or spell. And as you work, you'll discover that each creative step is itself an important, active meditation and way of making magic.

Unfortunately, too often newcomers, and even some long-term practitioners, think the magic of Witchcraft is achieved by following spells to the letter, just as if they were following a recipe for baking a cake. The creation of an effective and powerful Wiccan ritual or spell, even for the most pragmatic of purposes—such as getting a new job—requires that you understand the spiritual contexts of these aspects of Witchcraft. As we discussed in Chapter 8, Secrets of Spellcasting, it's impossible to really understand or make effective use of the many potions, props, and tools that are so much a part of Wiccan practice without that understanding.

To put all of these raw materials to best use, you need to engage their true magical power, and to know why Witches use them to practice the art of making magic. Just as magic is not a mechanical process, neither is working with any of the magical aids. Though a potion may be filled with power, as long as you think mechanically, the power remains outside of yourself, and it just won't work properly. And a magical tool, such as an athame, wand, or chalice, may be an evocative symbol, and can indeed hold a magical charge of energy, but it can't make magic *for* you. You can, however, learn why and how they make magic *with* you.

The Real Power of Props and ❊ Potions, Tools, and Talismans ❊

Witches have developed a sophisticated artistry based upon the magical energies of herbs, oils, stones, crystals, elements, and many other items used in magic. Quantum physics has shown us that, ultimately, everything is energy. So, for example, we know that herbs are energy, and certain herbs have specific energies—there are medicinal herbs, herbs for cooking, herbs for helping tell the future, herbs for helping shift your consciousness. Similarly, Witches work with colors, which are different wavelengths of light (energy), and each color has specific properties and effects. For example, modern Witches work with red as a color of power and of passionate love, and psychologists have discovered that people who spend time in a red room will feel invigorated, sometimes to the point of getting confrontational! It also has been proven to stimulate the appetite! Blue is associated with peacefulness and healing, and indeed, studies show this wavelength of light has precisely that effect on human beings.

The system of energetic relationships between all of the objects, aids, and tools we work with is usually referred to as "Correspondences," and is most often organized around the four elements and four directions. We'll be exploring these correspondences throughout the chapter and you'll find a Table of Correspondences in Chapter 3, Nature, on page 78. This system of correspondences is a remnant of ceremonial magical traditions—particularly that of the Masons and the Golden Dawn, reworked by that creative spiritual artist Gerald Gardner. The shamans of Europe probably did not work with this exact system, though there may be some similarities. However, contemporary Wiccans have found it useful and effective for organizing and working with a diverse range of objects and energies. And I believe one reason that it has taken such firm root in Europe, Australia (with a few variations based on geographical and seasonal differences), and the United States is that it basically coincides with the essential geographical and seasonal realities with which we live. In the United States it's also profoundly similar to the spiritual wisdom and practices of this land—for many Native American tribes not only worship in circles, but also honor the four directions and the powers associated with them. What is most important is the current function and usefulness of this system.

Everything is energy, and so Witches work with a wide variety of energies, and their material forms, to manifest and enhance their magic. Thus, a spell for love will not only use your own emotions, physicality, mental focus, and spiritual energy, it will also employ a wide variety of items that lend their energy to yours.

MAGICAL PROPERTIES

It's empowering to know that science has proven the qualities of many magical aids that Witches have always appreciated. Crystals are now used by computers to preserve information, as they have been used by Witches to preserve memories, spells, and spiritual information. The oils, incenses, potions, and baths that Witches use—which engage us through our sense of smell— have now been shown by aromatherapy lab experiments to have precisely the effects we work with (for example, the smell of

Magic and Color Correspondences

White—Peace, purification, protection, healing, the Moon

Pink—The Goddess, women's mysteries, friendship, beauty

Red—Power, courage, passion, love

Orange—Success, healing, power

Yellow—Success, beginnings, inspiration, the Sun

Green—Prosperity, growth, fertility, creativity, money, Earth

Blue—Peace, healing, emotional healing, water

Lavender—Spirituality, meditation, psychic gifts and dreams

Brown—Justice, Earth

Black—Banishing, rest

Gold—The Sun, success, prosperity, insight, the God

Silver—The Moon, inspiration, transformation, intuition, the Goddess

peppermint will perk you up and lavender's scent will relax you). I watch with regular delight as one herb after another is "discovered" and welcomed into mainstream culture and medicine. St. John's Wort, long used by Witches in potions and rituals to improve mood, is now all the rage, having been scientifically proven to have chemicals that indeed improve a person's disposition.

A great deal of herbal lore survived the Witch hunts, including our knowledge that all the creatures of the Earth have gifts to share with us. Witches also remember that although much has been handed down from generation to generation, originally there was no lab to provide herbal information to our predecessors. And I sincerely doubt that the village healer was engaging in trial-and-error experimentation! Even today, if you ask shamans how they know about the healing power of a certain plant, they will probably tell you that the plant spoke to them. Though their predecessors may have taught them which plant cures and which kills, and how to prepare and administer natural medicines, shamans are also taught how to listen to the spirits of all things, particularly when seeking to work with them. Your capacity to listen to the teachings of Nature is critical to your spirituality and your ability to make magic with Her gifts.

ADVANCED EXERCISE:
LEARNING THE MAGICAL POWERS
OF THE EARTH'S CREATURES

Return to Chapter 3, Nature, and practice the unnaming process. Work with the plants in your place of power. Ask who they are, what their purpose is, whether they need anything from you, and learn to listen for the answers.

Write down what you learn.

Compare what you learn from the plant with what you find in a good plant book.

The medicinal and culinary benefits of herbs seem sensible enough, but what about the magical powers ascribed to herbs, oils, and other items? It seems a stretch to say that a plant can help bring about love—indeed, Witches are often belittled because their potions and concoctions are thought by many to be the products of superstition.

The spiritual/magical properties of herbs, oils—and crystals— may never be proven in the same way we can scientifically establish medicinal purposes. But we are only just beginning to discover the hidden gifts of a quantum universe. Experience has taught us to honor what the plant world teaches us—and so, if a plant tells you it can heal a physically injured heart, and we know scientifically that it can, why can't a plant be right when it tells you it can heal a heart that's been "broken" emotionally? Remember, everything is energy, and everything is interconnected in the quantum energy field—including your broken heart and the emotionally and physically healing energies of plants.

And just as it makes a difference whether you ingest a medicine or apply it topically, it makes sense that there would be a difference between smelling the plant, ingesting it, or grinding it up and using it in a potion, etc. It also matters which parts of the plant you use, because in a single plant one part might be medicinal while the other is deadly poisonous. So, there is an entire study of herbal wisdom, or green magic, that Witches seek to master.

But while an herb, potion, oil, or crystal has inherent power, it does not contain the magic you are seeking. It contains the *potential* for the magic. In other words, it's not the magical or quantum energy of the herb called *damiana* that will make your love spell work. The herb itself has no power to affect the outcome of your love life *until you interact with it*. It is your intent, your desire, and most of all, your appreciation and respect for the assistance given to you by the herb or other aid, your reverence for it as an embodiment of deity, and your actions that *activate* its power.

It's easy for us to understand this principle in terms of scientifically proven healing properties. Here's an example of how we must interact with a plant to take advantage of its healing powers: The beautiful flowering plant digitalis (which I have planted all over my yard) is the source of a medication that is critical to heart patients. But the healing power of digitalis first had to be discovered (which happened long before there were scientific labs). And today when it is used, before the healing power can begin to work, the plant has to be properly harvested, prepared, and ingested by the patient—in other words, the patient has to interact appropriately with the plant. Similarly, the herbs and oils used in magic (whether in incense, baths, teas, magical pouches, or other forms) have no power to effect change until you interact with them—and not just by mindlessly following some recipe in a book! Quantum physicists now realize that there is an astonishing interface or interaction between consciousness and matter—and *it is this interaction that catalyzes or activates the power inherent in the object you are working with.*

It is not quite as simple as saying your potion will work because you believe it will, but as we know, in a quantum universe your beliefs and expectations will affect the outcome of events. Charge the potion with your intent and you unleash its power to work as intended. (If it doesn't, you need to reread in Chapter 8 about the magic of spells that don't manifest.)

Like a car that cannot go anywhere without a driver, all the potions and props in the world are powerless without the practitioner. Ultimately the power that makes all magic work originates not from the ingredients used but from the awakened divinity of you, the individual, working reverentially and consciously with the divinity of your ingredients or tools.

Paint by Numbers, or Discover ❋ *Your Inner Michelangelo* ❋

Crafting a ritual or spell, or creating the items you'll use such as a potion, incense, carved candle, or other aid, is an aesthetic and a spiritual activity. I've long marveled at how the form of Wiccan rituals is so similar to that of other spiritual works of art such as Buddhist mandalas and Navajo sand paintings. All three forms of religious art are rituals in which the process of creation, not the end product, is important. The mandala and the sand painting are both swept away when they are finished, just as a circle is closed once the spell has been cast, or the ritual completed. They are all about the infinite and perfect divinity of the moment experienced through the creative process.

As with any art, you need to master the fundamental knowledge and skills of working with the spiritual medium of ritual and spellcasting—Picasso spent many years being classically trained as a painter before he launched a revolution in the world of art. So, learn the correspondences, the symbols, and the energetic properties of herbs and colors and minerals—and you'll learn them best by working with them.

BASIC TO ADVANCED PRACTICE
MAKING MAGIC WITH A POTION

Decide what you'd like to accomplish—finding love, obtaining more money or better health, breaking an old habit, etc. If you're not sure what you need, or what type of spell to cast, use divination to help you. Decide if you are going to make a potion for an incense, a bath, or a bundle you'll carry or keep on your altar until your magic manifests.

Turn to the list of herbs and oils at the end of this chapter and look at the spells throughout this book. Choose a spell that addresses your goal or, if you cannot find one for your specific goal, look to the herb and oil lists and let your intuition guide you in choosing four herbs and one oil to produce your potion. Gather the herbs with respect and gratitude.

Write a four-line rhyming spell that addresses your goal.

Add three tablespoons of each herb to your mortar and pestle and grind the herbs together in the appropriate direction (see the Tips section at the end of this chapter) while carefully adding a few drops of oil. (If you're making incense, don't add too much oil or it won't burn properly.)

Chant your spell as you grind, carefully adding ingredients until you're happy with the fragrance. Then stop, thank the herbs for their gift of power, and declare your potion complete! Bind and set your potion's power with the words *"As I do will, so mote it be!"* And don't forget to write down your formula for next time. Use it in your spellcasting.

The world is your painter's box, filled with all the colors and textures of the rainbow, and more! At first when you are creating spells (and rituals), it's natural and appropriate to follow the paint-by-numbers instructions that you will find in this book, and certainly in countless others, just as painters literally copy the works of other painters to learn these artists' techniques and to discover their own. A great deal of research, care, experimentation, and generosity has gone into the creation of the potions, teas, incenses, oils, and spells you will find here and elsewhere.

However, it's equally important for you not to fall into the trap of mechanistic thinking that can accompany the temptation to rely on the work of someone else. So, learn from others, master the basics, and then, as soon as possible, strike out into the realm of your own divine creativity.

ADVANCED PRACTICE
WORKING PROPLESS

For those of you who have been creating rituals and casting spells for years, or even months, I'd like you to try an entirely different approach to making magic. You will find it easier to work outdoors, and an interesting challenge if you must work inside.

Spend the next lunar cycle practicing without any tools, aids, potions, candles, wardrobe, altar, etc. Instead, work directly with the elements themselves, in as natural a form as possible (which is why it's preferable to work outdoors). Bathe in a lake, stream, or ocean—or in your tub. Hike outside, or work in your garden, or go work for a farmer—or exercise. Fly a kite or just listen to the wind in the trees—or do long breath meditations. Let the sun bake you—or go to your kitchen and bake some bread.

Write about your magic in your Book of Shadows or magical journal.

✳   *Your Palette*   ✳

From reading this and other books with all the spells and their ingredients, it may seem like creating potions requires an overwhelming amount of stuff. It's impossible to do justice to the vast subject of herbs, oils, and all the rest of it in this single chapter, and there are many wonderful books now available (you'll find suggestions in the Resources), but below you'll find the basics.

HERBS

Herbs are used in magical potions for all sorts of goals, both spiritual and practical—for inspiration, love, healing, prosperity, protection, peace, and banishing bad habits and bad love affairs, to name a few. Decide upon your goal and you'll be able to find or create an herbal potion to help you. Herbs and herbal potions can be used as incense, bathing elixirs, magical pouches, poltices, teas, ingredients in magical food, and offerings.

The basic herbal apothecary here will allow you to creatively combine them yourself, and to figure out what to substitute if you can't find a particular herb. You should be able to acquire most herbs at the local herb or health food store (check out the herbal tea section if they don't carry them "loose"), and certainly at any Wiccan shop. You'll even find most of them at the grocery store, the farmer's market, and best of all, you can grow them in your yard, or in pots on your windowsill. But don't get overly ambitious, empty your kitchen cabinets, and fill them with herbs (like I did when I first started out!), because it's best to work with the freshest herbs possible. And devote a mortar and pestle exclusively to working with your herbs (be sure to clean it out between uses).

A GOOD HERBAL APOTHECARY

Cleansing, purification, relaxation: Chamomile, calendula, comfrey, lavender, eucalyptus, carnation, olive, patchouli, rosemary, sage, sandalwood, valerian, vervain, mint, rue. Also, sea salt and Epsom salts.

Banishing: Bay leaves, cinnamon, myrrh, salt, red pepper, nettle.

Healing: Comfrey, lavender, patchouli, basil, rose, lemon.

Peace and protection: Lavender, lemon, orris root, cardamom, thyme, vervain, basil, rue, frankincense, cedar, rosemary, sage, valerian, "dragon's blood powder" (palm tree resin).

Dreams, divination, enhancing psychic abilities: Mugwort, chamomile, sandalwood, sage, lavender, dittany of Crete.

Love and passion: Rosewater, rose petals, damiana, galangal root (an Indian spice), lavender, patchouli, powdered orris root, vervain, cinnamon.

Prosperity and success: High John the Conqueror root, bay leaves, cinnamon, vervain, anise seeds, orange peel, coffee.

Tip to speed up any spell: Add a dash of cinnamon and a dash of red pepper!

If you're just starting to work with potions, here's my A-list of what herbs you should have because they are used in so many spells and formulas:

The A-List: Lavender, vervain, sandalwood, bay leaves, chamomile, rose petals, frankincense, myrrh, rosemary, cinnamon, sage, patchouli, mugwort, "dragon's blood powder" (palm tree resin). And don't forget the salt!

OILS

Oils play an important part in Wicca. They are used to anoint yourself and your tools, and lend a powerful charge depending upon the properties of the oil. As aromatherapists know, the fragrance of an oil, like an incense or herbal potion, has the power to utterly transform your consciousness. They can be worn on your body, worked into an incense, rubbed onto magical tools and candles, burned over a candle—and you will undoubtedly discover other creative magical uses. And a few drops of oil can be used instead of the herbs from which the oil was extracted.

One of their most valuable uses is to seal your various pulse points. When you dab oil here, the oil enters your body through your skin and bloodstream, then helps hold your energy in your body until you are ready to direct it toward your magical goal. To find your pulse points, press your fingers against the following spots and feel for your heartbeat: your neck, throat, underarms, crook of your arm, wrists, groin, behind your knees, and your ankles.

WITCHY WARDROBE

"It's all about the clothes," my women friends and I always say with a laugh. While performing rituals, Witches may wear robes, special gowns, shirts and trousers, or just street clothes. Then again, to quote my Australian Witch pal, Fiona Horne, "Naked is sacred." A lot of Witches work without any clothes at all, or "skyclad." My circle does all of the above, depending on the ritual.

Working skyclad is probably one of the most singular religious aspects of modern Witchcraft. For Witches, the body is holy and sacred,

A GOOD OIL APOTHECARY

Here's a list of commonly used oils.

Almond oil—for love and prosperity.

Bergamot oil—for prosperity and protection.

Eucalyptus oil—for cleansing (be careful, because it's a powerful astringent and can irritate your skin and eyes!).

Frankincense oil—see all the uses for frankincense listed in A Good Herbal Apothecary, above.

Jasmine oil—for love and sexuality, for the Goddess.

Lavender oil—see all the uses for lavender in A Good Herbal Apothecary, above.

Patchouli oil—for love and all the uses in A Good Herbal Apothecary, above.

Sandalwood oil—see all the uses in A Good Herbal Apothecary, above.

utterly without sin, and a magnificent expression of divine beauty and genius. Working in the nude is a symbol of truth—and the fact that we are all naked before the Divine. Then too going skyclad really helped me, and lots of other women I've worked with, overcome the horrible pressures put on us by a patriarchal culture to conform to impossible standards of attractiveness. Together we realized that all women are incredibly beautiful, no matter what we look like. Men have their own body image issues, and I think they too find working skyclad a deeply liberating and empowering experience.

New folks sometimes worry that working skyclad in a mixed-gender coven will raise all sorts of sexual issues and tensions—in fact, I've found it has just the opposite effect. It is an expression and reflection of the profound trust and respect we all have for one another. In my circle, we tend to reserve working skyclad for the occasions when we are doing serious ritual and making major magic because it enhances the power, enchantment, and uniqueness of the experience. We also have special clothes that we use for public ritual, but we keep it simple—the women prefer beautiful gowns and the men often wear poets' shirts, or velvet robes in winter. Because we are a public coven that is dedicated to fighting the negative stereotypes about Witches, we don't wear black to public rituals (and we don't wear it in private circles either, except at Samhain, or if we're in our street clothes). And we work a lot in our street clothes because our tradition is about our lives being our magic—we don't make the usual distinction between mundane and sacred, trying instead to discover the Sacred within the "mundane."

We all have jewelry, and we generally wear our pentacles and other symbols, such as Goddess necklaces, in public. While every piece I own is precious to me—especially my grandmother's elegant cameo of the Goddess Aurora in her chariot, my mother's Athena necklace, and my green-and-gold David Webb snake pin—the power's not in the jewelry, it's in me. And though I have a moon crown, I only wear it on very special occasions.

In summary, when it comes to ritual clothing and jewelry, I think you should do what feels best. When it comes to jewelry, I follow my mother's advice: less is more! And remember, you don't need to wear an expensive, and often cumbersome, robe or flowing cape with a huge pentagram to be a Witch.

TOOLS

Witches have very deep, personal, and spiritual relationships with the "tools of our art." As with herbs, oils, and other aids, the power in the tools cannot replace your own, but can enhance it. When you work with them in ritual or spellcasting, the magic is unmistakable and deeply moving. Also, the way in which you find your tools is often charged with magic, and deity.

TIPS FOR WORKING WITH
POTIONS AND NOTIONS

- Herbs for magic involving increase or manifestation should be ground deosil—the direction in which the Sun moves (in the Northern Hemisphere this is clockwise; in the Southern, counterclockwise).

- Herbs for magic involving banishings should be ground widdershins—opposite to the direction in which the Sun moves (counterclockwise in the Northern Hemisphere, clockwise in the Southern).

- "Oiling" a candle increases the power of both flame and oil, and your magic. To oil a candle, dab your finger with oil, then rub the oil onto the candle, starting from the center and moving toward the wick end, and then from the center to the base of the candle.

- Keep your herbs in airtight jars, away from the light. It's cheaper and easier to buy herbs in larger quantities, but remember that freshness matters. Also, if you can, grow your own.

- Keep your oils in dark bottles, preferably cobalt blue or brown, also out of the light.

- Label everything carefully.

- Don't reuse candles that you've already used for candle magic for another spell or ritual. Let them burn completely down, someplace safe where they can't start a fire. If you must put them out, relight them while focusing on your intent. You may reuse the four candles that mark each of the directions ("point candles") at the edge of your circle, and the three candles you use for fire and illumination on the altar.

- Treat all of your aids with appreciation and respect.

- Remember: Safety first! Don't leave candles burning unattended; don't hold on to the incense charcoal once it starts to burn; use a pot holder with your brazier; be careful with long and flowing clothes around burning candles; don't get oils in your eyes or mucous membranes; if you're going to make a tea and ingest an herb, make sure you know that it isn't poisonous and that you aren't allergic to it. (Don't I sound like your mother?)

One of the members of my circle, Jefferson, has a wand he fashioned from a willow branch that he found while on a trip to Ireland. It has special meaning for him because of the magical way it came to him—a raven, a symbol of the Goddess, broke the branch off the tree as it took flight. The branch fell into the water of a well that was sacred to the Pagans who had lived on the land years before. But Jefferson also brings to this tool his own energy, as a person who was awake to the gift the Universe was providing for him.

BASIC PRACTICE
GREEN MAN MAGIC—FINDING YOUR WAND

Study the magical power of trees and the qualities they are associated with (a few examples of trees and their gifts are: willow—Moon, love, visions, enchantments; oak—strength; holly—wisdom; birch—rebirth; rowan—life and magic). In particular, research the trees that grow near where you live. Then take a hike in Nature and bring a pocketknife or small saw with you. Ask the Green Man to guide you to your wand. Pay attention to the sound of the wind in the trees, and watch the birds and the squirrels for signs. Look for a fallen branch that calls to you, or listen for a tree calling to you or sending you a sign. You can also bring along your favorite divination tool and use it to guide you—periodically asking it for advice, such as, "Is this the right tree?"

When you find the tree—by sign, divination, or attraction—ask the tree if it would like to work with you and provide you with a wand. If you feel a positive response, sit with your back against the trunk of the tree, ground and center, and feel yourself joining with the tree. Feel the tremendous power that runs through it. Listen as the tree speaks to you and teaches you.

When you are ready, open your eyes and ask the tree which branch you may take. Observe whether it has "suckers": small branches that grow low on the tree or on larger and lower branches, and which sap the strength of the tree. Pruning these helps the tree's health. Cut close to the base of the sucker. Offer a prayer of thanks to the tree, and the Green Man, before cutting. Hold the wand to your heart, and feel your energy, and the tree's energy, flowing through you and the wand. Hold it up to the Sun, down to the Earth, and to each of the four directions. When you're ready, offer one last thanks, leave your offering, and take your wand. Also take a leaf from the tree, and look carefully at the bark so that when you get home, if you need to, you can identify the tree and research its special magical properties. (Druids have extensive wisdom regarding the spiritual and magical gifts of trees.)

Wiccan tools are repositories of profound spiritual power, helping us connect to the divinity of the world, and the deity within ourselves. And as Jefferson's story shows, they can also connect us to the myths and magic of the past. A tool can be very evocative because it comes to you in a magical way, like Jefferson's wand did, or simply because you work with it and come to understand and truly appreciate its symbolism.

Many of these tools reflect the influence of ceremonial magical traditions on contemporary Wicca and the many traditions of Witchcraft. Several made an appearance in the Magician card of the first Tarot deck— the (Cary-Yale) Visconti deck—which appeared in Italy in the 1500s. (By this time, the magic of Europe was transforming itself as it moved from farm to city, men and women to just men, shaman to ceremonial magician.) But were these tools actually used by the practitioners of European shamanism? The sword certainly wasn't common, since they were so costly that only wealthy and powerful warriors or nobility owned them. However, the role of natural elements—air, fire, water, and earth—were

A WITCH'S TOOLS

There are several basic tools that Witches work with:

The athame (a-'tha-mee), or ritual knife, is used to guide and direct energy. In my tradition, it is never used to physically cut anything. Traditionally, the blade should be double-sided, and the length should be the distance from the tip of your third finger to your wrist; the handle should be black and may be inscribed or painted with the Witches' runes and/or your name. The athame corresponds to the direction of east and represents the element of air. Each side represents an aspect of wisdom: intellect and intuition. The double edge is also said to better conduct energy.

The wand is typically made from a magical wood such as willow, oak, or ash. The wand is the symbol for fire, which in the Northern Hemisphere corresponds to the direction of south; in the Southern Hemisphere it corresponds to the direction of north. A candlestick, with a candle, is also placed on the altar, to represent the element of fire.

The bowl or cup, often made of silver, could also be a large shell. It represents the element of water (on your altar, it holds the water you will use in ritual) and corresponds to the direction of west.

The pentacle, usually made of copper, is a round disc in which a five-pointed star has been inscribed. It is the symbol of earth, corresponds to the direction of north in the Northern Hemisphere and south in the Southern Hemisphere, and is also used for charging objects, jewelry, potions, talismans, and all sorts of other magical items. It's also used to invoke the God, by placing it on the forehead, and third eye, of the individual Drawing Up (or Down) as the invocation is made.

The chalice is a bowl or large cup, usually of silver, though sometimes ceramic or even glass is used. It is the symbol of the Goddess and in my tradition is placed in the center of the altar. People also often use a cauldron as a symbol of the Goddess (read the stories about the Celtic Goddess Cerridwen and her magical cauldron, the probable origin of the association of Witches with cauldrons and spellcasting). It is a symbol of the Divine Womb of life, and the Goddess's powers of nourishment (cauldrons are cooking pots) and rebirth.

The sword is also a symbol of air. It is generally used for casting the circle, and like the athame, is never used to cut matter. Unless you're a Priestess or Priest, or love to live large, you won't need a sword—an athame is more than enough.

The boline is a knife with a white hilt and is your working tool. You'll use it to carve candles, clean out candlewax, cut a cord or an apple (after you've cleaned off the wax!), and all the sundry magical crafty things you'll need a knife for.

The brazier, or incense burner, holds a special charcoal used for religious purposes on which you'll burn your incense. You may wish to put some sand in the bottom, and a pot holder or heat-absorbing surface beneath it, as the burning charcoal gets very hot. Obviously, since it's for incense, this tool works with the element of air.

You'll also need a few things to represent the four elements on your altar. Incense, which is burned in the brazier, represents air, and a burning candle represents fire. In addition to the water bowl or shell, you will also want to have a bowl with salt, which represents the Earth (I like to mix grain and seeds into my salt).

an integral part of life and were undoubtedly a part of shamanic practice, just as they are in other indigenous traditions.

And in fact, the four elements as spiritual aspects or qualities date back to Pythagoras and Goddess worship. We also know that the Grail (and its counterpart the cauldron) is a very ancient Celtic symbol of the Goddess, as is the stone (represented by the pentacle). The stone was an ancient British symbol of the Goddess Sovereignty. And along with the sword and spear (or wand), these four tools symbolize profound mysteries of the premedieval, Arthurian, and Grail legends of Britain. The tools we use today are very potent symbols and reminders of the divinity of these natural elements, as well as the Goddess and God, with which we make magic. And when they hold a charge (described in the practice below), tools become an extension of your psyche, and your magical powers.

Choosing Your Own Tools

So, where do you begin acquiring tools that are truly special to you? I was taught that you should never bargain about the price of your magical tools, so shop wisely. Years ago you really had to search for black-handled knives to use as athames; now all you have to do is go online, or find a Wiccan shop, conference, or catalogue! I'm old-fashioned—I think you really should hold and feel your magical tools to determine if they are meant for you.

My first tool, which came to me magically, was a chalice. The three tools I would suggest you acquire first are a chalice and an athame—because together they symbolize the Goddess and God—and a cauldron, since it has so many important uses in making magic. But take your time and don't worry—there are members of my circle who, after four years, are still looking for just the right athame. You can use your hand to point and direct energy, and dedicate a cup or bowl for ritual use.

BASIC PRACTICES
PURIFYING, CONSECRATING, AND CHARGING YOUR TOOLS

Purifying and Consecrating

All of your tools should be cleansed, charged, and consecrated, and any tool previously owned by someone else also requires purification. One method is to bury it while the Moon is waning, and retrieve it when the full Moon appears. Remember to ask the Earth for permission to bury it, and give thanks for its assistance. If you're a city dweller, you can use a pot of earth, or just purify it with the method below.

While the Moon is full you should also purify, consecrate, and charge your tools with each of the elements. Make a purifying incense of sage and sandalwood, or use a sage smudgestick, which is easy to acquire. On your altar you should have a brazier, or something to hold the smudgestick or burning charcoal for your incense, a white candle, a bowl of water, and a bowl of salt. Pass each tool through each element beginning with air (through the incense), then fire (over the flame), water (sprinkle it with water), and finally earth (rub it with salt—don't leave the salt on a silver chalice or blade as it will damage and discolor it). As you work with each tool and element say: *"I purify and consecrate this tool of magical art: My* (athame/chalice/etc.), *my instrument of* (air/water/etc.—state the element that the tool symbolizes) *with the element of (air/water/etc.*—state the element which you are using to cleanse and consecrate the tool). *May it aid me and bless my work in a sacred manner."*

Charging

After consecrating your tool with each element, hold it to your heart. Close your eyes. Ground, center, then draw the energy up through your body and run it through your heart and into your tools. As you feel the energy passing from you into your instruments, say: *"I charge this* (athame/chalice/wand/etc.) *with the divine power that dwells within, with the divine power that surrounds me, with the Goddess within and without, with the God within and without, and with all the love that is in me. I charge this* (athame/chalice/wand/etc.) *to aid me as I practice my sacred art. So mote it be."*

Your tools should be kept on your altar, or carefully stored in a special place, preferably wrapped in soft cloth like silk (never use an inorganic fabric as it blocks the circulation of energy). And a quick note of etiquette—never pick up or handle someone else's tools without their permission. Your tools will accumulate a powerful magical charge from working with you regularly. I'll never forget how I discovered this. One of my best friends in my first circle had the same athame that I did, with a long, black, double-edged blade and wooden handle; we even had the same leather case. We hadn't seen each other for two weeks and my friend arrived very agitated. "I somehow took your athame, along with mine," she said. "It was on my altar, but I didn't work with it."

"I'm sure it's fine," I said, pulling it from its sheath. I looked down at the knife and almost dropped it—the black had disappeared from the first three inches of the blade, and dark gray metal now appeared like a streak of lightning from the tip down the blade. The power of being in another Witch's force field had marked it, but I never minded because of who it had been with, and the lesson it taught me.

YOUR ALTAR

An altar is the focal point for your energies when you are making magic and, as it is something very personal that you will craft, it is also an embodiment of your divinity and an expression of your creativity. In my tradition, the altar is generally placed at the center of the circle, facing east, although I also have a permanent altar set up in my home, which is placed against a wall so it won't be disturbed. A traditional Wiccan altar also usually contains your magical tools and the four elements. The elements are arranged in the order in which we generally use them.

Creating a personal altar is a wonderful, magical experience. You can create one that you erect and take down after the completion of each magical circle you cast. If you are working with a particular element, you may wish to set the altar up in the corresponding direction. You may also wish to devise an altar that remains up as a permanent, sacred focal point for your daily meditations and magical workings. If so, find a spot that's private and won't be disturbed. Cleanse the area with some burning sage and salt water. If you leave your altar up, you must not neglect it—you cannot let it grow dusty, or let the flowers you bought for a ritual wither. A permanent altar demands and deserves daily attention, and unless you

Layout for a Wiccan Altar

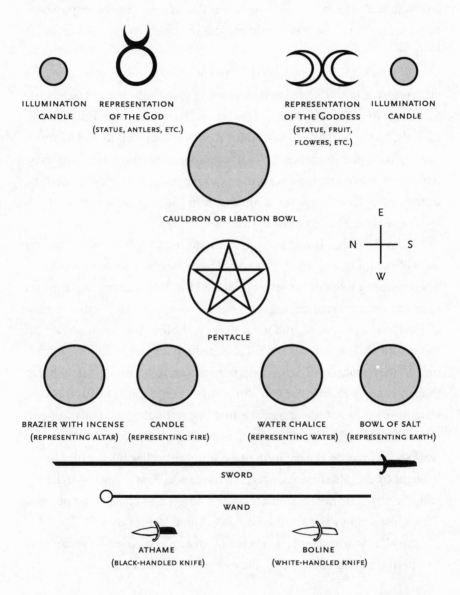

ILLUMINATION CANDLE

REPRESENTATION OF THE GOD
(STATUE, ANTLERS, ETC.)

REPRESENTATION OF THE GODDESS
(STATUE, FRUIT, FLOWERS, ETC.)

ILLUMINATION CANDLE

CAULDRON OR LIBATION BOWL

E

N ─┼─ S

W

PENTACLE

BRAZIER WITH INCENSE
(REPRESENTING ALTAR)

CANDLE
(REPRESENTING FIRE)

WATER CHALICE
(REPRESENTING WATER)

BOWL OF SALT
(REPRESENTING EARTH)

SWORD

WAND

ATHAME
(BLACK-HANDLED KNIFE)

BOLINE
(WHITE-HANDLED KNIFE)

are prepared to make a commitment to daily work (which I highly recommend!), you should set up your altar only when you are going to cast
a circle and take it down when you are finished.

I travel a great deal giving talks and workshops and so I have made a
traveling altar that I take with me. Everything is quite small and light-

weight, including the statues of deities. It gives me a great deal of pleasure and spiritual energy—especially when I'm in some stuffy, impersonal hotel room. Traveling has taught me the spiritual wisdom of keeping it simple!

Above all, an altar must speak from your heart, and to your heart. It is an expression of the Sacred and an offering to divinity. It must be beautiful—with fresh flowers, fruits, objects from Nature such as shells, stones, crystals, and bones. All of these natural objects are symbols and forms of the Divine—for example, a shell can represent the Greek Goddess Aphrodite, while a pair of deer antlers can represent the Celtic God Herne or the British God Cernunnos. You may also wish to have statues and images of Goddesses and Gods on your altar.

A personal altar is also a place for you to contemplate and charge objects of meaning and power for you. These may be a piece of jewelry, a photograph, a work of art, or a childhood toy. When they are placed on your altar, you are recognizing the tremendous spiritual importance these objects have in your life, and what they symbolize. You can meditate on them, and their meaning. Think about the issues, challenges, and triumphs they evoke. And, with time, they will accumulate a greater charge that you can work with for transformative magic. You can also make an altar devoted to a single magical effort or personal transformation you are undertaking, like writing a book or having a baby. One of my favorite workshops involves the creation of a community altar filled with objects brought by the participants, which all have special meaning for each person. We share stories, cast circle, raise energy, and charge our objects. Though seemingly simple, this ritual is always deeply powerful.

An altar is also the place where you dedicate yourself to your spiritual path. You will find a self-dedication ritual in the Epilogue.

YOU ARE THE ALTAR

Magically, when you cast a circle, your altar is not just at the center of the circle, it's at the center of the Universe. It is the point where spirit and matter unite. It was said that long ago the priestess was the altar, and in a very important and real sense, whether you are a woman or a man, you are the altar. *You are spirit and matter conjoined, the miracle of transformation—you are the divine magic of life.*

In my tradition—the Tradition of Ara —you must fully explore and cultivate and work with *yourself* as an altar of the Divine. I think this truth has been with me since the moment of my birth, which occurred as the constellation Ara, the sacred altar, appeared at the horizon. I realized it was to be the name of my coven during my first trip to Italy. I made a pilgrimage to the three magnificent temples in Paestum, built during the Magna Greca, which are remarkably preserved.

I walked through the temples, awed by their beauty, but found myself drawn to a spot in a field behind them, where I decided to journey. The drumming tape on my little tape recorder did its work and I was soon moving between the worlds. In the presence of the ancient Goddess, I asked for direction and was told, "Build My temples." For weeks afterwards I struggled with Her direction. I didn't have the resources to build temples—what was I to do?

The answer came to me during a circle with my first coven as a Priestess. Looking at the beautiful women sitting with me, I realized that the work I was doing with them was building the Goddess's temples. Each of us is a temple of the Goddess, and the God—the Divine dwells within us, and our spirituality is about honoring that innate divinity, in ourselves, as well as in the world. That night I knew the name of my coven, which would finally become my tradition and temple—Ara. Each of us *is an* altar where spirit and matter conjoin in sacred union.

ADVANCED PRACTICE
BE THE ALTAR

During the same lunar cycle that you work without tools or aids (see the Working Propless practice on page 221), work without your usual altar. Take it down. Cleanse, bless, and thank each of your tools, your symbols, your statues, your personal objects. Wrap them carefully and put them away.

Try to work outdoors as much as possible during this cycle.

As often as you can during the month without external forms, cast your circle and stand, sit, or lie at its center. Ground and center yourself. As you do, you will find the practice has more power, and meaning, than you have ever experienced before. Feel all of the elements within you—air in your breath, fire in your heart and belly, water in your veins, earth in your bones and all of your body. Revel in the clarity and perceptiveness of your mind, the passion that fuels your life, the love and all the emotions that flow through you, the strength of your body. Sing, dance, laugh, be silent. Pay attention to your feelings, for it is in your heart that you build a temple to the Divine. *Feel* the Sacred that resides within you, that *is* you, and that surrounds you.

During this cycle, please take time to integrate your physical and spiritual realities—attend to your health, eat properly, exercise, get enough sleep, laugh a lot, go dancing, play and have fun, and reconsecrate your sexuality. Your body is sacred. It is not merely a structure that holds deity, it is the embodiment of deity. Honor yourself fully.

At the close of this cycle, you may wish to devise a ritual to rededicate yourself as an altar of deity. You may also wish to reconstruct and rededicate your old altar, or set up a new one. I hope you will find the process charged with new meaning and power.

Your life is your magic, live it like an artist—create!

You are crafting yourself as a Witch —and to do so you'll need energy. There's an unlimited supply waiting for you, and there are more ways of finding and working with it than you may realize.

Energy

Magic, like everything else in life, can't work without fuel. How many days could you live without eating? And just how far will your car get without gas in the tank? How long would your marriage last if you didn't love each other? Everything requires nourishment, including your spirituality.

Raising energy supplies fuel to your magic, but I'm not going to take the usual "how-to" route to working with magical energy. Instead of the crowded, five-lane superhighway to instant spell success, I'd like you to take the scenic path. If you want to make real magic, you've got to work with real power—the infinite, abundant power that won't run out and leave you stranded on the side of your spiritual road.

WAND MAGIC AND GRAIL MAGIC

Without exception, every book on Witchcraft has a section on raising energy in order to make your magic work. They discuss the most common forms—chanting, dancing, drumming, running, and sometimes they'll even talk about raising energy through sex. These are all useful and powerful techniques and we will be discussing them shortly.

But there are a few problems with this universal approach that actually limit your ability to craft effective spells and powerful rituals. *Witch crafting is about working with the infinite potential of the Universe to manifest your destiny, your desire, and your highest and sacred self.* You need a wider, deeper, richer approach to working with energy, one that will move you beyond limitations to your true spiritual fulfillment.

Raising energy, and sending it off to manifest your goals, is the usual way of working with energy to cast a spell or make magic. I call it "wand magic" because it's a phallic image—energy shooting out into the womb of the Universe to inseminate the realm of infinite potential. So what's wrong with this approach? On its own, it's incomplete. Remember, the Universe is only half "masculine," the other half is "feminine" and they require each other for the generative, fertile process of life to exist. The conjoining of "masculine" and "feminine"—their "courtship"—is the energy that moves, transforms, and creates the Universe. Wand magic works best when you combine it with its feminine counterpart, grail magic: the practice of drawing in or receiving energy.

GRAIL MAGIC

When you practice grail magic, you open up and fill yourself with sacred energy. In my tradition, we energize ourselves and abide in the ecstasy of communion with the Numinous. Sometimes we send this energy outward, but often it remains within us, working its own sacred alchemy in our souls, bodies, emotions, dreams, and lives. *You are the Grail, the cauldron, the cup into which the divine life force is poured.* And as that energy fills you, it nourishes, energizes, heals, and transforms you. It crafts you as a Witch. Filled with the Divine, you realize one of the greatest spiritual truths of Witchcraft: *Your life is your magic!*

Grail magic helps you to discover, feel, and benefit from the magic the Universe is making in and through you. Even the smallest events take on meaning, and struggles become paths to empowerment. You begin to notice synchronicities—patterns of coincidence that you realize are not random or accidental. In these synchronicities, you find profound mythological parallels and deep spiritual meaning, and they direct you to your purpose, your unique gifts, and your destiny. In *Book of Shadows*, I wrote about crafting myself as a Witch, but at the same time I told a larger, archetypal story. I saw that my life was following the pattern of the Persephone myth of journeying to the Underworld and coming back to life. And I realized it was a story lived by most women. There are mythic stories playing out in your life too and with grail magic, you will start to recognize them.

The Energy Source

There's another simple but important problem with just raising and sending energy: If you're not hooked up to the main power line, you're draining your own batteries! Recently at a large Wiccan gathering, a healthy young woman who could dance circles around me, stay up all night, and then look as if she'd just gotten back from a spa, was completely exhausted after participating in a big ritual. Yes, she assured me, she had grounded. She'd raised all the energy she could by dancing and chanting around the bonfire all night, and then she had sent it off to create her dream. And the next day she was completely wasted, feeling as if the life had drained out of her.

It had! Well, of course, you're thinking, "I'd be wasted too if I'd been up all night dancing around a bonfire!" But I had been at the ritual also, and had danced and chanted just as vigorously, and yet I was fine the next day. In fact, I felt even better than I had the day before. Why? Because I had begun the ritual connected to the Divine—in myself, in the Earth, and in the world all around me. I had taken the time to fill myself with that sublime force, I had remained ecstatically connected throughout, and I'd ended the ritual still connected to the sacred source. The energy flowed *through me*, instead of just flowing *from* me.

The secret of success is being a conduit through which sacred energy flows, receiving and filling yourself with it, letting it work its magic on you, and *then* guiding and directing it to your purpose. Hook yourself up to the source, and you'll never run out of energy—you may get tired, but you won't be depleted.

BREATH

With each breath you are doing more than just inhaling oxygen; you are bringing into your body and soul the *élan vital*, the life force, what the Hindus call *prana* and the Chinese call *chi*. Conscious breathing enables you to *feel* the Divine flowing into and through you. You can use it during and after you've cast circle, and at any time during your daily life.

Air is the element of inspiration. The dictionary says that inspiration is "1 a) a divine influence or action on a person believed to qualify him or her to receive and communicate sacred revelation; b) the action or power of moving the intellect or emotions; 2) the act of drawing in—specifically, the drawing of air into the lungs." *Inhale and you are drawing in the Divine. Exhale and you are sending out the Sacred.*

PRACTICE
BREATHING THE SACRED

Basic

Return to Chapter 1 and review the meditation instructions. As you practice this technique again, focus upon the feelings of being filled with divine energy. Pay attention to how the energy flows into and out of you, and how your breathing unites you with the plants in a divine cycle of interdependent life.

Advanced

Begin each day with five, slow, conscious breaths. End each day the same way.

GROUNDING AND CENTERING

This practice is probably one of Witchcraft's most powerful. Most circles begin by grounding and centering, but it's not enough if you're not paying attention to its purpose—once again, understanding *why*. Far more than a rudimentary beginner's exercise, grounding and centering is an essential means of connecting yourself to the sacred power residing in the Earth.

The divine energy of the Earth can remain within you and be directed to parts of your body or emotions that need healing or strength. People often remark that everyone in circle looks radiant when we've finished grounding and centering as part of our grail magic.

Working with this energy source helps you keep your "batteries" charged while making magic. When we ground at the beginning of circle, after running the energy through ourselves, we run it through the circle that joins us together, and we always end the grounding by holding some of the energy in our hearts and our stomachs (the power center). This energy is drawn upon when we cast a spell, or conduct our rituals.

PRACTICE

GROUNDING CONNECTION

Basic

- Review the grounding and centering practice in Chapter 1. Now as you practice this technique, focus upon the feeling of being filled with sacred energy. Hold it in your heart, stomach, muscles, and bones. Feel how revitalized and joyful you are. Pay attention to how the energy flows into and out of you—and how grounding unites you with the Earth in a divine cycle of interdependent life.

Advanced

- Use your grounding technique to establish connections between specific aspects of the Earth and specific parts of your body. Work with a single boulder, a tree, a leaf, or a low-growing plant and run the energy through your hands, your feet, or other parts of your body.
- Try grounding and centering in the hollow created by the roots of an old tree that has blown over in a storm. You must ask the tree's permission—if it agrees, sit in the opening of the Earth and ground your-

self. It will be one of the most powerful experiences you ever had, as the spot is already charged with all the energy exchanged between the tree and the Earth for many years. Be sure to leave an offering. Ask the tree if you may take a branch to work with as a wand.

INVOKING DEITY

Drawing Down the Moon or the Sun and other ways of invoking deity are some of Wicca's most extraordinary practices for filling yourself with the Sacred. Although this form of trance work can leave you feeling somewhat "spaced out" and requiring food, drink, rest, and grounding, it is also one of the most profound sources of empowerment and magic.

Covens frequently raise energy and perform their magic after the Drawing Down. Why? Invoking the Goddess and God opens your circle and yourself to Their presence and Their energy—the energy with which all magic is made. *Real magic is a cocreative process of divine manifestation,* and it just won't work without the cocreator.

It's not necessary to direct this energy anywhere. Just having it within you changes your perceptions about reality, yourself, the world. *You become increasingly aware of your innate divinity.* Divine energy flows into and through you and your authentic self begins to emerge, finding itself in a sacred landscape that is alive with magic. Open yourself to this holy energy and the Universe begins making magic in you, conjuring and crafting your sacred self.

PRACTICE
INVOKING THE GODDESS AND THE GOD

Basic to Advanced

Use meditation and divination to determine what kind of energy you need for greater balance in your life. Do careful research to find a Goddess or God who embodies this energy. Find out all you can about Her/Him and use what you've learned to create a ritual to invoke the Goddess or the God: Write an invocation, prepare your altar, make an appropriate offering, incense, oil, etc.

Cast your circle and invoke the Goddess or God. Take all the time you need to feel Her or His presence in your circle and your self. Welcome the Divine. Open yourself: Reach out your arms, feel your heart opening like a flower or a green plant to receive the Sun and rain. Become the chalice into which deity pours itself. Concentrate on your feelings: intuitive, emotional, physical. Celebrate the deity's presence: Sing, dance, write, do whatever you feel moved to do. Hold the energy in your heart, and your stomach. Ground any excess energy. Give thanks and when you are ready, close your circle.

Advanced

- Following the basic procedure above, invoke a deity of opposite gender from yours into your circle, yourself, your life.

- Following the basic procedure above, invoke deity that is without gender (after all, the grass isn't male or female, and neither is the air, or the rocks—but they are divine). You may work with any of the elements to facilitate this, and working outdoors in Nature will also help you have a powerful experience.

❋   *The Energy of Love*   ❋

There are people who say they are practicing Wicca and who claim that the energy they work with is neutral. They say that it is like electricity: You can use it to play your stereo or to fry someone in an electric chair. The energy itself has no innate quality except power and you can use it as you choose.

Whenever I hear someone describe magical energy in this way, I know the person making these assertions is someone who isn't opening him/herself up to the energy that powers real magic. They're thinking in the old, patriarchal terms of the world lacking innate divinity. Certainly, if people are just projecting their energy out into the Universe in that manipulative, instant gratification, gimme-the-goodies approach to magic, they've probably missed the whole point anyway.

But when you become the Grail, there is only one word that approaches the true nature of the power you experience—love. *The energy that Witches work with, the energy that makes magic, that powers spells, fuels rituals, and crafts a Witch, is the energy of the Divine. And the energy of the Divine is love.*

But what about those destructive Goddesses and Gods? I can hear you wondering. They're certainly not the ones I invoke for a love spell! And what about disappointment, illness, death—the dark aspects of life? No, it's not sugary love, wrapped up in lace like a box of Valentine chocolates. But the energy is still filled with love. It's a lot more like tough love, but it's love nonetheless.

I learned this lesson in one of the hardest, most painful ways that life inevitably presents to us. My mother's mother lived with us from the time I was three until her death. Every year, when the little crab apples from the trees in our back yard had ripened, she would make applesauce, and I would help her. It was painstaking work that took days: She would gather hundreds of little apples, wash them, then sit at the kitchen table for hours, carving out the bad spots, getting rid of worms, cutting the stems and seeds away, and dicing what was left. Impatiently, after an hour I'd run off to play.

After days of preparation, she would cook the apples for hours and hours, adding what seemed like pounds of sugar. When it was finally ready, she would carefully spoon out two cups of the most glorious, delicious, vivid pink applesauce from her pot. I remember how it never filled more than half a jar left over from commercial applesauce. Gratefully savoring our precious portions, we knew that it was worth every bit of time and effort.

My mother, like her own mother, was an extraordinary woman: Mom was smart, elegant, a professional when women weren't welcomed in the workforce, an activist for social justice, and as focused and hardworking as my grandma (the apple not falling far from the tree). The last three years of her life were brutal, because she had Parkinson's and Alzheimer's. She broke both of her hips, and gradually began to slip away into a strange, frightening, and narrow world. It took tremendous effort, time, and patience to get the smallest response or recognition from her. At first I was overwhelmed by the painfulness of it all, and then one day, when I least expected it, she reached out and took my hand and told me how much she loved me.

When my mother was ill and dying I learned the lesson of my grand-

mother's applesauce: The greater the struggle the more cherished its rewards; and the magic of challenge is that it turns us toward the Sacred
(something we often forget when life is good), which always greets us
with love. When you're tested, you remember where your strength comes
from. The presence of divinity, so available to you through practices, provides consolation, wisdom, peace—and always love, and that is one of the
Universe's greatest gifts.

Focus first upon the true source of your empowerment, and you will
practice magic based on divine communion, co-creation, and the power
of love. You will craft a Witch who lives with joy, freedom, and authenticity. You will craft a Witch who knows that real magic is not about the love
of power, but the power of love.

✳   *Raising Energy*   ✳

Begin by filling yourself with the Divine and you'll have no problems raising and directing energy. And you'll be amazed at how much more successful your spells and rituals will be. At the heart of all being, there is
nothing but a dance of ceaselessly moving energy; raising energy is a conscious and deliberate way of participating in this dance. The way that I
work, raising energy is a rapturous, very physical way of directing the
flow, of choreographing the quantum and sacred dance. *Raising energy to
make magic is your creative way of contributing to and shaping the sacred
energy of the Universe.* And you may raise and direct energy toward any
one of your goals or necessities—healing, love, prosperity, clarity, inspiration, growth, security, maturity, strength, and my favorite, the pure experience of divine, joyous ecstasy.

You don't raise energy by imagining it. You have to feel it! And the
stronger your passions and your exertions, the more energy you'll raise.
Shamans, mystics, and Witches use a number of similar practices for raising energy, altering consciousness, and creating a state of ecstatic
communion with the Sacred— techniques known as core shamanic techniques. These practices are found in indigenous cultures and Earth religions all over the world.

SOME OF MY FAVORITE WAYS
TO DO GRAIL MAGIC

There are all sorts of wonderful ways of becoming the Grail and receiving divine energy. Here are a few of my favorites:

- Work with the elements and let them teach and bless you: Breathe fresh air, feel the Sun on your skin, drink water, eat well.

- Get a massage from a good, healing massage therapist. Let her or him send healing energies deep into your muscles, and your spirit.

- Go to a sauna, especially one with eucalyptus vapor.

- Lie in a "Witch's cradle": a simple blanket that everyone in your circle lifts and rocks slowly, while chanting your name and expressions of love, magic, and friendship.

- The next time someone compliments you, really take it in.

- Listen to your favorite music.

PERCUSSION

One of the most powerful ways to alter consciousness and raise energy is with the use of steady percussive rhythm—by drumming, rattling, clicking sticks, or other methods. Drumming has become an increasingly important part of Wiccan ritual, particularly at large Wiccan gatherings.

Drums draw up energy from the Earth, from your body, from the drum itself, and from spirits who are called by the drum (this is particularly true in African traditions and Voudou). Depending on the rhythm and tempo, percussion can stir hundreds of people to a night of rapturous dancing (which raises yet more energy) or one of stillness and deep trance. Many Native Americans refer to the drum as the heartbeat of the

Mother Earth, or the shaman's horse, carrying her/him on a journey into nonordinary reality.

The Priestesses of ancient Egypt are often depicted in sacred ceremonies shaking *sistrums* (a particular kind of rattle) and the use of drums is as ancient as humanity itself. There are many wonderful books, tapes, and classes on drumming, and every Witch should have a drum and a rattle to work with. There is an etiquette of drumming with others which should be observed—drummers work together, they don't try to drown each other out, and drummers who are learning follow the lead of their elders. They also play for dancers, not just themselves, and are nourished by the dancers' energy. (If you're observing, remember to express your thanks by bringing them water.)

DANCING AND THE SPIRAL DANCE

Dancing, one of the most ancient forms of spiritual celebration, is a great way to raise energy! That dancing is one of our central practices speaks volumes about Wicca as a joyous spirituality. Sadly, very few segments of the dominant patriarchal religions of the West, in which most of us were raised, incorporate dancing into their worship. Dancing is joyful and physical, and you don't have to be Fred Astaire or Ginger Rogers to do it effectively; you just need to do it with passion. And whatever purpose you're raising energy for, one of the fringe benefits of dancing is how blissful it makes you feel!

If you are working alone, cast your circle to contain the energy you're going to raise, and go for it! Use music or drumming or your own chanting and you've got energy!

The most ancient of all dancing was most often done in circles, for spiritual celebration and community building, and today all covens use dancing to raise energy. Dances are usually performed while holding hands, in order to keep the energies of the group connected, and the dancers move deosil around the circle. Some dances use particular steps, like the grapevine or the hora, but most tend to be quite free form. When you dance in a group, move faster and faster until you reach a crescendo.

Stop the circle and direct the energy toward your visualized goal, object, potion, or the person you wish to affect. Don't be shy when you dance with others: No one is watching or judging you. Remember, movement and enthusiasm are contagious; start and others will be inspired to dance along. And in fact, not only does dancing raise energy, it blends and unifies it. Dancing together is a jubilantly bonding magic.

One of the most wonderful dances corresponds to the way in which energy actually moves: in a spiral. We represent this movement, and think of it, as waves, but waves are actually two-dimensional representations of a three- (or more) dimensional form. And so the spiral dance is one of our most powerful and magical ways of raising energy.

We begin by dancing in circle, holding hands, and then the Priestess, Priest, or designated leader of the dance lets go of the hand of the person in front of them and begins to lead the dancers into a clockwise spiral. Everyone dances, holding hands, winding inward toward the altar. When the Priest/ess has reached the center of the circle (where the altar is usually set up), s/he turns around and begins leading the dancers counterclockwise back out. Dancers are now passing one another, some still moving inward and clockwise, and others moving outward and counterclockwise. This creates a great deal of energy and exuberance as people laugh, smile, and often kiss one another in passing, while also being careful not to crash into one another! You can really feel the energy building.

When the entire circle of dancers has unwound back out and is moving counterclockwise around the circle, the Priest/ess again turns around and begins moving, and leading the dancers back into a clockwise/deosil dance moving inwards, or at least back into a large deosil circle again. Once everyone is back in circle, the energy, which is quite palpable at this point, is directed toward its goal.

One of the most important aspects of raising energy while dancing is to push through the first wave of exhaustion to find tremendous and euphoric new levels of energy to draw upon. I think you'll find the results are astonishing, both in terms of the magic and the realization that you are capable of far more than you think you are. That discovery will empower your daily life as well as increasing the magic in your circle. Dancing to raise energy also reminds us that magic is joyful and should be celebrated!

RUNNING

Dancing often turns into a simple circular run—you'll be astonished at how much energy this raises! Just be sure that, if you're working with others, everyone in your circle is up for it. If they're not, they can drum, chant, or sit in the center of the circle where they'll catch a buzz that will have them humming for days!

CHANTING

It's impossible to drum and to dance without wanting to sing, and chants and songs are powerful ways to raise energy. Chanting does not require music—you can simply repeat a few lines, such as when you chant a spell. Or you can do a free-form associational chant: It might start as "grow strong" and someone else will chime in with "grow free," then "grow wise," then "wise one" (it's natural for free-form chants to mutate as you do them). You can also hum one tone, or chant a single word such as a Goddess or God name, or "Om." Chanting is a universal spiritual practice, and repetitive chanting is an ancient and effective means of altering consciousness.

When people first start practicing Witchcraft they often don't think of singing as a way of making magic, but it is one of our most exquisite practices (remember the origin of the word "enchantment"). Sacred songs of power, healing, and magic are part of a shaman's tools. In fact, the word Witch has its roots in the Scandinavian word "vitke," a singer of sacred songs. We sing songs and chants that have been part of our spirituality for many years, and it's wonderful to go to a large gathering or conference where Witches from all over the world and from all different traditions,

beginners and advanced practitioners alike, are all singing the same songs.
There are now many chants and songs that Witches sing, and you can learn
them at workshops, conferences, from tapes, and even books.

When you work alone, as with dancing, you're free to sing as loudly as
you like, or as off-key! The important thing is to sing with feeling. When
folks begin working in circles, they are often very self-conscious about
singing. I was certainly like that when I began years ago, and the circle I
am now working with was also surprisingly shy when it came to singing.
The coven's Maiden (the assistant to the Priestess) is a professional singer
who has a beautiful voice, but the rest would barely whisper "Om." Gradually, they began to realize that when a group sings together, everyone
sounds wonderful! And now they sound incredible—we've been able to
fully enjoy the magic of mixing voices: creating harmonies, blending
voices so perfectly that you can't tell your voice from others, one person
leading and the rest following, and then that leadership shifting, or someone setting up a counterpoint. And I love that moment of perfect unity
when a chant suddenly stops. There is always that sense of magical, divine
presence that a coven creates together, where the whole is greater than the
sum of its parts.

Creating chants is a natural part of being a Witch, and we often begin by coming up with a few simple lines that are easy to remember—this
is particularly important because you're going to start shifting into an altered state of consciousness where elaborate lyrics will only distract you
and keep you in a beta state. Remember, when creating a chant, or a
power song, keep it simple! And rhyming also helps you to remember it
and provides a natural rhythm.

Songs and chants can come in dreams, or spontaneously as you are
working in circle, or in other magical ways. They are especially likely to
come when you are doing air magic. One of the purposes of journeying is
to find sacred songs of power. Using drumming, we shift consciousness,
enter nonordinary reality, and ask our power animals and spirit guides to
assist us in finding a chant or song of power and magic. But you don't
have to journey to find such a magical gift. I got one of my favorite songs

while spending hours harvesting a huge crop of chamomile I had planted in my garden. It came from the flowers, and from my heart, and the Sun, and I wish I could sing it for you now, but here are the words: "*Thank you all, thank you all, thank you all/For the feeling and the healing of the Sun.*"

This is a song I use whenever I work in my garden, and often when I'm cooking, especially during the summer, with fruits and vegetables from my garden and local farms.

MUSIC

Music is the culmination of drumming, rattling, chanting, and singing, and it certainly makes dancing more joyful. Like chanting, it's been used in many faith traditions because of its power to evoke feeling, and particularly a feeling of divine presence. It's one of the most effective and powerful means of raising energy, and all by itself, as you have undoubtedly experienced, music *is* magic.

You can use tapes or CDs of all sorts of music to help you to raise energy: New Age, classical, ethnic, Wiccan, rock 'n' roll—whatever stirs your soul. A good friend made me a tape of positive pop songs about Witches and magic to take along on my first book tour, and I can't begin to tell you how much it helped raise my spirits and my energy! And you can learn to play an instrument—making music is as natural as birds singing.

WORKING WITH THE ELEMENTS TO RAISE ENERGY

Every element is a form of energy, and can be worked with in order to raise energy. By working in Nature, and working with various forms of elemental magic, you'll learn to appreciate and work with the different kinds of energies inherent in each of these elements. For air, you might take a bicycle or motorcycle ride (be sure to wear a helmet); for fire, sit inside a circle of candles, or cook; for water, dance in the rain or go white-water rafting; for earth, ride a horse or go camping. See Chapter 3 for more ideas on how to work with these divine energies.

❊   *Directing Energy*   ❊

When you are connected to deity, you remember that you live within an organic reality. By raising and directing energy, you are co-creating reality with the Divine, and just like sex, our procreative process, projecting energy must be based upon mutual consent, respect, and pleasure. Instead of commanding the Universe to do your bidding, open your heart and soul to it and commune with it. The experience will be one of ecstasy, directing energy will be a process of inestimable joy, and the results will be magical!

Once energy has been raised, it can be directed in any one of a number of ways. One of the simplest is when you are directing it into something on the altar (such as jewelry, tools, a potion, or a talisman), or toward a person who is in the center of the circle. You simply stretch out your arms toward the altar, object, or person, and as you feel the energy moving through you, direct it through the palms of your hands. You can plunge your hands right into a bowl of herbs, or place them on the person or object being charged.

The Laying on of Healing Hands

This technique of "laying on hands," described above, is an ancient healing practice used in many faith traditions and even in some modern hospitals. It is one of the most powerful techniques for healing magic. It is important to note that working with sacred energy should not be substituted for medical care—practitioners of indigenous religions have always worked not only with energy, but also with healing, medicinal herbs, providing the foundation for much of what is used in pharmaceuticals today. Modern medicine has come a very long way since our Pagan forebears and should be fully utilized. But adding divine magical energy to a healing process can speed recovery, and help overcome seemingly impossible obstacles.

Healing magic is also facilitated by working with particular herbs that are used to create an incense and potion (please note, you shouldn't ingest anything without first checking with your doctor, as herbs can have a powerful effect, and can interfere with other medications). Cast your circle, invoke Goddesses and Gods of healing (such as Brigid and Asclepius), and be sure to ground and center. Then raise and direct the energy with your hands into the individual who needs healing (s/he should sit or lie in the center of circle, if possible). You can also specifically direct energy into areas of the body that most require healing. After doing healing work, you should always be sure to ground the energy, and recharge yourself by eating.

The person who needs healing does not have to be present to receive the energy you raise for them. Visualize them well and healed, and chant their name. (See the Cone of Power practice on page 257.) I like to add candle magic: I use a yellow or blue candle carved with the person's name and words such as "healthy" and "healed" and burn it for at least seven days. Each day, pray, visualize, or do magic for the person's health. You don't have to cast a circle—just ground, center, and send healing energy.

I am blessed to have several friends who have survived deadly illnesses long beyond their predicted demise. We know that, in addition to getting the best medical attention, magical healing energy has helped them. But remember, you should only do healing magic for someone if you have their consent. (An exception would be if they cannot give their consent due to their condition.)

I worked with this simple but powerful practice just recently at a workshop with a group of fifty women who decided that they wanted to do healing magic. We had spent the morning telling our stories, getting to know one another, and creating bonds of trust, compassion, and appreciation. And in the process, we summoned the Goddess into the world. We also purified with a bowl of salt water, cleansing herbs and oils, and placed objects of personal power on the altar.

In the afternoon, we began by casting circle hand to hand, grounded and centered, ran energy around the circle, and chanted and called to Goddesses of healing. Then the women who wanted to be healed stood in a circle around the altar, facing outwards. The healers stood in a circle facing them, and a third group of women remained in the outer circle, drumming, chanting, and sending energy to the healers. The healers worked with each woman, directing energy to them with their hands and hearts. We ended with a celebratory spiral dance, which delighted many of them who'd never done it before, and also recharged their batteries. All of us stood in a circle once again; we stretched out our hands and sent energy into the articles on the altar. It was a wonderful, healing, and deeply moving ritual.

As you direct energy, you may be able to visualize the light streaming from your hands into your subject. You'll also feel a tingling sensation and warmth in your hands, and possibly your entire body. And if you are directing the energy into a person, they will feel a wonderful surge of power, often accompanied by a release of pain, sadness, and tears, followed by a profound sense of being loved.

BASIC TO ADVANCED PRACTICE
DIRECTING RAISED ENERGY INTO AN INDIVIDUAL

This practice is designed for work with a group or coven. However, you can also adapt it for use on your own to energize yourself.

Cast your circle and invoke the Goddess and God. Ground, center, and raise energy. Then, one at a time, each member of the circle should stand in the center of the circle. As you all dance around her or him, chant her or his name. Let the energy build, and as it peaks, direct it into the person. Have the person rejoin the circle, and as someone else enters, start dancing and chanting the next person's name. Continue until you've charged everyone in circle with the energy you've raised.

You'll be amazed at your ability to push past fatigue. My coven devoted a circle to this one night, and it was quite an undertaking! By the time we had finished raising energy and directing it into everyone we were exhausted. We thought we were all done and were laughing, ready to collapse, when Webster calmly walked into the center of the circle, stared up at us, and made it very clear that he too expected to have energy raised for him! He was absolutely right and we were happy to oblige!

If you do this on your own, direct the energy into yourself by laying your hands on your head, heart, stomach, and groin to charge yourself.

Be sure to ground your energy and recharge yourself before you close your circle. And be sure to eat, and rehydrate (no alcohol).

CONE OF POWER

This is one of the most best methods of directing energy. The energy that is raised is visualized or shaped into a cone, the point of which is high above the center of the circle. The energy is directed to spiral upwards, deosil, into the cone's apex, where it is then directed either downward into a person or object, or up and out into a person, object, or most often, a visualized goal. Generally, when it is directed downward, it "falls," and when directed outward it is sent with a powerful blast of energy, like a cannonball shot from a cannon (there's that phallic image!).

The directing of the energy may be done by everyone working together sending and visualizing, or by one individual working alone, or working with the group's energy. In many groups, the Priestess or Priest is often responsible for directing the energy, but each member of a coven should have an opportunity to practice this technique as part of their training. In my tradition everyone usually directs energy together.

> **BASIC TO ADVANCED PRACTICE**
> ## RAISING A CONE OF POWER

As you are raising energy, feel it and see it rising from you in a deosil spiral that spins upward through and around and above the circle. It may appear, or you can visualize it, as white, gold, blue, or other colored light depending upon the purpose of your magic.

Feel the energy moving through you and from you, see it swirling into a cone above the center of the circle. With practice, you'll be able to feel the energy building to a crescendo, and as it peaks, the person leading may shout, "Now!" or a key word pertaining to your magic, such as "Heal!" or "Prosperity!" If you're dancing or running, the circle stops, hands fly up, and the energy shoots from you into the spiral, which spins off to accomplish your magic. Everyone visualizes the goal being accomplished, feeling and knowing it as certainty.

It's a good idea to then drop to the ground, placing your palms against the ground and letting any excess energy return to the Earth whence it came. Some people may need to recharge by grounding. And again, don't forget to eat and rehydrate.

Several years ago, a mathematician who is one of the world's leading experts on wave theory told me that he and his colleagues had discovered something fascinating. When several waves from different sources are directed toward a common center point, they create a cone of energy that is greater than the sum of its parts—the waves cross over the tip of the cone creating a reverse cone where the energy is greater! I was astonished, for this is what Witches have been doing when they raise energy with a cone of power!

BALANCING ENERGY

As I mentioned above, raising energy can be depleting, but with practice you will become more skilled at letting energy flow through you rather than just raising it from within yourself. It's important to recharge yourself by reconnecting to deity, grounding, breathing, eating, and resting.

It's also important to give back, for Nature teaches us that not only is it the nature of energy to flow, it must do so in balance. Energy cannot always move in one direction—in fact, its movement is cyclical, and in this way it is constantly replenished. This is also why working with energy to make magic should involve both grail and wand approaches. When you work with the energy of divinity—your own, the Earth's, the Universe's, the Goddess's and God's—it is essential to reciprocate in thanks for what you have received.

TIMING, FLOW, AND OTHER PARTICULARS OF
WORKING WITH ENERGY

Much of our magical work is about attuning ourselves to the natural ebb and flow of energy in the world. And so the cycles of Nature are a very important part of how and why we make magic. The natural movement of energy will help determine the timing, approach, and content of your ritual—of how you will work with energy and whether you will raise it and in what manner, or simply internalize it.

For example, the energies of the full Moon differ greatly from those of the dark Moon. I would not undertake a prosperity ritual when the Moon is dark, but I would turn inward, doing divination, trance, and journey work, or do a spell to banish poverty. Similarly, there's little point invoking the Green Man and raising lots of energy for expansion during the dead of winter—the energy of growth is dormant, as it should be during this phase of the cycle. During the winter I can see my neighbor, a fisherman, mending his nets, for this is the seasonal aspect of his work. If you pay attention to and learn from Nature, you will discover how to work with the natural cycles of energy, thereby empowering and transforming yourself and your magic. And this energy is always available to you, whether you work with others, or as a solitary practitioner.

Solitary Practice

The path that each of us takes on our quest for divine magic is unique, and ultimately whether you work alone or in the company of a coven, you and only you will be the judge of whether you have walked it well. One of the central principles of Wicca is that *each of us is capable of, and responsible for, experiencing our own direct encounter with the Sacred. At the moment of revelation and communion, every Witch is a solitary.* Even if you are working in a coven, it's important to set aside time to pursue personal magical practice.

If you have been feeling isolated because you are practicing on your own, remember that working solitary is perfectly in keeping with Wicca as a shamanic spirituality devoted to personal communion with the Divine. It's true that for the first thirty years or so of the modern Wiccan revival, there were very few solitaries. In fact, one of the most heated debates back then was whether someone practicing alone could even *be* a Witch, since at the time, the dominant traditions of Gardnerian or Alexandrian Witchcraft required a practitioner to undergo training and initiation by another trained and initiated Witch. Many considered these two processes necessary to distinguish a Witch from a Pagan, and some still do.

But the debate over whether someone can be a Witch by practicing alone is mostly long over. Some estimate that the majority of Witches are now solitary individuals practicing in the privacy of their homes, their gardens, or their retreats into field and forest.

So how can a solitary practitioner, who by choice or circumstance works alone, learn the Craft? Where can you find guidance into the deeper mysteries and meaning of this richly rewarding spirituality? How can you develop the confidence, skill, and wisdom to craft yourself as a Witch, and to make real magic?

You are going to have to become your own guide.

It will probably be the most exciting adventure of your life. Taking responsibility for your own spiritual journey is the first and most important step in freeing yourself from the bondage of history. It also helps you to reject two disempowering fallacies: that someone else knows your connection to the Divine better than you do, and that you are not worthy of discovering your own innate divinity or encountering it naturally.

There are many who approach Witchcraft thinking that the power that makes magic work is to be found in a spell, the correct invocation, the secret potion, the God or Goddess—in something outside themselves. But the Charge of the Goddess reminds us: "*If that which you seek you find not within yourself, you will never find it without, for behold, I have been with you since the beginning, and I am that which is attained at the end of desire.*" You are never alone. *The Divine is always with you.* All of your ability to make magic flows from your connection to the Sacred, and that presence is going to help you be your own guide.

Establishing Your
✳ Spiritual Practice ✳

One of the first things you will need to do as a solitary is to set aside time for your spiritual practice on a regular basis. You will have to create your own structure; you can't simply wait for the "spirit" to move you. Good magical practice requires self-discipline, regularity, and consistency. It also requires common sense—a prominent Wiccan teacher tells a very funny story about how she was so determined to become a skilled practitioner that she spent every day meditating, practicing her skills, studying, writing, preparing for and casting spells and doing rituals, which left her completely exhausted and without a minute left over for a "normal" life! Her magic quickly evaporated as her life lost its balance.

While you may have to accommodate your work schedule, or the needs of roommates or family members, the ideal time to do your magical work is in correspondence to the phases of the Moon—new, waxing, full, waning, and dark—and the Sabbats, which correspond to the seasonal cycles of Earth and Sun. This will greatly enhance your magic because you will be working in harmony with Nature's cycles and rhythms. In fact, this is one of the keys to the success of Wiccan magic.

Wicca is a spirituality that rejoices in the divinity of everyday life, so it's good to have at least one daily practice. This can be something as simple as greeting the Sun and the Moon as they rise every day and night, spending time meditating in front of your personal altar, acting in accord to make your magic manifest, a daily divination, or one of my favorites, spending time in Nature.

Using simple techniques like grounding and centering, deep breathing, divination, and meditations in the presence of Nature will all enhance your ability to tune in to and be guided by the Divine. *The ultimate teacher is the God/dess inside you and in the world around you.*

Because of this great truth, there's a key to confidence and success on your solitary path. The way to evaluate all of the material you will read, the practices you will learn, and the teachings you will hear, is to ask yourself: Are they helping me to experience my connection to the Divine? Is the Sacred present in my life, and can I feel and see and understand how it is guiding and empowering me?

When you are just starting out, it's natural to feel overwhelmed by everything there is to learn and master. In a group you have the advantage of learning by repetition and osmosis, but on your own you will need to memorize a lot, so it's important to start simple and keep it simple. Begin by fully feeling and appreciating one aspect of casting circle rather than trying to perform the entire ritual complete with lengthy invocations, archaic language, and lots of movement and props that can force you into your head. Focus on mastering one practice at a time and you'll find yourself learning easily, with a lot less stress and a lot more fun. Keep your eye on *why* you're doing this. And pay attention to what you're feeling and experiencing rather than worrying about doing everything according to script. Be patient; it takes time to become comfortable with all the aspects of ritual, but it's worth it.

❋ Crafting Yourself ❋

The way that you will craft yourself as a Witch is by mastering the practices of Wicca. But how does a Witch alone learn them without the support and guidance of skilled Priestesses or Priests and colleagues in a circle or community?

First, you should realize that a great deal of wisdom will come to you intuitively, because it already exists within you! All Witches must learn to respect and cultivate these intuitive faculties.

EXERCISE:
CULTIVATING YOUR INTUITION

We all have powerful intuition, but just as if it were a muscle, if you don't use it, you will lose it. It's time to start exercising your intuitive muscles: You're going to begin by paying attention! For the next few weeks, keep a special notebook for this exercise, and try to carry it with you at all times as you begin to cultivate your intuitive talents. As soon after it occurs as possible, write down each incident where you sensed something was about to happen. Do you have a feeling that somebody is going to say a particular thing? Do you sense that the bus is going to round the corner, or that the phone is going to ring and it will be a friend you haven't heard from in months? Not everything you sense is going to manifest, but it's important to write down each premonition as a way of learning to pay attention.

Notice too whether you experience physical feelings such as tingling sensations, an internal jolt, or a feeling as if a door within you were being opened. Do you feel yourself growing hot, or your heart beating faster? (When I know what someone is about to say, my mind gets very quiet and clear and then I feel as if a curtain is parting in the front of my forehead.) Note too if you experience sudden mood shifts from "out of nowhere" (I often sense the strong emotions of others—feeling their sadness, joy, or love). These sensations can become your cue to the arrival of an accurate intuition.

Write down what you sense. Were they bad things, or good things? Unusual things? A synchronicity? Timing (the bus will come right now, even though it's scheduled to come five minutes from now)? Someone else's thoughts, feelings, or mood? Things that relate to a close relationship (for example, your normally cheery friend is calling because something is upsetting her, or your mother is hiding the fact that she is in physical pain, etc.)?

How did you feel when your intuition was borne out? Were you scared? Proud of yourself? Surprised? When your instincts have proven correct, take a look back at what you wrote. As you become more familiar with the sensation of intuition, you will know when it is happening, pay closer attention to what you are learning, and trust your instincts.

EXERCISE:
INTUITION GAMES

I think you'll find these little intuition games fun, which is very important because, as the Duke University PSI (psychic phenomena) experiments prove, boredom leads to a shutting down of psychic sensitivity. But repetition is important in developing your talents, so keep playing these little "games." You might want to record your results in a journal to see if you are becoming more intuitive.

- If a song or title of a song comes into your head, turn on the radio—odds are excellent that somewhere on the dial that song is playing, or is about to be played.

- Get a digital clock and start thinking about time in numerical patterns, such as 11:11, or 12:34, or 6:54. Be still for a moment, and think about what time it is. Check the clock. You're going to find that you're increasingly precise in looking at the clock at the exact moment of your time pattern.

- When the phone rings, before you answer it, take a moment to think about who it is that's calling. (No cheating—it doesn't count if it's your boyfriend or girlfriend calling you for your regular before-bed love chat!) You're going to find that you're increasingly aware of who's calling.

- Working with a partner you love increases your psychic/intuitive skills. Notice when you finish each other's sentences, sing a song that was in his/her head, start a sentence out of nowhere and discover s/he was thinking about exactly that subject.

- Keep a dream journal. Be sure to go back and note all dreams or parts of dreams that turned out to be prophetic.

Learning to be guided by your instincts will not only enrich your psychic skills, it will enable you to be guided by the Divine that lives within you and that is expressing itself all around you. If you keep in mind that your greatest teacher is this divinity, you can let go of any fear that you will be misguided or taken down a path that makes you feel uncomfortable. You can feel confident that you won't make irreparable mistakes casting spells, or get into a practice that feels inauthentic or violating, or be misguided by erroneous books or the wrong "experts." This perspec-

tive will help you to evaluate the information and sources that you are going to seek out.

✳   *Finding Your Way*   ✳

Unlike in the past when Wicca was hidden in the back of the broom
closet, today it's possible to find a wealth of information in a wide variety of public and increasingly mainstream places: on the Internet (you
can even be a part of performing rituals online!); at workshops and lectures presented in Wiccan, metaphysical, or feminist bookstores or centers; at Wiccan/Pagan and women's festivals and conferences that occur
all year long all over the country; at New Age conferences and local universities; and even at mainstream bookstores and adult learning centers.
Information previously available only through the oral teachings and
Books of Shadows of the rare, established covens has now been published.
Hundreds of books reveal or reinvent practices, and these titles can be
found at bookstores and libraries everywhere. And the Resource section
of this book will guide you toward these many avenues for expanding
your knowledge and skills.

With all the information that's out there, how do you choose what
will be most useful for you? Begin by using your intuition and be sure that
wherever your journey starts, you feel enthusiastic (a word that comes
from the Greek *en theos*, and appropriately means "to be filled with the
Divine").

One of the problems, however, is that many books and teachers often conflict with one another. At a recent lecture I was approached by a
young man who had been working on his own for about a year. He knew
Wicca was the path for him, and he wanted to practice, not just read
about it.

"But I'm confused," he said, obviously frustrated. "One book says
place my altar in the north, another says the east. There's another one that
has these really cool invocations of the four directions, but it says I should
bow when I'm finished. I don't know, I tried bowing, but it doesn't feel
right. Some of these books say you have to follow word for word, and oth-

ers say it's okay to make it all up yourself as you go along. Which one's right?" He shook his head.

What's a solitary to do? When you read about or use the practices set forth in a book, ask yourself: Where is the Divine, the Goddess, and God in all of this? What's the author's point of view? Are they providing a list of formulas to make more money, or are they grounding me in the experience of the Sacred, from which all magic flows? And trust your feelings, your judgment, and yourself. Notice and read the books the Universe leads you to, ask other Wiccans what they think, and check the background, expertise, and reputation of the author, lecturer, or website. Don't rely on just one source, and whenever you can, go to the original source. In short, do your research.

PRACTICE, PRACTICE, PRACTICE

All the Wiccan guidebooks in the world, including this one, are useless if you don't use them. You *must* move from information to experience, because it is only through practicing that you can begin to determine if the information, perspective, guidance, and tools work for you. If they don't, try a different approach. If a book tells you to bow after calling a quarter, and you feel awkward and uncomfortable—don't bow. If you're missing an ingredient for doing a spell, find a substitute, a different recipe, or another way of making your magic.

Also, remember that what works for someone else may not work for you. One of my dearest and oldest friends has a very difficult time journeying, but she loves to drum and so she became our group's drummer. I love to create spontaneous ritual, but I have students who need detailed scripts to guide their rituals. Just because a particular approach doesn't work for you doesn't means it's invalid or that there's something wrong with your response to it. It's just that each of us has singular interests, capacities, and inclinations. The goal is to find what works for you.

Wicca is not about information—it's about transformation. You should experience feelings of awe, reverence, and revelation; you should *feel* your heart and determination swell when you call to the spirits of the south.

You should *feel* the electrical surge of energy when you ground and center. You should begin to dream more vividly and psychically. You should become more intuitive, more compassionate, more sensitive to the Earth that gives you life. You should begin to recognize divine magic in the events of your life, long to be in Nature, and be able to sense the Sacred all around you. If you're in your head and not your heart, it's time to move on to another book, workshop, or website.

As you evaluate the effectiveness of the techniques you are practicing, especially if you are working solo and relying on books, keep in mind that crafting a Witch can be a slow, elegant, unfurling process of personal and spiritual growth that takes time and patience. Understand and accept the organic nature of change; you can't make the plants grow faster by tugging on them. Magic isn't necessarily instantaneous, and it does not always take the form that you intended, wanted, or expected, but it always provides what you most needed. Understanding this, and the spiritual meaning of events in your life, is what it means to truly become a Wise One.

BE HONEST AND PRESENT

When performing a ritual, try to escape the artificiality and constraints of the theatrical as soon as possible. A ritual is not about acting *as if* the Sacred were present, it is about actually *experiencing* the presence of the Sacred. In your heart, you will know the difference because one is pretend and the other is the most profound reality you will ever experience. And pretense is an impenetrable barrier to the manifestation of divinity. Magic is real, not make-believe.

BASIC JOURNAL EXERCISE: PATIENCE AND HONESTY

This is an exercise that you should record in your magical journal.

Think back on some of the magic you may have done already. How did it work out? Did you expect immediate results à la "abracadabra"? Did you get what you anticipated? Did something else occur? What did you learn from your experiences? Be sure to write it down! In the future, pay attention to these questions and most importantly, pay attention to experiences in which you felt the presence of the Divine, whether it comes to you in the middle of a magical circle or the middle of the street. Be honest with yourself, for without that there can be no magic.

THERE ARE NO MISTAKES

Frankly, it doesn't matter if you memorized every pantheon of every tradition, hundreds of spells, and countless rituals if you've never experienced the presence of the Divine. Wicca is not about the head, but the heart. Yes, there are ways of doing things correctly, but in a very real sense, *there are no mistakes!*

One of the things I've learned over many years is that when I or someone else does something "wrong," for example, calls the name of the wrong Goddess or forgets part of the ritual, two wonderful things usually occur: There's a sudden release of energy with an eruption of laughter, the person's nervousness about making a mistake evaporates and they start having fun! "Mistakes" give us a very important opportunity to laugh at ourselves, and to learn.

Mistakes can also be very magical! My dear friend, Fiona Horne, who's been practicing for fourteen years, cast a circle here in New York City recently for a large crowd, and something utterly magical happened because she "made a mistake." She faced the south (the direction a Southern Hemisphere Witch begins casting circle with, and which, Down Under, is associated with fire) and said, "I call upon the ancient and mighty powers of . . ." and out of her mouth popped "air"! Her eyes flew open in complete shock. "Where did *that* come from?" she exclaimed. I smiled and replied, "*We* were all thinking the element we begin with—'air.'" We got a good laugh at how she picked up on our collective thought; we had all just made real magic!

Approaching this work with reverence but also with light-heartedness and a sense of humor is one of the finest postures of a good student.

I can always tell a skilled practitioner by her or his sense of humor and joyfulness.

So, don't worry about mistakes. The way out of the mechanical, patriarchal trap of mindless devotion to the rules of ritual is to understand *why* you are doing what you are doing, to trust your instincts, and to open your heart. This will change the inner dynamics of the energy work you are actually doing, and that is what makes all the difference in the quality of how you make magic.

THE LANGUAGE OF RITUAL

Working from the heart and not the head will greatly enhance your magical endeavors. But there are several very important reasons for mastering specific language, at least in the beginning. Memorization sharpens your mind and focuses your concentration. Vibration of sound is also a form of magical energy and there is a resonance that accumulates in the repetition of certain sacred names, prayers, and tones that increases their power and effectiveness and therefore your own. These are certainly the ideas behind the use of ritualistic language in many magical systems, including the Cabala and ceremonial magic (which have had a strong influence on the development of contemporary Wicca). The Navajo are famous for the exact precision with which extremely long and complex prayers, some of which go on for days, must be delivered. Any mistake, even a single word, can negate the entire effort.

Memorizing language has other magical purposes that I think are even more important than mental focus and accumulated resonance. In my tradition, *the most important reason for memorizing and repeating specific language is to help you overcome self-consciousness.* We are constantly standing outside of ourselves—watching, judging, criticizing, wondering if we are good enough. When we focus on our self-doubt, we separate ourselves from the experience of the moment and inhibit our innate divinity from expressing itself. In order to practice magic effectively, we must be aware of and remove self-doubt, anxiety, and fear from our work.

When you memorize specific words and use them repeatedly, you are able to forget yourself, to stop judging and doubting. When the criticizing voice recedes, when the egotist gets bored, the Divine part of yourself emerges and is able to *feel*, to recognize, commune, rejoice, play, and to be creative and spontaneous. You are liberated from the trap of self-judgment, and your magical dance with the Sacred can truly begin.

RITUAL LANGUAGE: EXERCISE #1

As soon as possible, you should begin to memorize the invocations and ritual language used to create sacred space. Concentrate on working with one aspect of casting at a time, while you are also memorizing the language that accompanies it. Repetition and practice will also help you remember.

- Purification and consecration of the elements and the circle within the elements

- Casting of the circle

- Invocations of the four directions

- A simple invocation of the Goddess and the God

- Banishing or thanking of the four directions

WRITING FROM THE HEART

The moment I step into a room in which an altar has been beautifully prepared and decorated, with the fragrance of incense perfuming the air and candles casting their golden glow, my consciousness begins to shift toward the Divine. And when the first familiar words are spoken—"I purify and consecrate this element of air, so that all good may enter herein in the name of the Lady of the Moon and the Lord of the Dance"—a thrill of anticipation shoots through me, my mind opens, the magic begins, and the God/dess manifests. I have entered sacred space, the space where two worlds meet, where spirit and matter are one, and I have shifted into sacred consciousness and I know that all is holy and full of enchantment.

One of the reasons that this technique works is that because the language has meaning to me—it helps shift my consciousness. If I didn't understand the words, if they didn't speak to my heart, they would not have power. Remember, your goal, in reciting from books, is to begin focusing on your feelings rather than your insecurities or ego. There's a reason we call memorization "by heart"—because that's where and how we unlock the power of our true feelings. And without your feelings, you can't make real magic.

The next step in crafting yourself as a Witch is perhaps one of the most important: It's time to start trusting yourself! You are going to create your own language for consecrations, invocations, blessings, and banishings. You can draw upon the inspiration of others, integrating phrases or ideas that speak to you emotionally into your own ritual language. As you write, you will begin to discover that it is the intent—the meaning and feeling behind the words—rather than the words themselves, that matter.

A Buddhist monk and I were discussing this very idea just a few weeks ago. "If I were to say the Lord's Prayer it would probably have little effect on me," the monk explained to me, "as it is not part of my spiritual frame of reference. But when I chant—well, I am reminded that all is One, including the Lord's Prayer."

A fascinating example of the opposite relationship to the power of words is the reaction many of my Catholic friends had when the mass was translated into English from Latin. They complained that the ritual had lost its beauty, its mystery, and power. But what both of these examples of sacred language have in common is that the real power of words is their ability to stir our emotions. For the Buddhist monk, familiar words and chants evoked powerful feelings for him, while it was the mysteriousness of Latin that provoked religious awe in many Catholics. If language does not arouse our emotions and our spirits, if it does not inspire us, it has failed.

Many solitaries have questions about the style of language that is used in many Wiccan rites. One reason some Witches use language that is archaic, or poetic, is that for them these styles feel magical. My own preference, developed over many years of working in the realm of core shamanism, is to use simple modern language that comes from my heart. It may be poetic, but it doesn't have to rhyme. *Writing your own words will help you uncover the wisdom in your heart—what you truly feel.*

RITUAL LANGUAGE: EXERCISE #2

Write down your own invocations of the four directions. Read them aloud when working in circle, and when you are ready, memorize them. (You can use the Table of Correspondences, page 78, to help you craft your words.)

Next, write down your own words for casting circle. Again, read them aloud as you cast, and when you are ready, memorize them.

Do the same with the invocations of the Goddess and the God.

Once you have written and memorized these words, return to your magical journal. How do you feel about this new language? What did you experience using these words instead of traditional ritual language? Remember, there is no "right" answer to these questions. You may now want to add your words to your Book of Shadows.

By doing this exercise, you may have discovered new language that engages you more fully in your ritual. Maybe it feels a little better to use your own words, but you still have to search for just the right ones that really speak to, and from, your heart. Then again, maybe you will discover that traditional or archaic language works best for you after all.

As you discover and create invocations, prayers, spells, and rituals that resonate for you emotionally and spiritually, add them to your personal Book of Shadows. When you write, you are making magic and creating an offering to the Sacred—and you are expressing your own innate divinity. Cultivating this aspect of your creativity is, perhaps, one of the single most important reasons for writing your own Book of Shadows.

SPEAKING FROM THE HEART

Finally, it is time to be completely present in the moment and open yourself up to the Divine as it fills you, and speaks through you. This is what Priestesses do when they Draw Down the Moon, and the Goddess speaks through them; it is also what priests do when they Draw in the God. This sacred communion—learning how to open yourself up so that the Divine can speak to you and through you—is one of the greatest goals of all Wiccan spiritual practices. My favorite moment in all circles is the offering of the libation. I am always awed by the wisdom, honesty, beauty, and power when my circlemates speak spontaneously from their hearts.

As you learn to pay attention, to see the Sacred, you will become a Wise One, because that capacity exists within you. Honor it, cultivate it, treasure it. It is the best part of our humanity, and it is the proof of our divinity.

Groups and Covens

A quest for divine magic can be lonely—the path to the Sacred often leads through a dark wood, and there are dragons of self-doubt and uncertainty. The divinity that supposedly dwells all around you is nowhere to be seen. But no matter where your odyssey began, or how long you've been on the road, as you journey toward self-awareness and empowerment, real magic and revelation, you'll discover that you're traveling with kindred spirits. Seek to craft yourself as a Witch and you'll find companions who provide support, counsel, humor, perspective, and one of the most wondrous gifts of all—an expression of divinity.

Starting Your Own
※ Study Group or Coven ※

An increasingly common way for people to begin practicing Wicca together is to start a study group that may evolve into a coven (traditionally, a coven isn't formed until a group has been together for a year and a day, through every season). This more casual format will allow all of you the opportunity to get to know one another, to see who is serious about pursuing the more committed relationships required by a coven, discover your group's dynamics, and experience the natural attrition that occurs with any group, but which will be much easier to deal with in a study group. It will also provide an opportunity for you to explore a variety of approaches to Wicca to determine which tradition, or traditions, you would like to pursue more seriously.

One of the best ways to find people for your study group is to post a flyer with a brief description of what you'd like to set up. You may want to interview people before the group first gets together, or simply arrange for everyone to meet simultaneously to discuss your interests and goals as individuals and as a group. By interviewing people, you are acting as the group's organizer or leader, and you may or may not choose to take on this role permanently. And the group may decide to share leadership responsibilities.

Because some people are more comfortable speaking than others are, I suggest you create a structure in which everyone gets an equal opportunity to speak without interruption for a specific and limited time period. Start by sitting in a circle so that everyone can see each other and begin working within this spiritual structure. Someone should act as timekeeper to assure everyone gets to speak. Introduce yourselves, share your stories, and talk about your interests, expectations, and goals. Early on, it's important for any group—a new study group, coven, or workshop that will be meeting regularly, and especially any group working with *Witch Crafting*—to discuss the most important spiritual principles of Wicca. How will these principles guide your spiritual work as a group? And as individuals?

You will also have to decide how often to meet and whether to meet on a specific night or in harmony with the phases of the moon. While the latter is very desirable, you may find that it is easier, and therefore more productive, for everyone to meet on a given night. People often begin with great enthusiasm, but find that it's difficult to attend as often as they had hoped. As a group, you should agree upon a realistic schedule for all.

How will you divvy up responsibilities for calling each other, hosting the group, bringing refreshments, etc.? It's important to have agendas for your meetings and to agree on how you will all share the responsibilities of facilitating discussions and working together magically. And make sure that there's always time for socializing—my circle usually spends an hour catching up before we begin, and an hour or more afterward, during our feasting, to socialize and conduct business. During the fourth year of elder projects, many of our meetings are devoted entirely to business, but even so we begin and end with a simple joining of our energies, usually by casting and closing hand to hand.

The lessons you learn in the study group will serve you in forming a coven.

✳ *Covens* ✳

Once covens were as rare as a butterfly in winter, and finding one to work with was nothing less than a miracle of destiny. Certainly that was how it seemed to me over twenty years ago when I discovered my first circle. Today, they're almost as easy to find as the Sun in the summertime—you can even find covens meeting at mainstream chain bookstores in the "Bible Belt"!

Many people find the word "coven" as disturbing as the word "Witch" because they know nothing about Witchcraft, but *Webster's Dictionary* explains that it simply means: "1) a collection of individuals with similar interests and activities; and 2) an assembly or a band of usually thirteen witches." (sic) It comes from the Latin word *convenire*, which means "to come together" and the Middle English *covin*, which means a "band" or "group." I use the word interchangeably with "circle."

The decision to join a coven will be one of the most important of your life. There are now plenty of books and Internet sources that explain traditions of Witchcraft, and that can help you find (or start) and run a coven. It's impossible for me to provide all of the advice that would be helpful in one short chapter, but I would like to begin by providing a perspective that is critical in your quest to find, or create, and work with the right group for you:

Beneath all the questions you must ask and research you must do, beyond reading and meeting, networking and interviewing, the most important way to begin your search for a coven—whether it is an existing group, or one you start yourself—is to know what a coven really is and understand how it relates to the underlying spiritual principles of Wicca.

WHAT A COVEN REALLY IS, AND SHOULD BE

What is a coven? It is a group of people drawn together by effort and by fate. Starhawk describes it as "a support group, a consciousness-raising group, a psychic study center, clergy-training program, College of Mysteries, surrogate clan, and religious congregation all rolled into one." Others describe a coven as "a mutually committed, closely bonded, small group of Wiccan initiates, good friends and family by choice, who gather to worship the Old Gods and follow the Old Ways." I believe a coven is all of these things and much, much more.

Just as you are a vessel or embodiment of divine energy, so too a coven is a cauldron or chalice into which the energy of divinity flows. A coven is a group of people who, whether they have realized it or not, are the hope for our future. They are summoners of the Sacred into a world whose divinity has been forgotten.

A coven is a holy gathering where humanity discovers its own divinity. It is a human crystal—each facet unique, yet reflecting the beauty of those that surround it. A coven is a place of safety where the impossible becomes possible, where the invisible is visible, and the Divine is embodied. *A coven is a group of people within whom the Sacred dwells.*

WHAT TO LOOK FOR IN A COVEN

Just as you evaluate a book by asking, "Is this material helping me to experience the presence of the Sacred in myself, in others, and the world?" as you look for covens, you should begin with the same question: "Does this group enable each individual member to experience the Divine within themselves and in the world?"

Do you perceive that the group demonstrates that very special energy that comes from experiencing immanent divinity? You will discover this by asking the right questions (see below) but also because, having experienced that communion yourself, you'll be able to recognize it in others.

People who use Wiccan practices effectively to discover immanent divinity can come from all sorts of backgrounds and experiences, but they have in common enthusiasm, integrity, curiosity, intelligence, openness, warmth, generosity—and a sense of humor. Encountering divinity doesn't inflate one's ego. In fact, just the opposite is true—it creates a permanent state of awe, respect, responsibility, and humility.

Folks drawn to the Wiccan path tend to be quite independent, adventurous, self-contained, and interested in this spirituality because it enables them to grow and lead richer lives. They are usually not the type to be dictated to, to sit back passively, or to allow themselves to be mistreated.

Similarly, because Wicca is a celebratory path, coven members should have a sense of joyfulness. You will also find that honesty, commitment, continuity, strength under pressure, compassion, and a desire to share the wisdom that has been learned and earned are all qualities of a coven, or an individual who is doing good spiritual work. And at the risk of sounding corny, you will also recognize a light that shines in the eyes of people who have kindled the flame of inner divinity and who have learned to see it in the world. And they'll be looking for it in you.

A shared interest in healing, a particular cultural or ethnic tradition, a preference for a single gender group, or an introduction by a friend may draw you to a particular group. Or you may find yourself with people with whom you seem to have little or nothing in common except the fact that it's the only group within driving distance of where you live. They may all be half your age, or they're all straight and you're gay, or you wanted to study Celtic traditions and they're into Egyptian magic. Common interests, backgrounds, and goals are wonderful bonds for any group. But personally, having learned from Nature that healthy ecosystems are based on diversity, I try to create covens that are diverse. This always precipitates challenges as the many dissimilar personalities learn to work together, but in the long run, it makes for a circle of tremendous dynamism, strength, and integrity. So don't judge based on surfaces.

What is most important to any coven is the group's *sensitivity to the Sacred*. Find that capacity, along with all of the characteristics listed above, and you have found a group that knows what it's doing.

The quest for your coven is like being the mythical hero/ine about to enter the dark woods; this perspective on what makes a coven work is rather like the magical cloak, stone, or word that can transform risk into reward. You've got to make the journey, but now you have what you need to emerge with the treasure.

EXERCISE:
BEGIN WITHIN

All spiritual journeys begin by looking within. You can't really choose the right traveling companions until you know where you're going.

1. **Meditation** Begin by meditating on what your path is. Write down any images that come to you—these may be signs that will help you recognize those with whom you are meant to work.

Now do an active meditation, preferably outdoors in your place of power. After becoming silent and still, ask yourself: "Where did my quest begin? How far have I come? Where am I headed?" Pay attention to your surroundings. Again, write down the answers that come to you, and carefully note any images or signs Nature sends you.

You may also wish to use a technique of divination to help guide you (see Chapter 2, Divination).

2. **Focusing on Your Interests** Ask yourself whether you are interested in working with a mixed gender or single-gender group. Do you want to work with a coven that focuses on women's mysteries and the Goddess, or one that works with the God as well as

the Goddess? Are you fascinated by herbs, gardening, and environmental issues? Do you want to explore ceremonial magic, or would you prefer a shamanic approach? Are you drawn to Celtic or to *Stregeria* traditions?

Read, take classes, and explore the various traditions and approaches, then make a list of your interests and the things that are most important to you in a coven.

COVEN LEADERS AND STRUCTURES

As I've explained, Witchcraft does not have a single leader or mystical prophet, nor does it have a hierarchy, dogma, sacred text, or an elite cadre of religious professionals required to interpret that text for the untrained masses. Rather, it is a participatory, individualistic spiritual practice, well suited to the modern temperament that has influenced much of its present form. Wicca is not a religion for passive congregations or audiences—in fact, we commonly describe ourselves as "practitioners."

Every member of a Wiccan coven is expected to master the techniques that will enable them to commune with the Divine, practice their spirituality, and make magic themselves. And the intimate structure of the modern coven—generally no more than thirteen—fosters this model of personal involvement, responsibility, and spiritual activism. (I was told when I was initiated that there are thirteen because of the thirteen full Moons in a year.)

For the last fifty years, Witchcraft has had two fairly distinct coven structures. The traditional coven is a small group of not more than thirteen initiates led by a Priestess and Priest (often referred to as a High Priestess and High Priest). The coven works together for approximately three years, and then the "elevated" initiates, as High Priestess and Priests (or elders) provides the leadership for additional, or "hived" covens. And some "hived" covens begin traditions of their own. I waited until close to twenty years from my ordination as a High Priestess to formalize my practice as the Tradition, and Temple, of Ara.

The other popular coven structure is the "self-started" group, also generally comprised of no more than thirteen practitioners, which may or may not have a leader. These covens often follow the model of shared leadership, initiate themselves and one another, and over the years, many self-started groups have become traditions themselves, many of which are often referred to as "eclectic."

Because there are more people interested in practicing Wicca than the thirteen-person coven structure can accommodate, many covens also sponsor study groups, workshops, "outer courts," "groves," conferences, lectures, and even seminaries (or, in my parlance, ovularies), and these are often points of entry into a coven itself.

PRIESTESSES AND PRIESTS

The coven tradition in this country began primarily with groups led by a High Priestess and/or Priest, who initiated and trained coven members, having themselves been initiated and trained by an initiated High Priestess and Priest. Historical research seems to have largely disproven the myth of the organized, unbroken, and hereditary initiatory tradition of Witchcraft stretching back hundreds if not thousands of years (see the excellent book *Triumph of the Moon* by Ronald Hutton, which should be read by anyone interested in Wicca). There are always individuals who claim otherwise, and the possibility remains appealing and mysteriously veiled, perhaps waiting for a safer future before emerging. But what is undeniable is that the traditions that have developed over the last fifty years have created the structure they believed once existed, and in the process have created a great deal of value, including initiations and the role of Priestess and Priest.

Priestesses and Priests are guides, not gurus. They are teachers who lead by example, sharing their experience and wisdom with those who are committed to learning. A good Priestess or Priest doesn't stand between an individual and deity. Rather, they teach the practices that enable all of us to experience the Divine for ourselves.

Because Wicca is now so accessible, and so many people are self-taught through books and practicing alone, there are "self-proclaimed"

High Priestesses and High Priests, Lords and Ladies. There is no central authority that confirms, or denies, the legitimacy of fellow practitioners. I have no problem with people starting groups after reading a few books—in fact, that's one reason I've written *Witch Crafting*. And there's nothing *intrinsically* wrong with titles, although personally I'm not thrilled with the use of titles of nobility like Lord and Lady (a Gardnerian tradition), which I stopped using long ago because of the class, economic, and social distinctions these terms connote.

The titles Priestess and Priest, however, do imply that one has been initiated and trained, and is ready to initiate and train others. While initiation and training may no longer be a prerequisite for the creation of a coven or circle of one's own, the title Priestess or Priest carries with it a public declaration of readiness to undertake the serious responsibility of guiding others on their spiritual quests. Whether awarded or self-proclaimed, these titles ought to be used only by those who have earned them through extensive experience—and who live up to them. The Tradition of Ara awards the titles of Priestess and Priest only to those who have successfully completed initiatory training, and uses the word "Witch" for those who are self-trained or self-initiated, as well as for those who have been formally initiated by a Priest/ess.

Though the traditional models of coven leadership often describe the Priestess as the absolute leader whose decisions are infallible, in fact few Priestesses exercise this kind of power. Rather, they solicit opinions and concerns, needs and issues; they counsel and console, arbitrate disputes, resolve conflicts, and above all, nurture and cultivate the gifts of their community. A Priest/ess earns, and deserves, the respect of the coven because of her/his wisdom, experience, compassion, sincerity, humility, sense of responsibility, and connection to the Sacred.

COVEN PARTICULARS

Costs. Traditionally, covens have not charged for initiatory training. Historically, this reflects the influence of the Witchcraft Vagrancy Laws of England which made charging fees for the practice of witchcraft illegal.

It has also ensured that the religion is not corrupted or exploited for pe-
cuniary or selfish purposes. However, the training of a coven by an elder
is a commitment of extraordinary generosity on their part—of time, energy, love, and immeasurable amounts of psychic and earthly energy. In
exchange for this, coven members are expected to approach the work
with commitment, seriousness, discipline, and a willingness to give back
in a variety of appropriate ways, such as helping to prepare, lead, set up
for, and clean up after rituals, bringing and preparing food and drink or
other items needed for circle, keeping coven records, and participating in
other coven activities, such as charitable, environmental, or community
efforts. Coveners also share in the expenses associated with running and
maintaining the coven, particularly when the Priest/ess has to travel long
distances, provide concentrated training, or work with communities of
large and growing numbers.

Many elders and covens seek to serve the expanding community with
rituals that correspond to the phases of the Moon, and the celebration of
the eight Sabbats, and elders often conduct workshops, classes, conferences, and lectures, and are now creating seminaries and programs of
study. Charging for these is expected to cover the costs of renting space,
mailings, flyers, transportation, insurance, etc. It is also appropriate for
those who are receiving the time, energy, and efforts of teachers to reciprocate.

Sexuality. It is common for covens to work skyclad (nude) at least some
of the time (though some traditions only work robed). This aspect of
Wicca is unique among Western religions and is an expression of freedom, a commitment to truth, and the deep trust that is engendered by a
coven, and that is required for the group to function properly. *Under no
circumstances does Wicca require members of covens to engage in sexual activities as part of their initiatory obligations or training. Anyone requiring
sex of a prospective or active member of a coven should be challenged and
brought to the attention of the Wiccan community.* Sexuality is considered
sacred within the Wiccan religion. Rites such as the consecration of wine
and cakes, aspects of divine invocation, and certain levels of magical ad-

vancement involve the symbolic expression of divine union, or sacred marriage, of Goddess and God. Sex magic is also an important aspect of Wiccan practice, but is conducted by consenting adults and generally by individuals who are working partners, and is done in private.

Minors. It is common among Wiccan covens not to take on members who are under the age of eighteen years, without specific, written parental consent. But that does not mean that teenage Witches can't start their own groups—and many of them have, much to the delight of their "elders." Wiccan youth groups are growing in numbers and popularity, often meeting in schools that allow religious afterschool activities. Teen Witches are on the front lines of the struggle for religious freedom, including their right to wear pentacles (the symbol of the Wiccan religion) to school. If you're a Wiccan teen, remember that you're not alone; there are many sources of support and you'll find listings in the Resources.

LOOKING FOR A COVEN

And so, as you begin your search for a community of like-minded and well-suited fellow travelers, you must exercise strong intuition, common sense, thorough research skills, divination, conversation, investigation, and a dose of destiny. There are extensive resources available to you if you want to find a coven to work with, and so many possibilities. So, where should you start?

If you know someone who is practicing, or who knows people who are, begin with them. Ask them about the coven they work with, or know about. Ask them to introduce you to the coven's organizer, Priestess, Priest, or members. Bookstores—particularly Wiccan, alternative spirituality, independent, feminist, and even mainstream bookstores—are wonderful places to find postings for covens. Recently, one of the librarians in the very rural and predominantly conservative community where my country house is located happily pointed out a flyer for a newly forming coven posted on the library's bulletin board.

Local colleges and universities are wonderful places to find covens, though they will probably not be covens of existing traditions that are run by elders, but rather new groups where responsibilities and learning are shared. There are also Wiccan publications that provide listings of covens. And, of course, there's the Internet. There are tens of thousands of home pages for Wiccan covens and organizations, many bulletin boards and e-lists, and several sites that provide extensive listings of covens, conferences, and events—see the Resources.

When you've done your research and found a group you're interested in, send an e-mail or make a phone call. Remember that it is an honor to be welcomed into a coven, and they will be just as interested in learning about you as you are about them. They'll be judging you by your energy, as well as by many subtle signs and psychic signals. If you go to your interview with enthusiasm and appreciation, openness and honesty, you'll be starting off the right way. You should make the time for a purification bath, and some meditation and grounding first.

When you meet, ask questions; they'll have questions for you too. Ask how long they've been practicing, individually and with this coven, where they received their training, and if they've worked with other covens. Inquire about the tradition of Witchcraft they practice and where you can learn more about it. Is it an initiatory tradition? What's expected of coven members? How long does it take to become initiated, what's required to become initiated, and how long is the overall training? What qualities are they looking for in potential coven members? Are they engaged in community activities or "in the broom closet"? Ask also about their diversity—is everyone the same age, race, gender, etc.? How many members are there? And be sure to inquire about the spiritual principles they embrace and what their focus is.

When asking and answering questions, intuitive impressions are very important. Don't ignore a gut reaction, no matter how positive the answers to your questions seem.

Anyone who takes the time to answer all of the questions above will have provided you with ample opportunity to evaluate their demeanor. Are they nervous, self-important, testy? Or are they warm, friendly, open, and curious about you? Be sure to answer their questions honestly, tell them what you're looking for in a coven, and thank them for their time. Whether this is the right group for you or not, you will have learned a great deal about what group is right for you just by exploring what's out there.

If you know members of the Wiccan community, it's always wise to ask about the reputation of the coven and its leaders. Be aware that jealousies and politics can shade people's perceptions, but don't ignore repeated reports of problems within a coven, of "Witch wars" and instability, or a prima donna Priestess or predatory Priest—or vice versa.

If you're satisfied with the answers to your questions, if your intuitive impression is positive, and you determine that the coven and its leaders have a good reputation, all you need is an invitation. Traditionally, covens open themselves for new members once every three years, in order to keep the group working at the same general levels of challenge and development. It's a common practice that once you reach a certain point (often after the first year and initiations), new people are not brought into the coven. This is because it takes time to establish trust and to create the interconnections that are necessary in making magic. Exceptions are always possible, and certainly covens do bring in new members to continue and to teach others—usually after the training period has concluded. So, you may be coming into a coven with a group of new folks, or you might find yourself a new member in a preexisting community. The dynamics of membership in a coven can be quite challenging and we'll discuss those shortly.

❈   *Creating Group Synergy*   ❈

Whether you are part of an existing coven or a newly formed coven or study group, you will find that all of the practical considerations discussed above are an important part of creating bonds of trust and friendship, out of which grow, ultimately, love and the ability to make magic together. Wiccan groups invoke, raise, and hold the most precious energy in life—divine energy. Working together, they make magic that draws upon a power far greater than any individual can raise and work with alone. And they create a ring of sacred strength. The coven becomes a cauldron in which magic is made for nurturing, empowerment, transformation, and love.

Wiccan practices are a critical part of the development of a group's capacity to summon the Numinous together. The practices in Chapter 10, Energy, are the foundation for this process of integrating our psychic, physical, and spiritual energies into a whole that is greater than the sum of its parts. As you work with your group, you will learn to join your individual energy with others, and to cultivate group energy. You will find yourselves dreaming about one another, providing divinatory guidance to one another, knowing when someone in the group needs help and providing that help. My friend Ally tells the story of how, shortly after she had left her coven and moved to another city, she fell strangely ill for a week. Her stomach pains were intense and she had trouble sleeping—and then, just as suddenly, the symptoms vanished. A few days later she heard from an ex-covenmate who said that she was leaving the coven after some very intense disagreements the week previous. She hadn't wanted to call earlier and upset Ally, but the powerful bond between Ally and her coven resulted in her being aware of the disturbance anyway.

By working together in circle, by making magic together, by using the practices throughout this book, you will come to recognize and honor the God/dess within others. And you will truly experience the interconnectedness of all life.

DECISION MAKING

Many Wiccan groups, especially those that are self-started, make decisions by consensus rather than by majority decision. Consensus requires more time and dialogue, but the needs of all participants are taken into consideration. A "facilitator" makes sure that each person has an opportunity to speak. S/he also restates the various opinions and keeps the focus on the process of integrating everybody's perspective.

CREATING A CLOSE-KNIT COVEN

Here are some ideas to help create strong and fun-filled bonds amongst your coven members.

1. Create a ritual of commitment to the coven.

2. Work magically together to find the name of your coven, then chant the name, raising and directing energy into it.

3. Create a coven symbol together.

4. Create an oath for your coven, which expresses the values you share, and which you can use to reconnect yourselves.

5. Devote a circle to acknowledging and honoring one another's contributions to the coven.

6. Incubate a dream together by sleeping in the same room.

7. Spend social time together and share in each others' lives.

During consensus building, it's helpful to go around the circle, as often as needed, and have each person speak for a specified amount of time, and then open the floor to general discussion. The goal is also to move away from processes that have a winner and loser toward a process in which everyone wins. This often requires some compromising, and almost always requires a great deal of time, but it's a very unifying process.

Some groups also provide for a veto—to be used only as a last resort, when someone in the group finds a resolution so morally objectionable that were it to be implemented they would have to leave the group. And some groups also provide for the use of a majority vote if they can't achieve consensus after prolonged and best-faith efforts. (See the Resources for more information on consensus process.)

Even traditional covens that are led by a Priestess or Priest are highly participatory, and the opinions, concerns, and needs of all the coven members are discussed and considered in the making of virtually all decisions—particularly after coven members have been initiated. Rather than impose their decision on a coven, Priestesses and Priests explain their reasons for a particular choice or recommendation. A mutuality of respect and trust between Priest, Priestess, and covenmates grows out of the most fundamental spiritual principles that should be the foundation for every Wiccan group.

THE CHALLENGE OF GROUP DYNAMICS

No coven, study group, or community is free from conflict—and in a coven, particularly a healthy, diverse one, it's inevitable that personalities will abrade one another. After more than twenty years, I've seen how often these conflicts are responsible for coven "hopping"—the peripatetic search for the perfect group—and even the destruction of many covens. A coven is by nature an intimate group in which every member, and his/her attitudes, personalities, problems, moods, likes and dislikes, has a significant impact. A skilled Priestess and Priest will try to select a group that is diverse but can also get along well. Until the coven actually begins working together, however, it is impossible to know how successful this process of integration will be. In traditional covens, it's the role of the Priestess and Priest, as the elders, to facilitate this unusual, sometimes difficult, and deeply spiritual process. And in all groups, it's the responsibility of all coven members to assist by bringing the right attitude and energy to the group.

It is a challenge for a coven to become an integrated community in which each individual's needs and personalities are respected and in which the well-being of the entire group is also a priority. Some people are gregarious, others quiet, some are highly organized and proactive, others tend to be more passive and require direction. Some will measure their progress by the number of spells they learned, others by the number of divine encounters they've had. There are those who will want to grind herbs, others will want to meditate. And then there are the inevitable personality conflicts that come from fascinating astrological oppositions and combinations. I'll never forget my discovery, during my first year of training, that whenever I sat opposite one of my Priestesses, who was a Leo, she would get a bit testy and overly dramatic, or at least so she seemed to me, an Aquarian. But when I moved my position so that I was at an angle to her, our energies blended beautifully! I've learned over the years to pay careful attention to the astrological makeups of my coven members. But there are things that are even more helpful than astrological charts in resolving conflicts within a coven or study group.

❋ *Perfect Love and Perfect Trust* ❋

"Perfect love and perfect trust": These watchwords from the Gardnerian tradition reflect a very important unifying and spiritual perspective. After many years of leading covens, I have come to understand that few of us can perfectly love or trust even the people with whom we share the closest and deepest bonds. But it's a noble standard and a goal toward which we strive.

A coven is an utterly human container: frail, flawed, and idiosyncratic. But as we struggle with our limitations and with the challenges that we pose for one another, perfect love and perfect trust function like a lighthouse in the darkness—we aim toward it, knowing that by keeping that beacon in sight, we will weather any storm that strikes and reach the safety of home. *Within circle we treat one another with perfect love and perfect trust, because we see the Sacred in each other.* I first encountered the Goddess not in myself, but in my covenmates. When I recognized Her in them, I began to realize that She was a part of me as well. This is an incredibly precious gift that members of a coven give to one another. When we say to each other "Thou art God/dess," we really mean it. And when we treat each other with perfect love and perfect trust, that is what we create.

WORKING TOGETHER IN HARMONY

Just as our ethics flow from our experience of living in a divine world, so too our treatment of each other in circle flows from our honoring of the deity within one another.

Of course, our lives are spiritual adventures, and so our troubles cannot always be left aside when we begin circle. There are times when we need to discuss them with our covenmates. Then too the unconscious behavioral patterns we all have, which are left over from childhood, can complicate matters. Being aware of this and honest about it will help create a healthy, positive emotional and magical dynamic within a coven.

WHEN CONFLICTS ARISE

Honesty is also critical to the resolution of conflicts. Criticism that goes on behind the scenes can be very destructive. Friendships, bonds, and alliances form and shift within a coven, and it is natural for grievances to be aired amongst friendly peers. But problems *must* be discussed openly and frankly or they cannot be solved. And unsolved problems create discord and distrust that can destroy a coven.

Over the years I've come to appreciate how difficult it is for people to work out their problems, for them to confront and understand one another, resolve their conflicts, and forgive. It's particularly difficult for people to criticize Priestesses or Priests, no matter how often they are reassured that they can do so, because we're taught not to question authority, to hold it in. Often our fears cause us to fall into destructive passive/aggressive behavior.

Coven elders or organizers have a special responsibility to create an atmosphere of safety in which conflicts can be addressed and resolved. They need to lead by example, engaging in honest self-examination and taking responsibility for their own limitations and failings.

There are many specific ways to engender an atmosphere of trust and safety and the Resources section contains recommendations for reading material on the subject. Rituals, exercises, practices, divinations, and simply working together magically can all facilitate resolution, but I've found that dialogue, initiated by the coven leader, or by any member of the coven, is the very best way to tackle a problem. *We should always begin by remembering that divinity is present in each of us—this ensures that we will treat one another with respect, that we will choose our words carefully, and that we will listen with equal care.*

There is a process of conflict resolution that I've found very helpful over the years. When there's a dispute or tension between two or more members of your coven:

- Call a special meeting of the parties involved to resolve it and allow plenty of time for matters to unfold.

- Acknowledge that you are all in the presence of deity, and that you, as moderator, wish to create an atmosphere of safety, love, and trust in which any problem can be raised and addressed.

- Clarify the disagreement by stating what has been/is being done and what responses and feelings these actions are eliciting. No one should make statements that can be interpreted as character or personality descriptions or blaming. Instead of saying "You're not dedicated," people should use "I" language: "When you leave the circle early all the time, I feel that you don't share my commitment to this group. I feel abandoned. I feel overburdened. I feel that I'm not important to you, and neither is this work. And I guess I'm resentful."

- Emphasize forthrightness and self-honesty.

- Do not let the disagreeing parties interrupt one another, chiming in with their side of the story. Keep listening and do not allow a dialogue between the parties to take place until later in the process, after all action descriptions and feelings have been expressed, identified, and *acknowledged*.

- Acknowledge what has been said by repeating it. For example, "Jack, I hear you say that you are feeling abandoned. Is that right?"

- Guide all parties to acknowledge, *without judging anyone's motivation*, that 1) the actions (*not* the intent) described are correct;

and 2) the feelings created are caused, at least in part, by the actions. Emphasize that you know that no ill will or malevolence is involved and that the parties need to see beyond the cycle they have created and recognize their mutual desire for love and trust ("perfect" is the ideal).

- Suggest solutions, such as, "Jack, I hear Jill saying that she would be able to help clean up and participate in circle longer if we began earlier. What do you think we can do to accomplish this?"

You can use this basic model of conflict resolution to address a wide range of problems. While the conflicts may be far more complex than the example given, what all efforts have in common is respect, love, trust, safety, honesty, directness, seeking solutions, and speaking from your own feelings instead of blaming and accusing.

Whether or not you take a leadership role in your coven, by being the beacon of nonjudgmental and objective light, and by having the motivation to restore positive balance, you will be a powerful force in the process of resolution. You cannot control other people, but by showing how you control yourself and providing a safe harbor for exchange, you will set an example and usually you can bring about a solution.

Conflicts allow us to transform negatives into positives, weaknesses into strengths. They are our challenges and our chances to live our spirituality. *A coven, a group, a community is where, together, we summon the Sacred into the world.* And whether we are alone or with others who share our spirituality, the Sabbats are some of our most joyful summonings and celebrations of the Sacred.

Sabbats

Working in harmony with Nature's cycles has tremendous spiritual power. I experienced this in two profound ways when I was writing my memoir and first book, *Book of Shadows*. The process went easily for me because the pace and timing of writing paralleled the changing seasons: I began at the Winter Solstice, as the Sun was returning, made my greatest strides during the late spring and summer, completed my writing just after the harvest time of the Alutumn Equinox, and edited during the winter months. The book was ready in March, just at the time of the Spring Equinox, the time of rebirth.

There was another cycle in motion at that time: I was in recovery from a life-threatening illness, and thus being reborn into life even as my book was being born. And yet at the same time, my mother was dying: She passed away just two months before it was published. Living through that cycle of life and death was one of the most painful times of my life, but the pain was eased by the deep wisdom of life's rhythm.

I still miss my mother. But the timing of these enormous events taught me that life and death are intertwined, balancing one another, and so beneath the pain I have a sense of peace and awe. After my mother passed away, I kept waiting for some sign or visitation from her and finally, on the first night of my book tour, she came to me in a dream, hugged me, told me she loved me, and that I shouldn't worry about her. There have been other, more remarkable signs since then, from both of my parents—signals that they are watching over me, and rejoice in my life.

The spirit survives, and many Witches have had experiences that convince them that your spirit returns to be reborn in this world, to experience and learn from other lifetimes. As Einstein proved, the energy of the Universe is constant: It cannot be destroyed. And though the physical form succumbs to the passage of time, the energy of someone's life force cannot be destroyed. This cycle of life—birth, growth, maturity, decay, death, rest, and rebirth—is always present in the world around us. The Wheel is always turning and when you observe the seasons changing from one into the next, you also see that the cycle is full of mystery and divine magic that is as true for you as it is for the Earth.

Call it the Divine, the Goddess, the God, or the Tao, it is the force that spins the Wheel. Witches work with the energy of this ceaseless cycle, with the enchantment of life changing its form. This great and sacred magic is honored in the seasonal celebrations, the eight holy days that we call the Wheel of the Year. These sacred days are called Sabbats, from the Greek *esbaton* meaning "holy day," and they are most often referred to by their Celtic names.

Four Sabbats celebrate the Earth's seasons of change: Samhain (pronounced *Sow'en* and popularized as Halloween), Imbolc (which has survived as St. Brigid's Day and Groundhog Day), Beltaine (or May Day, still celebrated in Scandinavia), and Lughnassadh (still celebrated in Ireland). And four celebrate solar events: Winter Solstice or Yule, Spring Equinox or Oestara, Summer Solstice or Litha, and the Autumn Equinox or Mabon. All of these holy days were appropriated by the Church and now the basis for the Christian calendar of worship. Sabbats occur approximately every six weeks, and are one of the reasons Wicca is such a joyful spirituality—there's no time for the blues! Life is always changing, and Witches are always learning from and celebrating those changes.

Modern Sabbats contain elements of Welsh, Celtic, Nordic, Italian, Babylonian, Egyptian, Greek, and other ancient mythologies and religious mystery traditions. They also incorporate modern adaptations, recent and old folk practices, ancient invocations and modern language, and most important of all, the wisdom of Nature.

Though some would like to believe that our Sabbat rituals reflect a pure historical continuity, the fact is that many of our current practices and interpretations of the holidays are far more modern than ancient. And even the mythological motif of the dance between the Goddess and God that accompanies and explains the Wheel of the Year, though drawn from ancient myths, seems to be a recent adaptation. And there's absolutely nothing wrong with that. In fact, it is evidence of how vital Wicca is as a modern spirituality—addressing the perspective and needs of contemporary practitioners. So, let's embrace the vitality of this remarkable spirituality, enjoy celebrating, and remember, we have the same teacher as our ancestors: Nature.

✳ *The Role of the Sabbats* ✳

Celebrating the Sabbats is one of your most powerful ways of connecting to the cycles of the Earth and the Sun. And when you get together with others to attune yourselves to these profound rhythms, you create a spiritual community with a shared reverence for Nature's divinity and wisdom. Our forebears lived close to the Earth, so Her cadences affected every aspect of people's lives, from their survival to their spirituality. And so when the community gathered, religious rituals organically reflected the natural world in which the people lived. The agricultural cycles, the Sun's "movements," and the responses of a community as it organized to live and work with these rhythms all gave rise to religious rites and metaphors.

Today, Wiccan Sabbats are ritual celebrations that help the community as a whole, and each of us as individuals, synchronize our minds, bodies, and spirits to the tempo of the natural and divine world in which we live. But even when we come together as a community and celebrate with poetry, music, ritual, exuberance, and reverence, it's not enough. We need to incorporate the Earth's and the Sun's innate spiritual wisdom into our daily lives.

There's tremendous power in living according to these great cycles, and that power can change your life, and the culture around you. As you ritualize and are guided by the relationship of the Earth and Sun, you discover the rhythm and spiritual meaning of your own life.

Unfortunately, that's often easier said then done. Most of us live in urban and suburban environments, cut off from Nature and Her seasons. The seasonal weather often seems more of an inconvenience than a source of spiritual enlightenment. But every once in a while, Nature asserts Herself so absolutely that even we modern creatures have to stop and pay attention to Her grace, power, and intelligence. It was wonderful, with spring just two weeks away, to watch the entire city of New York, and most of the Northeastern seaboard, grumpily grind to a halt as a huge snowstorm bore down on the East Coast, burying us in two feet of snow. For two days, winter reminded us of Her perfect purpose—the world grew quiet, the rushing about stopped, and we were wrapped in a snowy blanket of stillness and silence. As we should in winter, we put down our daily busy-ness and watched, stunned by beauty as the Earth turned inwards again, concealing Herself beneath a mantle of white.

You celebrate the Sabbats to recognize and learn from the Divine that resides in the world, and to express your gratitude. Sabbat rituals help you to see how divinity creates and transforms life—how it shape shifts—and why. Guided by the Sabbats, you begin to transform your own life. The Wheel reminds us that a Witch crafts her/himself not with a quick flick of a wand, but in a patient, certain, organic pace. As I already mentioned, you can't tug on a growing plant to make it grow faster, but the Sabbats teach you that you can assure a fertile harvest.

Because I lived in New York City for so much of my life, and particularly my life as a Witch, I always had to work hard at paying attention to Nature's presence and her wisdom. I had to walk blocks to get a clear view of the new Moon, and rush out into the first fallen snow before it was shoveled and plowed into giant dirt-covered piles on the sides of the city streets. I reveled in being able to celebrate Summer Solstice outside in Central Park after the longest Sun had set and the night sky was filled with fireflies, but could only do so in the safety of a group of fellow Witches. And how I wished I could dance naked beneath the full Moon on a warm summer's night!

As closely as I could, I paid attention to the lessons in the tempo of the seasons, but my life, like most people's, still required that I march to the beat of the society in which I lived. As an attorney, I had to be as productive during the darkest days of winter (when all I wanted to do was hibernate) as I was in the summertime. And when the breeze was warm and the Earth was exploding with life, I had to remain indoors working on tasks better suited to snowy days. Many people experience this same problem; as a Witch, the Sabbats provide deeply moving opportunities to re-attune your soul to the rhythm of the sacred.

It's not easy to live the wisdom of the Sabbats when you reside in a world that's largely disconnected from Nature, but it *is* possible—and it's worth every effort to do so. When you are able to harness these phenomenal forces for your own life, you will find that you are able to grow, change, create, and release the outworn with greater ease and fulfillment.

Wheel Magic

While some traditions adhere to a practice of celebrating the Sabbats without making magic, my tradition performs the magical "Great Work": awakening yourself to your innate divinity by living and working in harmony with Nature. The Sabbats help you to find your dreams, nourish them, and turn them into goals—dreams with a deadline—that you accomplish. Attuning yourself to the energies of Earth and Sun will empower you to make this journey of discovery and fulfillment. It's up to you whether you choose to make magic at a Sabbat or not, but these holy days are certainly charged with divine energy, and participating in them will change you in many extraordinary ways. This is just part of the blessing of the Wheel of the Year.

In this practice you are going to work with a full cycle of the Wheel of the Year in order to set and reach a goal. Begin at Samhain by finding a dream to fulfill—reflect on what would be a meaningful project or goal to work on, and start working on it during Winter Solstice, nurturing it through the changing seasons of spring and summer as you rejoice in your creativity and progress. Harvest your efforts at the Autumn Equinox, giving thanks for the blessings of a magical life, and letting go of those things you have outgrown during the last year. Begin seeking a new dream at Samhain. Be sure to record your process in your magical journal.

❋   *The Mythology of the Sabbats*   ❋

Joseph Campbell described a myth as the collective dream of a culture. When you participate in a Sabbat celebration, you are experiencing the Universe's dream of love as it comes to life in our reenchanted world. The Sabbat cycle expresses the myth that is the collective dream of our Wiccan culture.

There are a variety of myths and approaches to the Wheel of the Year, and a variety of interpretations of the meaning of the Sabbats. Some people focus on the Egyptian cycle, or the Greek Eleusinian Mysteries, or the Nordic or Celtic traditions, seeking to retrieve these ancient traditions and to practice them as closely as possible to their original forms. Or you can do what many modern practitioners do, and look to the deep pattern at play in the cycle of the seasons, while integrating aspects of these various traditions. Interestingly, though there is great variation depending on the geography and climate of a given culture, beneath all the versions of the Sabbat story is a similar archetypal theme. It is this theme that is emerging as the primary mythos now celebrated at the Sabbats: the courtship of the Goddess and God.

While many groups work only with the Goddess, and some feel strongly that both are necessary, we need to remember that the Goddess and God are our anthropomorphic metaphors to express the universal dynamic of polarity. Gender is our human expression of polarity, although in reality male and female aren't exclusive opposites. Each gender incorporates aspects of the other, and members of the same gender can also enact the dance of polarity. Thus, in my tradition we may refer to the relationship between the Lover and the Beloved instead of Goddess and God. And sometimes the cup symbolizes the Lover and the athame symbolizes the Beloved, and other times the cup is the Beloved, and the athame the Lover when consecrating the wine for libations.

The dance of Goddess and God, Lover and Beloved, is a dance of love, and that is the energy that spins the Wheel. Because polarities are irrevocably attracted to and require each other, their movement is a cycle of change and transformation. Something new always comes out of their interaction. Through the metaphors of Goddess and God, we can perceive, understand, and appreciate the rhythm of the dance of Earth and Sun. We can also see how it applies to our own lives, and how the energy we work with is love.

It is a dance that begins, interestingly enough, at Samhain (the Celtic New Year), when the Goddess or the God descends into the Underworld, the realm of death, and the world rests. This descent is also one of the most profound myths from the ancient Fertile Crescent, present in the stories of Innana, Persephone, and Isis, of Tammuz, Dionysus, and Osiris. At each stage of the journey, the two polarities interact, coming together in darkness (at the Winter Solstice) and in light (at the Summer Solstice) to create new life. The God and Goddess make love, and new life is conceived: the reborn Sun, the returning corn or grain, the flowers of spring, the God and Goddess as the force of new life emerging from death.

And at each stage during the turning of the Wheel of the Year, there is a bond or exchange between the Goddess and the God. Their roles in relationship to each other change—they are maiden and death, mother and son, lovers, crone and wise old man—but their love and their connection is constant as they move through the seasons of life. The Goddess is the womb of the Universe and the Earth, the God is the Sun and the seed. For most Witches, the Goddess is immortal, and the God is born, lives, dies, and is reborn through the Goddess. For others, both Goddess and God are immortal, and because divinity is also immanent, they also undergo transformations of time—being born, living, aging, dying, and being re-born. Whichever way you view the myth of the courtship of the Goddess and God and experience the Wheel, their relationship is the dance of life choreographed through the cycle of the seasons. Birth, growth, harvest, death, rest, and rebirth reveal the mystery of the spirit that ceaselessly changes forms, and is the mythological motif of the Sabbats.

As you work with this beautiful story, you must also attend to the wisdom of your part of the Earth, and you must learn from the spirits of place. The Wheel of the Year is rooted in the Earth's relationship with the Sun, in the growing cycles, and so it is only natural that your Sab-bats should reflect the reality of the Earth's rhythms where you live. It makes no sense to celebrate the Summer Solstice and the richness of the Earth and the power of the Sun in June if you are living in Australia where it is winter, and the Winter Solstice is occurring. Wicca is not an abstract theology and its rituals are not abstract either. We are an Earth-based spirituality, so you should celebrate your seasons when they ac-tually occur.

If you live in Florida, or southern California, or the outback of Australia, you may find the Sabbats you celebrate would be more mean-ingful if they were based not upon the Northern American or Northern European seasonal rhythm, but upon the Greek, Middle Eastern, Egypt-ian, or local Native American or indigenous seasonal holidays. It's im-portant to note here that Witches, in both America and Australia, seek to work with the spirits of place and their spiritual wisdom, but are also very respectful of the indigenous traditions. Given the terrible history of geno-cide and oppression, Witches are careful not to appropriate indigenous religious traditions, though they are also very willing to learn from their brothers and sisters.

Whether you celebrate alone or with others, the sacred mystery of this cycle and the ways in which it brings you closer to Goddess, God, and the divinity of the world is ultimately yours to experience and to interpret. What follows are my interpretations of these marvelous holidays drawing upon the core magical and celebratory practices that I've used with my community in rituals large and small, public and private, over the years. They are written for groups to work with, but are easily adapted by an individual. I encourage you to draw upon and modify the rituals as you create your own. The explanations for each Sabbat will be found in the ritual section called Declare the Purpose of Circle (see page 306 for the first of these).

Celebrating the Sabbats is a moving and joyous experience that all Witches share, for it unites us with the Divine, with the Earth, the Sun, our community, our essential humanity, and with love. As you rejoice and learn from Nature, the meaning of the Sabbats will become clearer and as the Wheel turns, and turns again throughout your life, you'll feel yourself growing, changing, learning to let go, and to begin again. You'll see yourself reflected in the story of the Goddess and God, and so you have yet another way of finding the Sacred that dwells within you. Joining the dance of the Earth and Sun, you craft yourself as a Witch by living in harmony *and* in rhythm with the Divine. And that is how you reenchant your life, and the world.

✳   *The Sabbats*   ✳

While each of the Sabbats is unique, they follow a similar basic structure. The following is a template that can be used in celebrating each of the Sabbats. The particular activities, dances, symbols, colors, Goddess and God aspects, etc., are provided for within each Sabbat ritual. There is also language for declaring the purpose of each Sabbat, but you should feel free to modify it or write your own. Remember, these are guidelines—the most important ingredients are your creativity, and your connection to Nature's divinity. If you're having fun, you're doing it right.

Sabbat Template

- Create a Sabbat incense that can be used at any Sabbat (to represent the element of air): Grind together equal parts of patchouli, sandalwood, orris, rose, fennel, thyme, rue, chamomile, and vervain. Add a few drops of benzoin oil, and a few drops of pennyroyal oil.

- As with all ritual, you should begin Sabbat celebrations by purifying yourself with a purification bath or smudging with sage.

- Set up your altar using the appropriate seasonal colors, fruits, vegetables, symbols, and images of the Goddess and God.

- Cast your circle. All castings should also include grounding and centering, connecting participants in the circle, and connecting to deity.

- Declare the purpose of the circle—the meaning of the Sabbat.

- Invoke the Goddess and God in their seasonal aspects.

❋ *Samhain* ❋
The Night When the Veil between the Worlds
Is the Thinnest and We Enter the Dreamtime

OCTOBER 31 IN THE NORTHERN HEMISPHERE; MAY 1 IN THE
SOUTHERN HEMISPHERE

People often wear black on Samhain, but in my tradition we also like to wear bright colors to express our joy in the presence of our loved ones who return to visit us. Prepare the altar with colors of black, gold, and orange. On the altar place pairs of black and orange candles, a pomegranate—the symbol of Persephone, the Greek Goddess who was the Queen of the Underworld—and an offering of food and drink for the spirits of the ancestors, and your divination tool (please do not use a Ouija board

- Celebrate with the appropriate activity/magic. This often draws upon surviving folk practices, and also usually includes dancing and chanting to raise and direct energy. Specific dances (such as the Equinox dances, the Maypole dance, and the spiral dance) and chants are described in the Sabbats below.

- Offer libations.

- Bless the cakes or bread.

- Tell stories, play games, or feast within the circle if you like.

- Thank the Goddess and God and close circle.

- End with parting words, "Our circle is open, but never broken. Merry meet and merry part and merry meet again," and hugs and kisses all around.

- If you are working outdoors, be sure to leave the place better than you found it.

- Remember, while I've written these rituals for a group, you can use them on your own as well.

as the results tend to be negatively chaotic). You can also place on the altar photographs of people you love who have passed over. As you work, please remember that this is a sacred day of remarkable power and we rarely find that the ritual proceeds as planned, for there are often very unusual and unexpected manifestations, strong emotions, and startling revelations.

Prepare a special Samhain incense and Hecate anointing oil:

Flying Incense (which enhances psychic powers and spiritual vision): Grind equal parts gum mastic, cinnamon, musk, patchouli, juniper, sandalwood, ambergris, Lo-John powder, and myrrh. Add drops of cedar oil and orris oil.

Hecate Oil (Hecate was Persephone's guide through the Underworld): Mix oils of Lo-John, cedar, dittany of Crete, musk, and ambergris. Put a small piece of frankincense in the oil.

Anoint the candles and yourself with the oil.

Cast your circle in the names of Hecate, Goddess of Magic and Transformation, Persephone, Queen of the Underworld, and the Lord of Death and Rebirth.

Declare the purpose of your circle: "*Samhain is the Celtic New Year, and has become the Wiccan New Year. This is the night when the Goddess enters the Underworld to confront the God in his aspect as the Lord of Death and Rebirth, the master of time.* The Wheel begins to turn, following in the footsteps of the Goddess [and/or God], who bravely descends into the realm of spirits. And so we begin by going deeply into ourselves, and into the dimensions of reality where the spirits live.*

"*Tonight the veil between the worlds is thinnest, and we honor the spirits of our ancestors. On this holy night we welcome them with love, for they are able to visit us and we are able to speak with them. On this holy night, we are free to move backward and forward in time—to see our past lives, and to find the dreams that will become our destinies*

"*On Samhain we seek to understand ourselves and our spiritual journeys as we enter the dreamtime. We let go of our old, outworn forms of living, and in the midst of realms of spirit where form no longer exists, we seek a dream, for all new life begins first with a dream.*"

Invoke the Goddess, as Hecate the Crone, and Persephone the Maiden, and the God as Lord of Death and Rebirth: "*Bless this time and this place and those who are here. We welcome You and bid You guide the way for our loved ones to return to this safe and sacred space place.*"

Draw an invoking pentagram in the west; this will help to open a portal through which the ancestors may enter. As you draw the pentacle, say: "*We ask you to open the portals between the worlds.*" As you do so, feel the veil parting and your loved ones coming to be with you as you continue speaking: "*Welcome, beloved Ancestors, who have gone before us. Join us in*

---

*And in some traditions this is the night when the God enters the Underworld, and the Goddess is the Crone. In our tradition, both are equally true, for it is the night of transformations, when the old forms give way and the mystery of new life begins.

this circle of light and joy, we honor you and your journey and rejoice in your return."

You may also wish to move three times around the circle widdershins, reversing the movement of time within the circle, before you open the portal.

After the portal is opened, sit and use your trance techniques to shift your consciousness to better sense your visitors. You might want to drum in the tempo of a heartbeat. Allow your mind to envision your loved ones who have passed over, concentrate on the sense of presence you experience, listen to what they say. You may also use your divination tools to communicate. Tell them what you are doing, ask for advice, and above all, express your love and share with them whatever you may have wished to say but didn't when they were alive. Listen carefully for their answers. When you're done, you may feel them withdraw from you and the circle; if so, thank them and bid them farewell. Or they may remain for the feasting and toasting that will follow shortly.

Now use your divination tools to seek a vision of your future. (You may also ask for a vision of a past life.) Ask for guidance in finding a new dream. Be sure to reread the message you receive for guidance in making magic between Samhain and Yule.

Place the pomegranate in the Goddess's chalice and with your athame, bless it as you would the libation. Open it and eat a seed as a symbol of your journey from immortality to mortality to immortality again. Honor the cycle of life and death and rebirth. Honor your ancestors. You may wish to share stories about them as you offer libations, toast, and feast in their honor (a very ancient, Nordic tradition).

When you are done, thank your ancestors and bid them farewell. If you have walked widdershins, walk deosil three times. Close the portal in the west. Thank the Goddesses and God for being with you and close the circle. And remember, all new life begins first with a dream.

❋ *Yule, or Winter Solstice* ❋
The Longest Night When the Goddess Gives Birth to the Light and the Sun Returns

DECEMBER 20–22 IN THE NORTHERN HEMISPHERE; JUNE 20–22 IN
THE SOUTHERN HEMISPHERE.

If you can, wash your face in snow to purify and use snow for water
on your altar. Work with the colors red, green, gold, and white. Decorate
the altar with pine boughs, holly, and mistletoe. Place a large yellow candle (the symbol of the God, the returning Sun, who is born of the Goddess) within your cauldron in the center of the altar. Around the cauldron
place additional candles, which you will light later.

Make a Sun incense of equal parts of frankincense and myrrh.

An advanced project, which my circle does as part of our public Yule
celebration, is to create a labyrinth of light (either candles for a private
celebration or connected strings of little lights for public). We light the
candles or plug in the string of lights after the invocation of the Goddess
and the God, and everyone walks the labyrinth. As they reach the center,
where the altar has been placed and where the Priestess and Priest stand,
each person lights his or her candle from the light burning in the cauldron, expresses their wish for the New Year, and then proceeds back out
through the labyrinth.

Cast your circle in the name of the Great Mother Goddess, the infinite womb, and the Child of Promise, the returning light.

State the purpose of the circle: "*Tonight is the longest night. The Sun
returns, born from the dark and nourishing womb of the Great Goddess. The
Lord of Death is the Lord of Rebirth, and darkness now gives way to light as
each day grows longer. On this night we remember that darkness is not
empty, nor frightening. It is the infinite potential out of which the light is
born. On this night, we rejoice, for the dreams we have found in the dreamtime now appear before us. On this night, we kindle the light of hope, for
light is returning and with it, new life.*"

Invoke the Goddess and God.

Light the candle in the cauldron and hold it high. Say: *"The Goddess gives birth. Behold the light is returned, the Sun is reborn!"*

If you have created a labyrinth, this is the time for everyone to walk it, lighting their candle from the cauldron on the altar. If you don't have a labyrinth, raise energy by dancing the spiral dance. When the energy is raised, light your candles from the cauldron. As you light your candle, speak your wish/dream/goal for the new year. As the circle becomes a circle of light, chant: *"See the Sun returning, feel the fire burning."*

Offer libations, close circle, and feast! This is a Sabbat that calls for much merriment. In fact you can appoint a Lord of Misrule who has a mistletoe wand and whose job it is to provoke laughter. You should also have lots of music. You might want to exchange gifts; in my circle, we usually do a grab bag. We also take up collections for worthy causes, or do a food or clothing drive. If you're alone, be sure to spend some time celebrating with close friends or family.

✸ *Imbolc, "In the Belly"* ✸
The Holy Day of the Goddess Brigid When We Rejoice in the Life That Grows Within

FEBRUARY 2 IN THE NORTHERN HEMISPHERE; AUGUST 1 IN THE SOUTHERN HEMISPHERE

Work with bright and sunny colors: orange, yellow, red. Have enough candles for each person present and place them around all of you as you sit in circle. If you are alone, have at least eight white, yellow, or orange candles with which to make a circle around yourself. In the center of the altar place a yellow candle in the cauldron to symbolize the Sun/Grain/God growing in the Universe/Earth/womb of the Goddess.

On Imbolc we honor Brigid, the muse to poets and artists; She is also a Goddess of fire, sacred wells, healing, and smithcraft (working with metals, which is symbolic of creating civilization). You may work with any of these aspects of Her, but the following ritual focuses on Her as muse.

Prepare an artistic offering to Brigid: a poem or any piece of writing, music you or someone else has written that you will play or sing, a painting, photograph, or any other form of artistic expression, including food you've prepared. Place it on the altar.

Cast circle in the name of Brigid and the God who grows within the belly.

Declare the circle's purpose: *"This is Imbolc, the night when new life stirs within the belly. The light grows stronger and the Earth is stirring from Her winter's sleep. The first signs of returning life are appearing and we are filled with hope. But the nights are cold and dark, and the days still bring us snow. Supplies grow low and we all have cabin fever! But the fire burns within to bring us hope and warmth, and so we come together to kindle from the fires that glow within us all, a great fire burning bright that will light the world with love and joy. We offer the brightness of our spirits to each other, and to the Goddess who nurtures the light within us all."*

Invoke Brigid and the God who grows within.

The candles on the altar should be passed around and each person should carve on a candle their name and the goal they are nourishing to fruition. You may wish to chant to raise energy as you carve: *"One thing becomes another, in the Mother, in the Mother."* Concentrate on your dream taking shape, like the God growing stronger each day, as you work and sing. Meditate on how you will nourish your dream to fruition, like the Goddess within whose womb all life grows.

When everyone is done carving, bring the chanting to a peak and send the energy into your candles while holding them to your heart. Going deosil around the circle, one at a time, each person should light her/his candle, and state what her/his goal is; saying it out loud enhances the power of your magic, so don't be shy! Place the candle in a holder behind you. If you are alone, carve your name and goal on a candle, chant, raise, and direct the energy, light the candle, and then light each of the candles placing them in a circle around you.

When the circle of light is complete, honor the fire by saying: *"We burn with the power of divine inspiration. We are light, sitting in a circle of light. When we come together as a community, the fire burns more brightly*

than when we are alone and there is warmth and illumination for us all. We
offer our light to the Goddess and the world."

Everyone should then share her/his offerings—reading, singing, playing, feeding everyone. This is a magic of light-heartedness and merriment, so feel free to joke and laugh. Close and seal the circle: One person
walks widdershins around the outside of the circle blowing out the quarter candles, as everyone blows out her/his own. As s/he walks s/he says:
"Fire seal the circle round, let it fade beneath the ground, let all things be as
they were since the beginning of time." Repeat until a full circuit has been
made and all the candles, including the altar candles, are blown out. You
may relight your personal candle later to complete your magic.

Oestara, the Spring or
✳ Vernal Equinox ✳
The Holy Day When Light and Dark Are in Balance,
When Life Emerges from the Great Mother Earth

MARCH 20–22 IN THE NORTHERN HEMISPHERE; SEPTEMBER 20–22
IN THE SOUTHERN HEMISPHERE

This is a wonderful Sabbat to celebrate outdoors if possible! The Earth
will be waking up and shoots of green will be appearing. The songbirds will
have begun to return, and the Sun will be warmer though the air is cool.

This holiday was named for Oestara, the Germanic Goddess of the fertile
Earth (whose name is the source of the word "Easter"), so place on your altar
Her symbols: eggs, images of rabbits, and lots of spring flowers. Use images of
the Goddess and the God as Maiden and Youth. Have a basket of seeds. If you
are working indoors, have pots filled with dirt so you can plant the seeds in
them; if you're outdoors, have some spades and tools nearby so you can dig in
the Earth to plant. Work with the colors of spring: green, yellow, purple, pink.

Create an inspiration and instigation incense for spring: Grind together equal parts pine, hyssop, verbena, clove, and galangal; add drops
of lily oil and hyacinth oil.

This ritual should begin after you and everyone participating has
done some major spring cleaning of home, office, relationships, and self.

Throw and give things away! Open the doors and windows and use a broom to sweep out the stale negativity! Speak your peace—stop holding things in—and then let it go! Commit to breaking an old bad habit.

Cast circle in the name of the Maiden and the Youth. Wait to do the grounding and centering as part of the ritual.

Declare circle's purpose; you can draw upon the following: *"Spring is here! This is the moment of perfect balance, for night and day are equal. But now the Wheel turns toward light, and life is reborn from the belly of the Earth. The Goddess emerges from the Underworld bearing new life in Her arms, the God grows strong: The Sun is warm, and the Earth is green again. The Maiden and the Youth return and we rejoice as our lives emerge from the dreamtime and take their shape. We plant the seeds of a new harvest, for the Earth is ready and the Sun is high."*

Invoke the Goddess and God together as Maiden and Youth.

Everyone should ground and center, filling themselves with the regenerating energy of the awakening Earth. When everyone is done, dance the Equinox dance, the dance of the balanced circles: One group will move deosil, the other widdershins, representing the balance between light and dark. Couples stand back to back, then reach out with their right hands to the person in front of them, moving as they go, then reaching out with their left hand to the next person, and so on. This is called the Grand Allemande and is an old circle dance.

A wonderful chant is: *"As we sow, so shall we grow, strong and free, in prosperity."* And chanting while planting is great!

As you dance you will raise energy; when it peaks, send it into the seeds. Pass them around and, if they are to be planted in pots, do so while stating what your goal is. If you are planting outside, have half the group remain in circle, chanting, while half leaves the circle to plant their seeds. Then switch.

When everyone is done planting, all should return to circle, chant, and send the energy to the Earth. Offer libations, give thanks, close, feast, leave seeds for the birds and squirrels, and spend the rest of the day outside. If you're planting in pots, each person should take hers/his and carefully tend it through the growing season.

❋ *Beltaine, or May Day* ❋
The Goddess and God Join in Love and the Earth Blossoms in Ecstasy

MAY 1 IN THE NORTHERN HEMISPHERE; OCTOBER 31 IN THE SOUTHERN HEMISPHERE

This one has to be celebrated with other folks; if you're alone, find a local group or get some friends together. You'd be surprised how many of your friends who may not be Witches will love celebrating with you. Get yourself outside and enjoy the gorgeous weather—in my circle, we've been doing outdoor Beltaine celebrations, many of them public, for almost twenty years and we only had rain once!

Work with spring colors. Women often make garlands of flowers to wear in their hair. Everyone should bring a ribbon, twenty feet long and one inch wide, the color of the magic they are working on (see the Table of Color Correspondences on page 216). Instead of setting up and using an altar, go find a Maypole—a straight branch or small fallen tree about eighteen feet long—to plant in the center of the circle. People whose goals require them to be active should fetch the pole; those doing introspective work should remain and dig the hole. Dig a hole deep enough to plant the pole in. Tie your ribbons to the top of the pole and decorate it with flowers and lay it carefully within the circle.

Cast circle in the name of the Lady of the Flowers and the Lord of the Dance.

Declare the circle's purpose: *"This is the celebration of the ecstasy and the power and the juice and the joy of falling in love. The Sun is warm and the Earth blossoms in beauty, and the dance of desire weaves destinies together. The Goddess and God (Beloved and Lover) join in the sacred marriage, and we join in the sacrament of love."**

Invoke the Goddess and God together as the Lady of the Flowers and the Lord of the Dance.

The active magic makers should raise the Maypole, and place it in the

---

*Please remember that Beltaine, as well as all Sabbats, can be celebrated by same-sex partners and single-gender circles and you should modify the language as you see fit.

hole, which will provoke lots of laughter. (My coven has an appropriately irreverent chant for this part of the ritual: The women chant, "Longer pole!" and the men answer, "Deeper hole!") Several people may have to hold the Maypole in place, which means they'll be getting quite a buzz of energy as everyone dances around them.

Everyone should find her/his ribbon (which always makes for lots of lovely chaos) then stand back to back with a partner, all circling the Maypole as far out as your ribbons stretch. Similar to the Equinox dance, but holding ribbons, the dance begins with those going deosil lifting their ribbons as they move forward, while the circle going widdershins ducks underneath the ribbons as they move forward. The deosil group then ducks under as the widdershins circle lifts their ribbons, switching when they encounter the next person coming toward them. Continue dancing and weaving ribbons over and under, over and under until the Maypole is wrapped in ribbons.

As you dance, chant: *"Corn and grain, corn and grain, All that falls shall rise again. Hoof and horn, hoof and horn, all that dies shall be reborn."* After a while you might want to begin a counterpoint chant, written by Deena Metzger: *"Isis Astarte Diana Hecate Demeter Kali Innana"* and then yet another: *"Pan Woden Baphomet Cernunnos Osiris."*

Let the power build and grow. Some dancers may wish to change places with the folks holding the Maypole. There's always lots of laughing as people get closer and closer to the pole. Everyone can also run deosil, holding their ribbons, when they become too short to weave. When the ribbons are all tightly wound around the Maypole, everyone stops, ties off their ribbons, puts their hands on the pole, and sends their energy into it; the energy then travels into the Earth and the sky, and into the future to manifest your magic.

Offer libations (everyone will need to rehydrate!), give thanks, and close.

This is a Sabbat that you can also celebrate by making love with someone you love when you've returned home from the ritual celebration. Each of you personifies the Goddess and God, the Lover and Beloved, for each other, and as you make love, you do so as the Divine couple, performing the sacred marriage. And don't forget to practice safe sex!

❊ *Litha, or Summer Solstice* ❊
The Longest Day When the Sun Is Strongest and the Earth Is Fertile and Abundant

June 20–22 in the Northern Hemisphere; December 20–22 in the Southern Hemisphere

This is another Sabbat to celebrate outdoors! If you can, get up as the Sun rises, and go outside again at noon when the Sun's power is greatest, and be outside once again to see the Sun set. You can cast your circle at sunrise, midday, or sunset. Wear colors of the fruitful Earth and shining Sun. Fill the altar with fruits, vegetables, and flowers of the season—particularly roses, for the flower represents the Earth and the thorn the pain of the Sun's departure. Everyone should bring an object that represents the goal they are nourishing.

Cast circle in the names of the Goddess of the Fertile Earth and the God of the Shining Sun—you can also invoke them using specific Goddess and God names (see the Table of Correspondences on page 78).

Declare the circle's purpose: "*This is the longest day of the year, the Sun is at its zenith, and the Earth responds to His power with fertile abundance. The two embrace, creating life. Though today the Sun's power begins to wane, as He begins his journey into winter darkness, the summer begins. And so we celebrate the loving union of Goddess and God. We rejoice in the richness of our lives, giving thanks for the fruitful blessings of the Great Mother Earth, and the Father Sun, without whom there would be no life. As the Earth transforms the Sun into life, so we transform the light within ourselves into goals that will grow as the Earth does.*"

Invoke the Goddess and God.

Then everyone should lie on the Earth and absorb the life-making energies of Sun and Earth. Try using a large gong (a fire instrument), or drums (earth instruments) as accompaniment. When you're ready, rise and raise yet more energy by dancing a spiral dance in honor of the Sun's descent and the Earth's fertility. Chant the name of a Sun God such as Helios and an Earth Goddess such as Demeter. When the energy peaks, send it into the objects you have placed on the altar (such as a green prosperity candle) and send it into the future to manifest your goals. Litha is also a powerful Sabbat for prosperity, so ask the Sun to carry obstacles and poverty away with him, and ask the Earth to richly reward your efforts.

There is a special consecration for the wine: "*Spear to cauldron, lance to Grail, spirit to flesh, flesh to spirit* (Lover to Beloved, or vice versa), *God to Goddess, Sun to Earth.*"

After libations, give thanks and close.

❋   *Lughnassadh, or Lammas*   ❋
The First Harvest

AUGUST 1 IN THE NORTHERN HEMISPHERE; FEBRUARY 2 IN THE SOUTHERN HEMISPHERE

Try to celebrate outside, preferably in farm country! Dress in yellow and green, the colors of the ripening corn. If you are working indoors, or in a backyard or park, use fresh corn, other fruits and vegetables of the season, and freshly baked bread (Lammas means "Feast of Bread"). Again, place your goal, or its symbol, on the altar.

Cast circle in the name of the Great Mother Earth and Lugh, God of the Corn, and, if you wish, the waning Sun God.

Declare the purpose of circle: "*We gather to turn the Wheel, to celebrate the first harvest. We honor the wisdom of the Mother and Her lesson of eternal abundance and generosity. We honor the blessings of the Sun God who journeys ever closer to darkness. We give thanks for the Corn God who has grown by the power and union of Goddess and God, Earth and Sun, and who now sacrifices Himself, so that we may live, and that He may live again. Though we grieve as the Goddess grieves for the Sun's parting, and the death of Lugh with the Corn's first cutting, we rejoice in the life that still grows. It is time to acknowledge our power to make our dreams come true, to fulfill the goals we set for ourselves. The first fruits of our labor nourish us, but we must also nourish patience, for the great harvest is yet to come.*"

Invoke the Goddess and Gods.

If you have musicians, have them play as you dance in circle. You can also chant: *"One thing becomes another, in the Mother, in the Mother."* Raise the energy, direct it to the corn, and the objects on the altar.

This is a great Sabbat for dancing and physical games—especially the ones we played as young children, like Duck, Duck, Goose, or London Bridge Is Falling Down. The Irish are famous for their horseraces, fairs, gaming, and dancing that occur on Lughnassadh. Let them inspire you to be creative in your celebrating. Offer your libations, pouring some onto the Earth, then give thanks and close.

❋ *Mabon, or Autumn Equinox* ❋
The Great Harvest

SEPTEMBER 20–22 IN THE NORTHERN HEMISPHERE; MARCH 20–22 IN THE SOUTHERN HEMISPHERE

If possible, go to farm country and see if you can participate in a harvest or go to a farm that allows you to pick your own fruits and/or vegetables. Actually harvesting can make this one of the most meaningful Sabbats you'll ever have! Work with the colors of the harvest: greens, oranges, yellows, reds. Pile the altar high with the fruits and vegetables of the harvest and autumnal flowers, and place some corn on their stalks by the sides of the altar. Place a sickle on the altar, and images of the Goddess and God as Crone and Wise Old Man. In fact, you don't need a formal altar—a simple pile of what you've harvested, some cornstalks, and the sickle is a beautiful and powerful center for your circle.

Use the Sabbat incense and add cypress. Cast circle in the names of the Crone Goddess Hecate and the Wise Old Sun, and declare the purpose of your circle: *"This is a moment of perfect balance, for day and night are equal. We gather to turn the Wheel, as the energies of life flow toward darkness and repose. Mabon is the ritual of rejoicing in the richness of the Earth, and the power of the Sun, without which we could not live. It is the time to give thanks for their gifts and rejoice in the bounty we have harvested for ourselves in our work, our relationships, our spiritual journeys. This is also the time we reflect upon those aspects of our lives that no longer serve our growth and happiness and we let go of them so that we may continue to grow. The Great Mother Earth has fulfilled Her promise of nourishment and life and now She becomes the Crone. The God who has danced with Her and loved with Her has bestowed His energy and power, and now He becomes the Wise Old God. We give thanks to Them for all of our blessings."*

Invoke the Goddess and God in the Crone and Wise Old Sun aspects.

Then raise energy by dancing the Equinox dance (as done in the spring) the Grand Allemande. As you dance, one circle should chant: *"Corn and grain, corn and grain, all that falls shall rise again. Hoof and horn, hoof and horn, all that dies shall be reborn."* The other circle should chant Z. Budapest's great chant: *"We all come from the Goddess, and to Her we shall return, like a drop of water flowing to the ocean."* When the energy is raised, send the energy into the corn.

The eldest woman, representing the Crone, should now harvest the corn. She should enter the circle, hold the corn stalks in one hand, the sickle in the other, and say: *"Blessed are we by the fruits of the union of Sun and Earth. Here is the mystery and the richness of energy encased in seed. Though the form changes, the energy of life is eternal. We recognize the mystery of the transformation of energy into matter, and matter into energy. We gather at this sacred moment when the Sun has gone into the seed."*

As she finishes, she should cut the corn from the stalk and hold it aloft, which is the cue for everyone to cheer.

Instead of the usual libation, pass the corn around the circle so that everyone gets a piece. Each person should husk the corn, and as they do so, say what they are harvesting—what they have created—and what they are releasing. Eat the raw corn—if it's fresh, as it should be, you're going to be in for a wonderful surprise!

Close your circle, and be sure to leave some corn as an offering for the animals.

So the Wheel turns. We end where we began, to begin again. The cycle is the same, but we are changed, and will change again, for this is the magic of the Universe, the spell of you, coming into being as a Wise One.

Epilogue

AHEAD OF YOU lies a world rich with spiritual adventures, a world charged with divine magic. You stand at a crossroads where history, the future of the Earth, and your own path converge. There is an ancient Goddess who presides at this place of decisions and destiny, and who has watched over your journey of Witch crafting. Her gifts are now yours—and with them you have the power to reenchant your life, and the world.

PERSONAL RITUAL

Personal ritual is one of a Witch's greatest arts. Other than graduation, marriage, the military, *Monday Night Football*, and funerals, we live in a world devoid of rituals. And half the population doesn't even have *Monday Night Football* (not that most women would complain about this particular loss).

But life is full of crossroads—they are the events that deserve, and require, rituals. They are the passages of life that will profoundly change who you are and who you will become. Some are undertaken voluntarily, others come by force of time or unexpected tragedy, triumph, or destiny. New phases of life commence. Children are born, important relationships begin and end, youth transforms into maturity, and the mature become elders. Jobs are lost and new careers are begun. Accidents and illness change your course, and synchronicities and epiphanies reveal sacred mysteries guiding your life. Each and all of these changes provide

319

CREATING A PERSONAL RITUAL

- Reflect on and make a list of the many reasons to create personal rituals. For example, the birth and naming of a child, or the ending of a pregnancy; onset of menopause; leaving home and getting your first home of your own; marriage, anniversaries, and divorce; moves and job changes; coming "out of the broom closet" as a Witch; fighting and recovering from an illness; achieving sobriety; death and other losses; the relinquishing of a dream; the achievement of a goal. And don't forget the "little" things like cleansing away the day's cares, or cleaning out your closets.

- Set time aside, and make a commitment to yourself to use the time, for your ritual.

- Meditate on your ritual's purpose and the meaning of the event in your life.

- Use divination to help you understand yourself at deeper levels, and to help you create a meaningful ritual.

- Determine if you want to work with a specific deity who can best help you, and draw upon what you have learned about

opportunities to discover and fulfill the magic of who you are, for a Wise One knows that life is crafting you as a Witch.

Wicca provides invaluable tools and sacred gifts for this journey of transformation. And among these is your ability to create rituals that honor all the magical moments, whether difficult or blissful. But the power of rituals, and their magic, is not just for the momentous. It is also for the simple matters of daily life, whether it's relieving the stress of a difficult day, finding solace or inspiration to make a difficult decision, or getting the energy to do your best.

Her/Him to craft your ritual. For example, work with colors, days of the week, herbs and plants, elements, symbols, images, and invocations of that deity.

- Consider which element would be most beneficial to your purpose. Integrate more "traditional" ways of working with the element, and devise new ones.

- Create an altar.

- Create safe and sacred space in which you can craft a ritual without interruption. Give yourself all the time you need to work without pressure.

- Always begin by connecting to the Divine—around you and in you.

- Work with the techniques and information provided in this book and others.

- Write your own invocations.

- Leave room for spontaneity and divinity.

- Use your intuition and creativity, and remember: Your life is your magic.

Whatever the occasion, great or small, here are steps for creating personal rituals. May they fill your life with magic.

Just as Sabbats bring our community together, we can also create personal rituals for one another. A very gratifying experience I had recently was helping the women of a New York City Unitarian Universalist church create a croning ritual honoring the elder women. It was celebrated first among the women themselves, and then with the full congregation. Honoring and assisting one another's passages creates a caring community grounded in the sacredness of our shared life. Rituals can welcome a new member into the community—honor a girl's first menstruation and passage into womanhood, or a boy's passage into manhood, and mourn the passing of others; celebrate the birthing of a child or the onset of menopause; and participate in the joining of a couple in a Wiccan rite of marriage (called a handfasting).

Rituals celebrate the accomplishments of our community, whether it's cleaning up a park or buying land, creating a Wiccan publication, organization, conference, or temple, or winning the right of Wiccans to practice their religion in freedom and peace. There are milestones being achieved every day in this struggle for tolerance, and they deserve rituals of honoring and rejoicing. I recommend to you a small piece of masterful filmmaking to experience the power of a community creating together: Watch the barn-raising scene about an hour and ten minutes into Peter Weir's brilliant film *Witness*. No matter how often I've seen it, I always weep with joy.

One of the most profound personal and community rituals you will ever experience is a Wiccan initiation. This is the traditional ritual of commitment to Wicca as your spiritual practice and to yourself as a Witch. Like the initiations of most indigenous religions, and those devoted to the Goddesses of the Fertile Crescent, the Wiccan initiation is a cathartic rite of passage, a ritual of death and rebirth. It marks the passage from a life of social constraints and conformity to an authentic life of self-discovery and spiritual fulfillment.

All religions have an initiatory tale or myth at their theological center, whether their adherents actually engage in rites of initiation or not. The stories of the Goddesses Isis, Innana, and Persephone, and the Gods Osiris, Dionysus, Odin, and Lugh, and those of the world's great spiritual teachers Lao Tzu, Moses, Jesus, Buddha, Mohammed, and Aradia are all stories of initiation. They are tales of a heroic descent into the Underworld to confront death, and an equally heroic return to the world with precious gifts of spiritual insight and inspiration. As the Wheel of the Year reveals to us, these stories describe not only the quests of mythical heroes, prophets, Goddesses, and Gods, but the very Earth and Sun as well. And perhaps most importantly, these tales have lessons for you about the sacred mysteries of your life—your journey of death and rebirth.

An initiation is a ritual in which you cross over a magical threshold from the past to the future, from a world that is devoid of divinity to one that is charged with it. Initiation is a rite of transformation from a self separated from the Sacred to a self that is part of the sacred Oneness of life present everywhere. It is not a commitment to a cult, a guru, or any external authority. It is a commitment to yourself and to your own divine magic.

Traditionally, when you felt ready for initiation and you had studied for at least a year and a day, it was your responsibility to request that your Priestess and Priest initiate you. For many years these rituals were a carefully safeguarded secret. Gradually, however, many of the rites of initiation for various traditions such as the Garnderian, Alexandrian, and Faerie have been published and much of the Wiccan movement has been influenced by these rituals as individuals have initiated themselves, and one another.

Though profoundly powerful, the ritual itself does not accomplish this extraordinary metamorphosis—*you* do, and your life does. The ritual of initiation is just the beginning. I warn the people I work with to expect the events of their lives to swiftly and even dramatically initiate them, once the ritual and the commitment have occurred. You may lose your job, become ill, have your marriage end—the Universe will strip away the things that mask and confine your authentic self and block your real power, whether you like it or not. Whatever happens, recognize that these changes are meant to serve you, for this is how the Universe begins to craft a Witch.

An initiation is a test of who you are and a trial for who you will become. The path of the initiated isn't an easy one, but it is extraordinary, glorious, and magical. What follows is a ritual of self-dedication—a rite of self-initiation. It is not a formal initiation into the Ara tradition of shamanic Wicca, which requires specific and supervised training. And in keeping with the tradition of ancient mystery schools, our initiation is secret, because the psychological, emotional, and spiritual impact is strongest when there is secrecy and surprise. However, this ritual provides a starting point, whether you are working as a solitary or with others, to make your commitment to the path of Wicca, and most importantly to yourself.

There's a wise expression that you shouldn't pick the people you're going to travel with until you know what path to take. Choose the right path, and the right companions will join you. The Ara community is exploring ways to expand the opportunities for people to study and be initiated. If it is the right path for you, and you are ready, we hope to provide ways of working formally within the tradition in the future.

It is time to return to the beginning of your quest: Open your magical journal and read the first pages in which you described what you were seeking. Reflect on and write about what you have found. The ritual of self-dedication honors how far you have traveled and how much you have achieved. I hope it is more than you expected as you craft yourself as a Witch.

TRADITION OF ARA RITUAL OF SELF-DEDICATION

You may use this ritual as presented or adapt it as you wish. I believe that the most moving and effective ritual you can perform will be one that you personalize, and that includes an oath that you've written yourself. I have also included language that dedicants of the Tradition of Ara use.

You may wish to perform this ritual in your place of power, or inside, with as few tools and items as your Book of Shadows, athame, and chalice, or a complete ritual altar.

Before you begin your ritual, write it in your Book of Shadows.

Organize all of the items you'll need for your rite.

Take a purification bath or shower. If you're at home, set up your altar as you wish. Inside or out, be sure to include your charged Moon water and charged Sun candle. If you're working outside, enjoy your walk to your place of power.

Place your athame horizontally across the threshold to your place of power or temple space. You should have your chalice and your Book of Shadows with you. Sit "outside" your sacred space in front of your athame and write down on a piece of paper the parts of yourself from your past that you wish to release, surrender, and banish. Burn the paper.

Pay attention to the shift in energies that has already begun. Meditate on your path: where you started, how far you've come, and where you wish to go.

When you're ready, open your eyes and stand up. Say, "*I am ready to dedicate myself to my true and sacred self and to this path of Wicca. I come to my future with perfect love and perfect trust.*"

Hold your Book of Shadows and chalice and step over your athame. Allow yourself to fully experience crossing the threshold into your future. Then pick up your athame and place your Book of Shadows and chalice in the center of your sacred space. Pour the Moon water into the chalice and light the Sun candle.

Cast your circle. Ground, center, and call upon the Goddess and the God: "*Great Mother Goddess, by flower and by fruit I invoke you. Great Father God, by hoof and by horn I invoke you. I welcome you to this sacred space, to the temple of my heart. Embrace me and transform me. Bless me and fill me with your presence. Accept my offering as I dedicate myself.*"

Feel the energy flowing through you. Take all the time you want and need. Feel the joy and peace that the Divine bestows upon you. Feel yourself coming home to your true self, to your destiny, and to the Sacred. When you are ready, read your oath.

If you're dedicating yourself to the Tradition of Ara path, you should also add: "*I open my eyes, my heart, and my soul to the Mystery of the Sacred, which is everywhere present in the world and in my life. I will draw my power from that divinity and, awakened to the magic of the world, I will give thanks each day for its blessings.*"

Consecrate yourself with the Moon water in your chalice by placing a drop on your third eye, your heart, and your groin, saying: "With the waters of life, I bless and consecrate myself as a Witch and dedicant."

Feel yourself filled and surrounded with love, and feel love flowing from you to the world, and the Sacred. Hold your Book of Shadows to your heart and charge it as a Witch and dedicant. You may also charge your jewelry or a power object that honors this rite of passage. Offer a libation to the God, the Goddess, and yourself, then thank the Goddess and God for blessing you and for accepting your oath of dedication.

Close your circle. If you are outside, as always, leave an offering for your fellow creatures in the sacred space.

Go forth into your new life, acting in accord.

The world that you reenter will be an enchanted one, for you have crafted yourself as a Witch and you have the skills and wisdom to live a life of embodied divinity. I hope that *Witch Crafting* has been, and will continue to be, useful to you in your ongoing quest for the real magic of life.

Thou art God/dess. Our circle is open, but never broken. Merry meet and merry part and merry meet again.

Resources

For a comprehensive listing of additional Wiccan resources, please refer to the Appendix, pages 295 to 302, of my first book, *Book of Shadows: A Modern Woman's Journey into the Wisdom of Witchcraft and the Magic of the Goddess*, also published by Broadway Books. The list below is only a partial list; exclusion does not constitute a statement of criticism—it merely reflects a limitation of space. Many of the items included were chosen because they will in turn connect you to others.

RESEARCH RESOURCES ON THE WEB

Classical Mythology Online: http://www.oup-usa.org/sc/0195143388/

Classical Mythology by Geography (Greek):
http://www.princeton.edu/~markwoon/Myth/old-index.html

Diotima (Materials for the Study of Women and Gender in the Ancient World): http://www.stoa.org/diotima/

Druidry and Paganism: http://www.goodnet.com/~merlyn/druid.htm

Encyclopedia Mythica: http://www.pantheon.org/mythica/

Greek Gods: http://www.geocities.com/Athens/Academy/4994/gods.htm

Greek Mythology Today (aka Myth Man):
http://www.thanasis.com/myth.htm

Horned Owl Library:
http://www.islandnet.com/~hornowl/library/library.htm

Magic and Mysteries of Ancient Egypt: http://www.verdenet.com/isis/

Mystery Religions page:
http://www.belinus.co.uk/mythology/Mysteryreligions.htm

Mystery Religions: Britannica.com:
http://www.britannica.com/bcom/eb/article/6/0,5716,115606+15,00.html

The Book of Gods, Goddesses, Heroes, and Other Characters of Mythology: http://raven.cybercom.com/~grandpa/gdsindex.html

Research Indexes

Anthro.net (contains bibliographic references and links to Internet resources for the anthropology of religion):
http://home1.gte.net/ericjw1/religion.html

Avatar Search Engine of the "Occult:" http://www.avatarsearch.com

Mything Links ("An Annotated and Illustrated Collection of Worldwide Links to Mythologies, Fairy Tales and Folklore, Sacred Arts, and Traditions"): http://www.mythinglinks.org/

Mythology, Folklore, and a little bit of Religion (compiled by Sarah Craig and updated by Russell Connell. A massive list of links to sites about mythology, folklore, and religion):
http://www.fas.harvard.edu/~folkmyth/fandmwebsitessarah.html

Myths and Legends: http://pubpages.unh.edu/~cbsiren/myth.html

Research Institute for the Humanities and Religion:
http://www.arts.cuhk.edu.hk/Rel.html

Resources for Studying Mythology (general, Greek/Roman, Middle Eastern, European, Asian, North and South American, African links):

http://www.dc.peachnet.edu/~shale/humanities/literature/world_literature/myth/myth.html

WICCAN CALENDAR OF EVENTS SITES

PagaNet News: http://www.paganet.org/pnn/Calendar_of_Events.html

The Wiccan and Pagan Times: http://www.twpt.com/calendar.htm

Calendar of Events Links Published by Larry Cornett, 9355 Sibelius Dr., Vienna, VA 22182; this website includes links to other calendars, etc.: http://members.aol.com/lcorncalen/CALENDAR.htm

Voices of Women: http://www.voiceofwomen.com/calendar.html

FORUMS/COMMUNITY

Aquarian Tabernacle Church, P.O. Box 409, Index, WA 98256; www.aquatabch.org or www.atc.org

Circle of Ara/Temple of Ara, H.Ps. Phyllis Curott, Box 311, Prince Street Station, New York, NY 10012: www.WitchCrafting.com

Center for Women and Religion, Graduate Theological Union, 2400 Ridge Rd., Berkeley, CA 94709

Circle Sanctuary, P.O. Box 219, Mt. Horeb, WI 53572; http://www.circlesanctuary.org/

Church of the Iron Oak, P.O. Box 060672, Palm Bay, FL 32906; (407) 722-0291; www.ironoak.org

Church of All Worlds, P.O. Box 1542, Ukiah, CA 95482; http://www.caw.org/

Church of Wicca, P.O. Box 103, Kelmscott, WA 6111 Australia; (08) 9430 6779

Covenant of the Goddess, P.O. Box 1226, Berkeley, CA 94704: http://www.cog.org/

Covenant of Unitarian Universalist Pagans (CUUPS), P.O. Box 640, Cambridge, MA 02140; http://www.cuups.org/

Earthspirit Community, P.O. Box 340, Williamsburg, MA 01096; http://www.earthspirit.com/

Fellowship of Isis, Clonegal Castle, Enniscorthy, Ireland; www.fellowshopofisis.com

Fiona Horne Website: http://www.fionahorne.com

Grail Directory: GPO Box 1444, Canberra ACT 2601 Australia; (06) 249 1313; grail@ozemail.com.au

Hidden Path: Windwalker, Box 934, Kenosha, WI 53141

Invisible College, P.O. Box 42, Bath BA1 1ZN, UK

MAMAROOTS: Ajama-Jebi (Afracentric Goddess), P.O. Box 16151, Oakland, CA 94610; (510) 238-9260; www.mamarootsweb.com

Michigan Womyn's Music Festival: (616) 757-4766; www.michfest.com

Military Pagan Network: P.O. Box 1225, Columbia, MD 21044; (410) 740-0561; www.milpagan.org

National Women's Music and Spirit Conference, Women in the Arts, P.O. Box 1427, Indianapolis, IN 46206; www.wiaonline.org/nwmf/

Nature Religions Scholars Network: http://www.uscolo.edu/natrel/

Ontario Consultants for Religious Tolerance: http://www.religioustolerance.org/

OzPagan Website: (Australian) www.vrx.net.au/ozpagan

Pagan Alliance: P. O. Box 823, Bathurst, NSW 2795, Australia; www.geocities.com/Athens/Thebes/4320

PaganPath: http://www.paganpath.com/

Pagan Educational Network: P.O. Box 585, Portgage, IN 46368;
www.PaganEdNet.org

Pagan Federation International (comprising Pagan communities in Belgium, Canada, Germany, Austria, Ireland, Netherlands, South Africa, and the United Kingdom): BM Box 7097, London WC1N 3XX, UK; http://www.hexhus.a.se/pfint/main.html; http://www.paganfederation.org

The Pagan Community in the United Kingdom: http://www.pagan-link.org/uk-info/

Pagan Pride: www.paganpride.org

PYRAA (Pagan Youth Religion and Arts Alliance) and *Crescent* Magazine, Khristine Annwn Page and Laura Schmidt: waxnwane@crescent-magazine.com & pyraa@crescentmagazine.com; http://www.crescent-magazine.com

Reclaiming: P.O. Box 14404, San Francisco, CA 94114;
www.reclaiming.org

Sacred Well Congregation (excellent help for Military Pagans): P.O. Box 58, Converse, TX 78109; www.sacredwell.org

SilverCircle (Dutch): Postbus 473, 3700 Al Zeist, Netherlands;
www.silvercircle.org

Spirit Online: http://www.spiritonline.com/main.html

The Southern Hemisphere Pagan Network Page:
www.poboxes.com/shpn

Teenage Pagan, Minor Arcana, P.O. Box 615, Norwich, Norfolk, NR1 4QQ, UK; http://www.members.tripod.com/~Minor

Teen Witch ("This is a website for serious teen witches. . . . NOTE: There is no relation between TeenWitch.com, the website, and *Teen Witch*, the book.): http://teenwitch.com/

Wiccan Church of Canada, 109 Vaughan Road, Toronto, M6C 2L9, Canada; www.wcc.on.ca

The Witches' Voice, P.O. Box 4924, Clearwater, FL 33758-4924; http://www.witchvox.com/—Always a great place to start any Internet search!

Witch/Pagan Resources: http://www.pagansunite.com/index2.shtml

Women's Spirituality Forum, (Z. Budapest): P.O. Box 11363, Piedmont, CA 94611; (510) 893-3097; www.zbudapest.com

Women of Wisdom Foundation, P.O. Box 30043, Seattle, WA 98103; (206) 782-3363; www.womenofwisdom.org

LEGAL ACTION NETWORKS

American Civil Liberties Union—www.aclu.org has contact information for state/local chapters, and check your local phonebook

Alternative Religions Educational Network: http://www.aren.org/

Committee of Legal Assistance of the Universal Federation of Pagans: UFP@tylwythteg.com:; http://www.tylwythteg.com/ufp.html

Earth Religions Legal Assistance Network: http://www.geocities.com/CapitolHill/5883/

Lady Liberty League—religious freedom support for Wiccans, Pagans, and other Nature religions practitioners worldwide, an international information and networking service sponsored by Circle Sanctuary, Box 219, Mt. Horeb, WI 53572; email: circle@mhtc.net; phone: (608) 924-2216; fax: (608) 924-5961; http://www.circlesanctuary.org/liberty/

Natural Religion Anti-Defamation Group of the Southeastern Pagan Alliance, Rebecca Martin: camozzi19@hotmail.com; http://www.tylwythteg.com/sepa.html

Public Interest Law Group, Clare Kelsey: cckelsey@Sover.net

Pagan Educational Network, Cairril Adaire: pen@bloomington.in.us; http://www.bloomington.in.us/~pen

Religious Liberties Lawyers Network, Phyllis Curott, Esq., National Co-ordinator, Kirsten Rostedt, Esq., Director; rllnhq@aol.com

Sacred Earth Alliance (An Alliance of Earth Religions Information & Assistance Leagues) c/o Larry Cornett, 890 Alhambra Rd., Cleveland, OH 44110; lcorncalen@aol.com; http://members.aol.com/lcorncalen/SEA-Homepage.htm

The CommonWealth Pagan, Kostya Branwen Sudice,: http://www.mindspring.com/~viragofreespirit/tcp.html

WLPA (The Witches League for Public Awareness founded by Laurie Cabot), P.O. Box 8736, Salem, MA 01971; http://www.celticcrow.com/

Witches Against Religious Discrimination, Inc., Christine Craft: ja@epix.net; http://www.cybergoddess.net/ward.html

Write Your Representative: This service is provided to assist you in finding and contacting members of the United States House of Representatives. Please note that the contact information accessible through this service is provided by each member office; http://www.house.gov/writerep/

World Pagan Network, Chris West: Ceile@aol.com: http://www.geocities.com/Athens/Aegean/8773/index.html

PERIODICALS, NEWSLETTERS, MAGAZINES, E-ZINES

The Beltane Papers (women's mysteries), 1333 Lincoln St., #240, Bellingham, WA 98226

Black Raven—A journal of myth and symbolic studies; http://www.motley-focus.com/~timber/raven.html

The Cauldron: http://www.ecauldron.com/index.php

Cauldrons and Broomsticks-ezine; www.cauldrons-broomsticks.net

Circle Network News, P.O. Box 219, Mt. Horeb, WI 53572

Chrone Chronicles, P.O. Box 81, Kelly, WY 83011

Connections Journal: The Official Journal of the Covenant of Unitarian Universalist Pagans: http://www.connectionsjournal.com/

Crescent magazine: www.crescentmagazine.com; email waxnwane@crescentmagazine.com or to order by credit card: 1.877.CC NOW-77 (877-226-6977)

Enchante, 30 Charlton St., Box 6F, New York, NY 10014

enLIGHTen Metaphysical E-zine—astrology, paganism, healing, music, Gaia's Light, P.O. Box 127, Altoona, FL 32702; (352) 669-6903: http://www.digiserve.com/gaia/archives.html

Esoteric Art—For additional magazines on the Internet: http://www.esotericart.com/fringe/ezines.htm

Gnosis, P.O. Box 14217, San Francisco, CA 94114

Goddessing/Goddess Regenerated, P.O. Box 73, Sliema, Malta, or P.O. Box 269, Valrico, FL 33595; email: goddssng@maltanet.net

Goddess Rising, 4006 First St., NE, Seattle, WA 98105

Green Egg, P.O. Box 1542, Ukiah, CA 95482: http://www.greenegg.org/

InnerViews—mix of pagan and New Age topics: http://www.newageinfo.com/articles/

Keltria—A Journal of Druidism and Celtic Magick (under construction at time of publication): http://keltria.org/journal/

Kindred Spirits Magazine, Foxhole, Darlington, Devon, England TQ9 6EB. www.kindredspirit.co.uk

Magickal Blend, P.O. Box 11303, San Francisco, CA 94101-7303

Of Like Mind, P.O. Box 6677, Madison, WI 53716; (608) 257-5858

Old Ways—a Journal of the Craft in the Modern Age:
http://www.oldways.com/

PagaNet News; PagaNet, Inc., P.O. Box 61054, Virginia Beach, VA 23466-1054; www.paganet.org/pnn

Pagan Times—published by Pagan Alliance, P.O. Box 823, Bathurst, NSW 2795, Autstralia

Pagan Path—Canadian journal published eight times a year:
http://www.geocities.com/Athens/9301/path.html

The Pomegranate—Journal of Neo-Pagan Thought:
www.interchg.uba.ca/fmuntean/

Psychic Times: http://www.psychic-tymes.com/

PanGaia/SageWoman—celebrates Goddess-loving women from around the world: http://www.sagewoman.com/PanGaia/SageWoman/Blessed Bee; www.blessedbee.com; www.sagewoman.com; www.pangaia.com; *PanGaia* Magazine/*SageWoman* Magzine, Blessed Bee, Inc., P.O. Box 641, Point Arena, CA 95468 (these three pubs are all owned by Blessed Bee, Inc.)

The Shaman's Drum, Box 2636, Berkeley, CA 94702

Spirited Women—articles on Goddess Spirituality, Dianic Wicca, Paganism, Feminist Christianity and Judaism: SisterSpirit, P.O. Box 9246, Portland, OR, 97207; http://www.teleport.com/~sistersp/magazine.html

The Web, 401 Cumberland Dr., No. Augusta, SC 29841

The Wiccan Rede—Dutch/English; www.silvercircle.org

Wiccan-Pagan Times Journal: www.twpt.com (e-zine only)

Widdershins—The Northwest's Finest Pagan Newspaper, Emerald City/Silver Moon Productions, 12345 Lake City Way NE, Suite 268, Seattle, WA 98125; http://www.widdershins.org/

The Wise Woman, 2441 Cordova St., Oakland, CA 94602

Witch's Brew—Journal of Wisdom: Witch's Brew Subscription Dept. 610 Turner Rd., Bluff City, TN 37618; www.witchs-brew.com

Witch's Trine—a publication of the New Reformed Orthodox Order of the Golden Dawn, 48 Page Street, San Francisco, CA 94102; www.NRODGD.org

The Witches' Almanac, P.O. Box 318, Milton, MA 02168

Woman of Power, P.O. Box 2785, Orleans, MA 02653

Yoni—a celebration of the feminine; http://www.yoni.com/index.html

RETAILERS AND E-TAILERS

For people who do not have herbal or Wiccan shops in your area, you will find lots of e-tailers online through any search engine.

These are catalogs, and also informative:

Magickal Blend: The Magical Blend Inc., 1928 Ste. Catherine Street West, Montréal, Québec, H3H-1M4 Canada; tmb@themagiccalblend.com

AzureGreen P.O. Box 48-WEB, Middlefield, MA 01243-0048; abyssdist@aol.com

A VERY SELECT SUGGESTED READING LIST

Please note that many of the authors listed below have written more titles worth reading.

Abracadabra: Lexicon van de Moderne Hekserij by Jan de Zutter. Atwerpen-Barrn, Hadewijch, 1997.

The Ages of Gaia by J. Lovelock. Oxford: Oxford University Press, 1988.

The Alphabet Versus the Goddess: Conflict Between Word and Image by Leonard Shlain. New York: Penguin, 1998.

ARADIA, or the Gospel of the Witches, a new translation by Mario Pazzaglini, Ph.D. & Dina Pazzaglini, with additional material by Robert Mathiesen. Custer, WA: Phoenix Publishing 1998.

Arthur and the Sovereignty of Britain, Kind and Goddess in the Mabinogion by Caitlin Mathews. London: Arkana, 1989.

Awakening Osiris, The Egyptian Book of the Dead. New translation by Normandi Ellis. Grand Rapids, Michigan: Phanes Press, 1988.

The New Book of Goddesses and Heroines by Patricia Monaghan. St. Paul: Llewellyn Publications, 1997.

Book of Shadows: A Modern Woman's Journey into the Wisdom of Witchcraft and the Magic of the Goddess by Phyllis Curott. New York: Broadway Books, 1998.

Buckland's Complete Book of Witchcraft by Raymond Buckland. St. Paul: Lewellyn Publications, 1986.

Celebrating the Male Mysteries by R. J. Stewart. Bath, Avon; England Arcania, 1991.

Choirs of the God, Revisioning Masculinity, edited by John Matthews. London: Mandala, 1991.

Covencraft by Amber K. St. Paul: Llewellyn Publications, 1998.

Drawing Down the Moon by Margot Adler. New York: Penguin, 1997.

Ecstasies: Deciphering the Witches' Sabbath by Carlo Ginzburg. New York: Pantheon Books, 1991.

Ecstasy: Understanding the Psychology of Joy by Robert Johnson. New York: Harper & Row, 1987.

The Elegant Universe: Superstrings, Hidden Dimension and the Quest for the Ultimate Theory by Brian Greene. New York: W. W. Norton, 1997.

The Hero with a Thousand Faces by Joseph Campbell. Princeton: Princeton University Press, 1990.

The Holy Book of Women's Mysteries by Z. Budapest. California: Wingbow Press, 1989.

Listening to the Oracle: The Ancient Art of Finding Guidance in the Signs and Symbols All Around Us by Dainne Skafte, Ph.D. San Francisco: HarperCollins, 1997.

The Magickal Formulary, edited by Herman Slater. New York: Magickal Childe, 1981.

The Master Book of Herbalism by Paul Bereyl. Custer, WA: Phoenix Publishing, 1984.

Meditation: The First and Last Freedom, A Practical Guide to Meditation by Osho. New York: St. Martin's Press, 1996.

Magick Made Easy: Charms, Spells, Potions, and Power by Patricia Telesco. San Francisco: HarperCollins, 2000.

The Pagan Book of Living and Dying, edited by Macha Nightmare. San Francisco: HarperCollins, 1997.

Practical Intuition: How to Harness the Power of Your Instinct by Laura Day. New York: Broadway Books, 1996.

Quantum Self: Human Nature and Consciousness Devined by the New Physics by Danah Zohar. New York: Quill/William Morrow, 1990.

The Rebirth of Witchcraft by Doreen Valiente. Custer, WA: Phoenix Publishing, 1989.

Reconnecting with Nature: Finding Wellness Through Restoring Your Bond with the Earth by Michael J. Cohen. Coryallis, OR: Ecopress, 1997.

Runes and Magic: Magical Formulaic Elements in the Older Runic Tradition by Stephen Flowers. New York: P. Lang, 1986.

The Secret Language of Symbols: A Visual Key to Symbols and Their Meanings by David Fontana. San Francisco: Chronicle Books, 1993.

Sibyls and Sibylline Prophecy in Classical Antiquity by H. W. Parke. London and New York: Routledge, 1988.

The Twelve Wild Swans by Starhawk and Hilary Valentine. San Francisco: HarperCollins, 2000.

Triumph of the Moon, A History of Modern Pagan Witchcraft by Ronald Hutton. Oxford: Oxford University Press, 1999.

The Way of the Wizard by Deepak Chopra. New York: Harmony Books, 1995.

When the Drummers Were Women: A Spiritual History of Rhythm by Layne Redmond. New York: Three Rivers Press/Crown, 1997.

Wicca: The Old Religion in the New Age by Vivianne Crowley. London: Aquarian Press, 1989.

Wicca Coven: How to Start and Organize Your Own by Judy Harrow, Secaucus, N.J.; Carol Publishing Group, 1999.

Wiccan Warrior: Walking a Spiritual Path in a Sometimes Hostile World by Kerr Cuhulain. St. Paul: Llwellyn Publications, 2000.

Wicca on the Web by M. Macha Nightmare. Publication forthcoming.

Witchcraft Today by Gerald Gardener. London: Rider, 1954.

The Witches' God, The Witches' Goddess by Janet and Stewart Farrar. Custer, WA: Phoenix Publishing, 1998.

Witch: A Hip Guide to Modern Witchcraft by Fiona Horne. London: Thorsons, 2000.

Witchcraze: A New History of the European Witch Hunts by Anne Llewllyn Barstow. New York: HarperCollins, 1994.

The Women's Spirituality Book by Diane Stein. St. Paul: Llewllyn Publications, 1987.